INTERNATIONAL DEVELOPMENT IN FOCUS

Political Economy of Education in Lebanon
Research for Results Program

HUSEIN ABDUL-HAMID AND MOHAMED YASSINE

 WORLD BANK GROUP

Contents

Boxes

Figures

Acknowledgments

This volume was coauthored by Husein Abdul-Hamid (Senior Education Specialist) and Mohamed Yassine (Education Specialist), both of the World Bank. The Research for Results (R4R) program was designed and executed by a World Bank team, in close collaboration with the Lebanon Ministry of Education and Higher Education (MEHE) and the Center for Educational Research and Development (CERD). The team was led by Husein Abdul-Hamid, Mohamed Yassine, and Noah Yarrow (Senior Education Specialist); and included Christin McConnell (Education Specialist), Mirvat Haddad (Program Assistant); Nadine El Franji (Consultant), Jocelyne Jabbour (Procurement Analyst), Rita Nasrallah (Consultant), and Reine El Khoury (Consultant), all of the World Bank.

The research was conducted under the guidance of H.E. Akram Chehayeb (Minister of Education), H.E. Marwan Hamadeh (former Minister of Education), and H.E. Elias Bou Saab (former Minister of Education). It was governed by a steering committee chaired by MEHE and a technical committee chaired by CERD. Fadi Yarak (Director General of Education, MEHE), chair of the steering committee, and Nada Oweijane (President, CERD), chair of the technical committee and member of the steering committee, provided close follow-up, guidance, and valuable feedback to the research process and outputs. The steering committee included Ahmad Jammal (Director General of Higher Education, MEHE), Therese El Hachem (Dean of Faculty of Education, Lebanese University), and Karma El Hassan (American University of Beirut), as well as representatives from the two donors of the program: the United Kingdom's Department for International Development (DFID) and the United States Agency for International Development (USAID). The technical committee provided valuable inputs to the research design, instruments, and outputs. It included Hilda Khoury (Direction d'Orientation Pédagogique et Scolaire [DOPS] Director, MEHE), Samia Abou Hamad (CERD), Nashaat Mansour (Lebanese American University), Iman Khalil (Lebanese University), Fadi El Hage (Saint Joseph University), Claudine Aziz (Education Practitioner), Hanadi Jardali (Education Practitioner), and Samir Costantine (Education Practitioner).

Furthermore, the research outputs benefited from inputs from Sonia Khoury (Reaching All Children with Education Program Management Unit [RACE PMU] Director, MEHE), Imad El Achkar (Director, MEHE), Amal Chaaban

(Director, MEHE), George Daoud (Director, MEHE), Hadi Zalzali (Director, MEHE), and Ghassan Chakaroun (Advisor, MEHE); and detailed review by Victoria Collis (Consultant, MEHE), Kawthar Dara (Consultant, MEHE), and Maysa Mourad (Consultant, MEHE). Iman Assi (MEHE) and Lynn Hamasni (Consultant, MEHE) provided administrative support for the implementation of the studies. The World Bank team extends its appreciation to all staff at MEHE and CERD who provided administrative and technical support to the program. The team would also like to thank Boutros Azar (Secretary General of the General Secretariat of Catholic Schools in Lebanon and Coordinator of the Association of Private Educational Institutions in Lebanon), Adla Chatila (Makassed Schools), Bassem Kandil (Makassed Schools), Rana Ismail (Mabarrat Schools), and Fayez Jalloul (Mabarrat Schools), who provided valuable inputs during the research process. The team would like to also acknowledge all stakeholders interviewed for the political economy study, including former ministers and CERD presidents, parliamentarians, teacher unions, school principals, and teachers.

The authors acknowledge the input of the research teams that contributed to the collection and analysis of data under R4R. In this volume, the literature review discussed in chapter 1 was conducted by a team led by Adnan El Amine. The public perception data presented in chapter 3 were collected and analyzed by a team from the Consultation and Research Institute (CRI), comprising Kamal Hamdan, Redha Hamdan, Rania Nader, and Lea Bou Khater. The political economy study was prepared by Ramzi Salame. Nada Mneymneh (President, Lebanese Association for Education Studies, LAES) provided valuable inputs to the literature review, public perception, and political economy studies. The textbook study was conducted by Nicholas Read (Icon4ed) and the Education Management Information System (EMIS) review was conducted by Namrata Saraogi (World Bank).

The studies under R4R were made possible through generous financial contributions from DFID and USAID. The DFID and USAID teams provided valuable inputs and comments to the research design, implementation, and the outputs of the study. The World Bank team extends its gratitude and appreciation to Deirdre Watson, Nathanael Bevan, Anfal Saqib, Miriam Light, Hannah Percival, India Perry, and Maya Doueihy of DFID; and to Zeina Salame, Christine Pagen, and Bruce McFarland of USAID.

Within the World Bank, the team is grateful for guidance and support from Saroj Kumar Jha (Regional Director), Keiko Miwa (Regional Director), Jaime Saavedra Chanduvi (Global Director), Safaa El Tayeb El-Kogali (Practice Manager), and Andreas Blom (Practice Manager). The team received valuable support and comments from Kamel Braham (Program Leader), Pierre Kamano (Program Leader), Haneen Sayed (Lead Operations Officer), Nathalie Lahire (Senior Economist), Kaliope Azzi-Huck (Senior Operations Officer), and Mouna Couzi (Country Operations Officer); as well as from peer reviewers Harry Patrinos (Practice Manager) and Samer Al-Samarrai (Senior Economist). The authors acknowledge contributions to parts of this manuscript by colleagues Anahita Hosseini Matin (Consultant), Mohamad Husein Mansour (Consultant), and Evelyne Karam (Consultant).

About the Authors

Husein Abdul-Hamid is a Senior Education Specialist at the World Bank. He managed education operations in Europe and Central Asia, the Middle East and North Africa, Sub-Saharan Africa, Latin America, the Pacific Islands, and North America, with a focus on education system reform, system solutions, education in fragile contexts, and learning in the face of adversity.

His professional career includes international development, academia, and government. He has more than 25 years of experience in the following areas of education: teaching, policy, reforms, systems approach, institutional effectiveness and system accountability, analytics and strategic planning, system intelligence, equality, and analysis of learning outcomes.

Before joining the World Bank, Abdul-Hamid was a Senior Administrator and Professor of Management at the University of Maryland. During his tenure, he pioneered policy research on higher education. He holds a PhD in statistics. His recent publications include *Data for Learning, From Compliance to Learning, Learning in the Face of Adversity*, and *What Matters Most for Education Management Systems*.

Mohamed Yassine is an Education Specialist at the World Bank. With more than 8 years of experience in international development, he has led the design and implementation support of large education programs in the Middle East and North Africa and the Sub-Saharan Africa regions. He has expertise in a broad range of education topics, including teacher professional development, student learning assessments, school-based management, refugee education, information management systems, and education technology.

Yassine has co-led several research programs in education, including rigorous impact evaluations. He has also worked on introducing innovative financing instruments in education sector development, including results-based financing approaches, public-private partnership models, and impact bonds.

He holds a master's degree in education from Stanford University and a bachelor's degree in computer engineering from the American University of Beirut.

Abbreviations

ALP	Accelerated Learning Program
CAS	Central Administration of Statistics
CDR	Council for Development and Reconstruction
CERD	Center for Educational Research and Development
CF	circonscription foncière
CRI	Consultation and Research Institute
CSO	civil society organization
DFID	Department for International Development (the United Kingdom)
DG	Director General of Education
DGE	Directorate General of Education
DOPS	Direction d'Orientation Pédagogique et Scolaire (School Guidance and Counseling Department)
ECE	early childhood education
EFA	Education for All
EGRA	Early Grade Reading Assessment
EMIS	Education Management Information System
ESCS	economic, social, and cultural status
ESDP	Education Sector Development Plan
GDP	gross domestic product
HOI	Human Opportunity Index
ICT	information and communication technology
IT	information technology
MEHE	Ministry of Education and Higher Education
MENA	Middle East and North Africa
NER	net enrollment rate
NETSP	National Educational Technology Strategic Plan
NFE	nonformal education
NGO	nongovernmental organization
NSSF	National Social Security Fund
OMSAR	Office of the Minister of State for Administrative Reform
PISA	Program for International Student Assessment
PMU	Program Management Unit

PPP	public-private partnership
R4R	Research for Results
RACE	Reaching All Children with Education
SDG	Sustainable Development Goal
SIMS	School Information Management System
SIP	school improvement plan
STEM	science, technology, engineering, and mathematics
TIMSS	Trends in International Mathematics and Science Study
TVET	technical and vocational education and training
UIS	UNESCO Institute for Statistics
UN	United Nations
UNESCO	United Nations Educational, Scientific, and Cultural Organization
UNGA	United Nations General Assembly
UNRWA	United Nations Relief and Works Agency for Palestine Refugees in the Near East
USAID	United States Agency for International Development

In this report, all dollar amounts are U.S. dollars, unless otherwise indicated.

Overview

THE VALUE OF SYSTEM-LEVEL RESEARCH AND THE POLITICAL ECONOMY APPROACH

Understanding the education system in its entirety was the primary objective of the Research for Results (R4R) program.[1] The program, launched in 2016, was designed to generate new evidence on the education system's foundations, assets, successes, and challenges, as well as student and teacher performance across school types. The program combined system-level analysis and stakeholder outreach with research on service delivery to create policy recommendations for strengthening the efficiency and quality of the whole education system. This approach aimed to align actors and build coalitions around a structured and systematic mechanism for research and to foster institutional capacity for conducting and using research.

R4R tackled two main areas of system diagnostics: (a) a political economy analysis of policies and institutions; and (b) service delivery research on teaching and learning in schools. This volume covers the political economy dimension, while a subsequent volume (i.e., volume 2) will cover service delivery in schools. The system-level analysis presented in this volume used a mixed-method approach. Qualitative and quantitative analyses were conducted based on a review and an analysis of more than 1,900 research papers/articles/books, laws and policies, expenditures, trends, and enrollment and outcomes indicators. Primary methods of inquiry were also used and included interviews, focus group discussions, and a household-based perception survey.

This volume used a political economy approach to study the drivers and factors that guide education operations to produce and utilize education outcomes. This included the study of context, stakeholders, and processes that shape education policies, institutions, and activities. It also aimed to identify enablers and constraints for policy change, policy implementation, and results achievement. In this context, the analysis encompassed how education policies are developed; how education consumables—such as curricula, textbooks, and learning materials—are produced, distributed, and used by learners; how education services are delivered and monitored; and how results are measured in terms of fulfilling learners' and society's needs and aspirations. It included the identification of the most influential actors in the education arena, as well as their vested interests. It also examined unfavorable frameworks of action that are likely to block the adoption of reforms and delay or derail their implementation through missteps at various levels of the implementation processes, thus undermining efforts to deliver education services in an equitable, efficient, and effective manner.

FEATURES OF THE EDUCATION SYSTEM IN LEBANON

Education service delivery

The private sector in Lebanon dominates education service delivery, enrolling 71 percent of Lebanese students in 2018. While most of the private sector is financed through tuition paid by households, there is a segment of the private sector, mainly affiliated with religious institutions, which receives direct subsidies from the government (i.e., direct fund transfer per student enrolled). These schools are known as "free private schools" as they use subsidies from the government to dramatically reduce tuition paid by parents. Out of all Lebanese students, 57 percent were enrolled in paid private schools; 14 percent in free private schools, and 29 percent in public schools (figure O.1). Moreover, for Lebanese students, enrollment trends in the past 15 years showed a steady increase in the share of private schools at the expense of public schools (figure O.2). The largest networks of private schools are religiously affiliated. In 2015, an estimated 41 percent of all private schools were officially affiliated with religious establishments. They enrolled 58 percent of private school students (both paid and subsidized) and 34 percent of all students in Lebanon (LocaLiban 2015).

FIGURE O.1

Distribution of Lebanese students by education sector, 2018

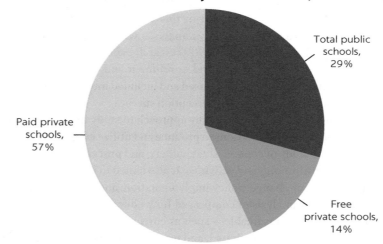

Source: CERD statistical yearbook 2017–18, Beirut, https://www.crdp.org/files/201908271242061.pdf (retrieved April 8, 2018).
Note: CERD = Center for Educational Research and Development.

FIGURE O.2

Number of Lebanese students by education sector

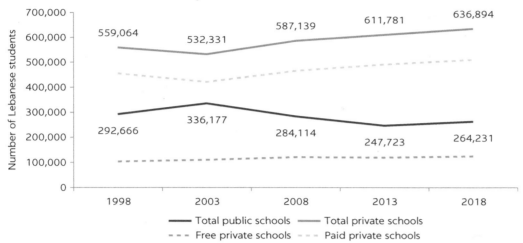

Sources: CERD statistical yearbooks, Beirut, https://www.crdp.org/statistics?la=en.
Note: Number of Lebanese students for 1998 and 2003 were estimated from the total number of students in those years based on the distribution of Lebanese and non-Lebanese students in 2005.
CERD = Center for Educational Research and Development.

Education financing

At 1.8 percent of the gross domestic product (GDP), the level of public expenditures on education is low in Lebanon compared to international benchmarks, but this is mainly due to high levels of private education provision and private households' out-of-pocket spending. In terms of public expenditures, the government finances education through multiple channels:

1. The Ministry of Education and Higher Education (MEHE) budget for the administration and operation of public schools, including general and vocational education;
2. The Center for Educational Research and Development (CERD) budget for teacher training, conducting research, improving curriculum, and other activities in its mandate;
3. The Council for Development and Reconstruction (CDR) budget for school construction;
4. Subsidization to a selected number of private schools based on enrollment figures;
5. Education allowances to civil servants to enroll their children in private schools;
6. Budgets of other ministries and public institutions as needed, such as the education inspectorate.

Data from the Lebanese Ministry of Finance indicate that from 2013–15, actual public expenditures to the general education sector—excluding vocational and tertiary education—were around 1.8 percent of GDP and 5.5 percent of total public expenditures.[2] Public expenditures on general education in those 3 years averaged around US$900 million. While the absolute number has doubled since 2005, the share of education expenditures as a percentage of total expenditures has nearly stayed constant (figure O.3).

FIGURE O.3

Public expenditures in general education over time

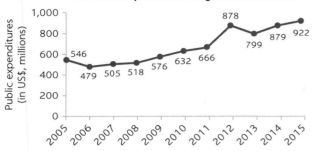

a. Public expenditures in general education

b. As percentage of GDP and total public expenditures

■ As % of GDP ■ As % of total public expenditures

Source: Data provided by the Ministry of Finance, Lebanon, in 2016.
Note: GDP = gross domestic product.

FIGURE O.4

Breakdown of government expenditures on the general education sector

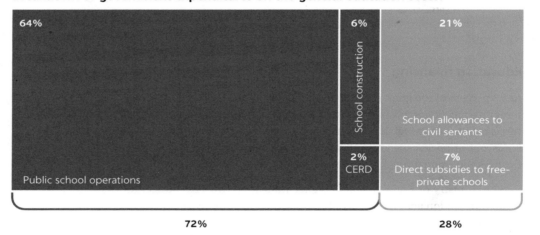

■ Expenditures to the public sector ■ Expenditures to the private sector

Source: Calculations using data provided by the Ministry of Finance, Lebanon, in 2016.
Note: CERD = Center for Educational Research and Development.

Figure O.4 shows an average breakdown of government expenditures on the general education sector. Out of all government expenditures on general education (approximately US$900 million), nearly 28 percent (around US$250 million) were subsidies to the private sector: either through direct subsidies to the "free-private" schools (7 percent) or through education allowances to civil servants (21 percent), to enroll their children in tuition-charging private schools. The remaining 72 percent (around US$650 million) were expenditures on the public education sector, including running public schools through the MEHE (64 percent), investments in public schools' construction through the CDR (6 percent), and investments in education quality (curriculum, teacher training, research) through the CERD (2 percent).

Conversely, the level of private expenditures on education (i.e., households' out-of-pocket cost) is high. The private general education sector had a market size estimated at US$1.6 billion, based on tuition data collected from the Ministry of Education.[3] Through education allowances to civil servants, the Government of Lebanon covered around US$200 million of the tuition market, while the rest (US$1.4 billion) was covered by private households' out-of-pocket expenditures. At 2.7 percent of GDP, private expenditures exceeded the government's public expenditures. When both types of expenditures are combined, Lebanon's total education expenditures reach 4.5 percent of GDP, a figure which is comparable to other upper-middle-income countries and in the OECD (figure O.5).

Syrian refugee education

While the public sector caters to a small share of Lebanese students, it has expanded tremendously during recent years to accommodate a large number of refugee children from the Syrian Arab Republic, who moved to Lebanon after the onset of the Syrian crisis in 2011. As of 2018, Lebanon enrolled 220,498 non-Lebanese children in public schools (figure O.6), a significant accomplishment, given that the public education system had to increase its capacity by approximately 77 percent in 6 years, with non-Lebanese students comprising 45 percent of total students in the public system in 2018. The expansion in formal education to Syrian refugees was made possible through the establishment of second shifts in public schools (figure O.7). In fact, in 2018, 70 percent of non-Lebanese students were enrolled in second shifts, uniquely dedicated to their instruction, while the remaining 30 percent were going to schools with their Lebanese peers during the first shift.

The Syrian refugee crisis introduced a parallel system of financing, which was sponsored by donor countries and aimed at responding to the Syrian refugees' need for education services. Donor financing to the public education system for the years 2014–18 had an annual average of US$250–US$300 million,

FIGURE O.5

Public and private education expenditures as percentage of GDP

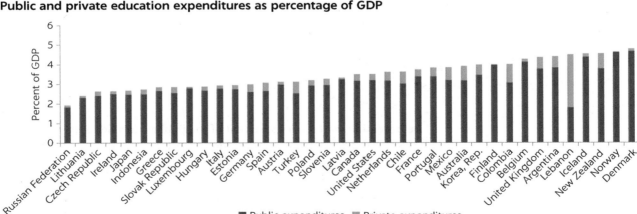

Source: Calculations using data from OECD 2019a, 2019b.
Note: GDP = gross domestic product; OECD = Organisation for Economic Co-operation and Development.

FIGURE O.6

Number of Lebanese and non-Lebanese children, ages 3–18, in public schools

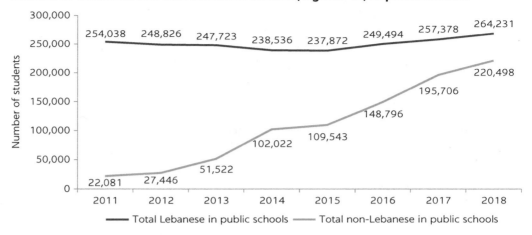

Sources: Data for Lebanese students: CERD statistical yearbooks, Beirut, https://www.crdp.org
/statistics?la=en; data for non-Lebanese students: RACE PMU (February 1, 2018).
Note: CERD = Center for Educational Research and Development; PMU = Program Management Unit;
RACE = Reaching All Children With Education.

FIGURE O.7

Distribution of non-Lebanese students across first and second shifts

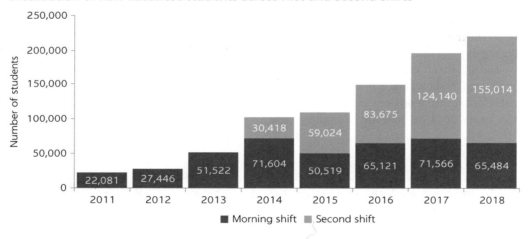

Source: Data provided by RACE PMU (February 1, 2018).
Note: PMU = Program Management Unit; RACE = Reaching All Children With Education.

representing more than 25 percent of the public education sector financing. Given that this financing was aimed to support the Government of Lebanon to enroll Syrian refugee students in public schools, and that the refugee population, as of 2018, exceeded 45 percent of the public student population, the level of donor financing was low, indicating that a significant share of the cost of education of Syrian refugees was absorbed by the Government of Lebanon and/or was partially offset by an increase in the efficiency of the system.

HOW IS THE SYSTEM PERFORMING?

Perception versus reality

When the general public was asked how the education system was performing in Lebanon, 76 percent of respondents had a positive opinion about the sector.[4] Satisfaction rates of education have been consistently high over the years. However, perception of education quality does not reflect the reality of the sector in Lebanon, as measured by learning outcomes, which are the determining metrics of success in education.

When considering harmonized learning outcomes (HLO) (Altinok, Angrist, and Patrinos 2018), Lebanon had an average score of 401 in 2015, based on learning assessments in reading, math, and science conducted in both public and private schools at different grade levels. This placed Lebanon approximately at the 35th percentile globally in terms of learning outcomes (ranking 92 out of 141 countries).[5] In contrast, using the Gallup surveys for cross-country comparison of satisfaction rates, Lebanon was approximately at the 75th percentile globally in terms of perception of education quality (ranking 37 out of 141 countries) (Gallup 2015). This large discrepancy between perception and reality of education quality is illustrated in figure O.8.

Learning outcomes

Student performance in Lebanon has been significantly lower than the international average, with a declining trend as measured by international learning assessments.

Results from the Trends in International Mathematics and Science Study (TIMSS), a large-scale standardized assessment administered globally and in Lebanon in both private and public schools, indicated that learning outcomes in

FIGURE O.8

Perception of education quality versus learning outcomes in Lebanon and comparator countries

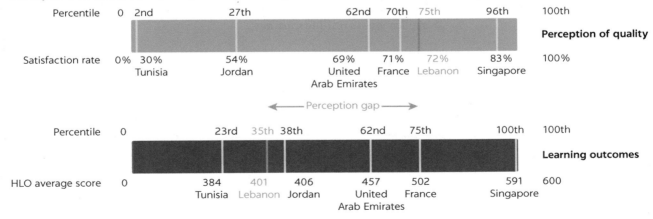

Sources: HLO scores from Education Statistics (EdStats) (database), World Bank, Washington, DC, https://datatopics.worldbank.org/education/country /lebanon; perception scores from Gallup (2015).
Note: HLO = harmonized learning outcomes.

math and science for grade 8 students have been decreasing since 2007 (figure O.9).[6] In math, while Lebanon's average performance was at the international average in 2007, by 2015, Lebanon's performance had significantly decreased below the international average. In science, Lebanon has been consistently performing significantly below the international average, and the gap between Lebanon and the international average has been widening. Comparatively, the average performance in the Middle East and North Africa (MENA) region has been consistently improving since 2007. In 2007, Lebanon's learning outcomes were significantly higher than the MENA average, but by 2015, the MENA average scores had reached or exceeded the Lebanon scores in both math and science.

Lebanon's low performance compared to the international average was also demonstrated through the Program for International Student Assessment (PISA) 2015 results. PISA, which measures learning outcomes for 15-year-olds in math, science, and reading, showed that Lebanese students were on average approximately 4 years of schooling behind students in the OECD countries (figure O.10) (World Bank 2016).[7] In Reading,[8] Lebanon was the worst performer among all 70 participating countries (OECD 2018).

While private schools performed better than public schools, results were significantly low for both sectors. For example, in science, private school students outperformed public school students by 64 points (CERD 2018a), which is equivalent to 2 years of schooling (figure O.11). However, Lebanese private school students still fell behind students in OECD countries by 75 points, equivalent to 2.5 years of schooling. Table O.1 illustrates the difference in performance in PISA 2015 between the Lebanese public and private education sectors.

It is important to note that in TIMSS 2015, there were no statistically significant differences in performance between public and private schools (CERD 2018b). In other words, grade 8 public and private school students had similar scores in math and science in TIMSS. A possible explanation for the absence of the private sector's lead in TIMSS compared to PISA is the different focus that each assessment has. TIMSS puts a greater focus on curriculum and require certain content to have been covered by the nominated grade; PISA, on the other hand, focuses less on curriculum content and more on skills and knowledge applications to real-life situations.

FIGURE O.9

TIMSS scores in math and science, 2003–15

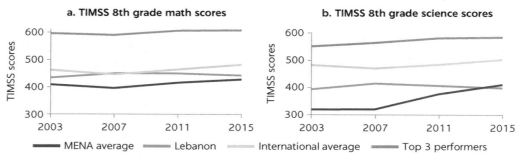

Source: Education Statistics (EdStats) (database), World Bank, Washington, DC, https://datatopics.worldbank.org/education/country/lebanon.
Note: MENA = Middle East and North Africa; TIMSS = Trends in International Mathematics and Science Study.

FIGURE O.10

PISA 2015 scores in reading, math, and science

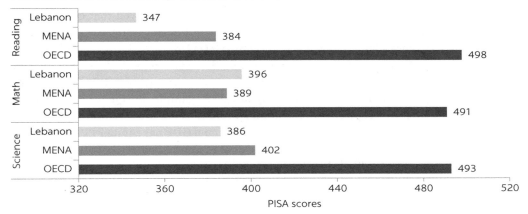

Source: World Bank 2016.
Note: MENA = Middle East and North Africa; OECD = Organisation for Economic Co-operation and Development; PISA = Program for International Student Assessment.

FIGURE O.11

Lebanon PISA 2015 scores in science by school profile

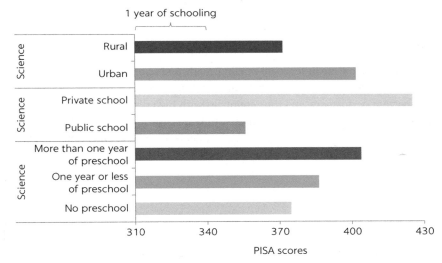

Source: World Bank 2016.
Note: PISA = Program for International Student Assessment.

TABLE O.1 **PISA 2015 results by sector of education compared to OECD average**

SUBJECT	LEBANON—PUBLIC SCHOOLS (PISA SCORES)		LEBANON—PRIVATE SCHOOLS (PISA SCORES)		OECD AVERAGE (PISA SCORES)
Reading (English)	329	+50	379	+119	498
Reading (French)	293	+99	392	+106	498
Math	361	+69	430	+61	491
Science	354	+64	418	+75	493

Source: Disaggregation by sector of education was retrieved from CERD 2018a.
Note: CERD = Center for Educational Research and Development; OECD = Organisation for Economic Co-operation and Development; OECD AVERAGE = average PISA score of OECD countries; PISA = Program for International Student Assessment.

The low PISA 2015 scores for Lebanon also highlighted alarmingly low levels of proficiency in math, science, and reading among Lebanese students. Using the PISA 2015 proficiency benchmarks, the results showed that 60 percent of Lebanese students did not achieve basic proficiency in math, 63 percent in science, and 70 percent in reading (figure O.12).

Compared to countries at a similar level of economic development (that is, similar GDP per capita public-private partnership [PPP]), Lebanon's performance was significantly low. For example, in science, at Lebanon's GDP per capita PPP, Lebanon's average score was 46 points below the expected score for a country with an equal GDP per capita PPP (figure O.13) (World Bank 2016); this is equivalent to approximately 1.5 years of schooling (World Bank 2018).

These figures point to a learning crisis in Lebanon, with nearly two-thirds of students at age 15 not reaching basic proficiency in reading, math, and science, placing them at a risk of exclusion from secondary school. Low proficiency in foundational skills has also been measured in Lebanon as early as in grades 2 and 3. In 2016, a nationally representative Early Grade Reading Assessment (EGRA) found that more than 83 percent of students in grades 2 and 3 performed at the lowest benchmark set by the Lebanese government education institutions.[9] In grade 2, 10 percent of children were not able to read a single word, and a total of 37 percent were not able to read more than 10 words (QITABI 2017).

Equity

In addition to low mean scores in reading, math, and science, Lebanon had a high dispersion rate. Dispersion rates measure the difference in scores between the top and bottom performers, and thus countries with high dispersion rates are countries where inequity is high, and there are large gaps in learning achievements between schools and between individual students. Figure O.14 illustrates the low mean score and high dispersion for TIMSS grade 8 science scores as an example.[10]

FIGURE O.12

Lebanon PISA 2015 proficiency levels in reading, math, and science

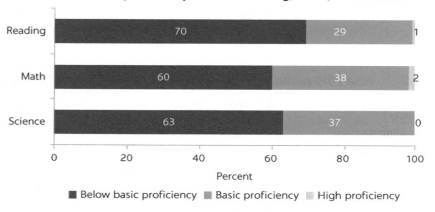

Source: World Bank 2016.
Note: PISA = Program for International Student Assessment.

FIGURE O.13

PISA 2015 scores in science as a function of GDP per capita, PPP

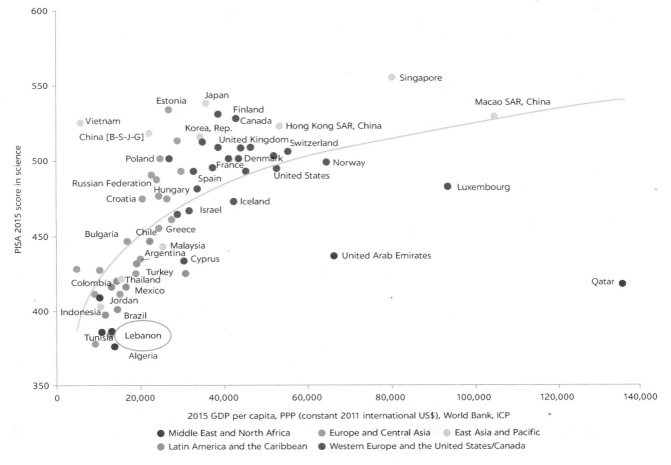

Sources: World Bank 2016; ICP (database), World Bank, Washington, DC, https://databank.worldbank.org/reports.aspx?source=international
-comparison-program-(icp)-2011.
Note: B-S-J-G = Beijing-Shanghai-Jiangsu-Guangdong; GDP = gross domestic product; ICP = International Comparison Program; PISA = Program
for International Student Assessment; PPP = public-private partnership.

Economic, social, and cultural status (ESCS) is a key factor driving inequity in learning achievement in Lebanon. In fact, in the MENA region, Lebanon has the highest gap in student performance between the top and bottom ESCS quintiles. As an example, PISA 2015 science scores showed a difference of approximately 2.8 years of schooling between the top and bottom ESCS quintiles (figure O.15) (World Bank 2018).

There is also evidence for regional inequity in terms of learning achievement. The EGRA 2016 data demonstrated that grade 2 students in Mount Lebanon performed significantly better in reading fluency than students in all other governorates.[11] The PISA 2015 showed that students in Mount Lebanon and Beirut performed significantly better than students in all other governorates (Bekaa, North, South, and Nabatieh) in science, math, and reading (CERD 2018a).

Another equity concern apparent from the study was the difference in education outcomes between public and private schools. Indeed, passing rates for national examinations in 2017 revealed that there are differences in

FIGURE O.14

TIMSS grade 8 science: Mean scores and score dispersion rates

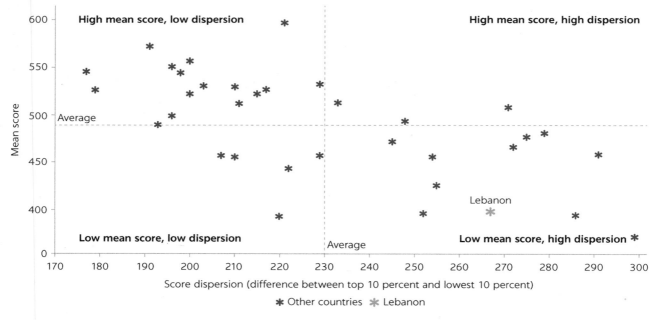

Sources: Education Statistics (EdStats) (database), World Bank, Washington, DC, https://datatopics.worldbank.org/education/country/lebanon.

FIGURE O.15

PISA 2015 science scores by top and bottom ESCS quintile in the Middle East and North Africa

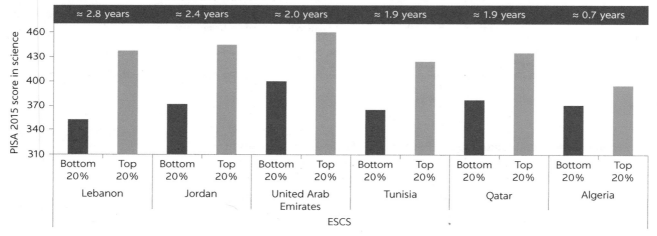

Source: World Bank 2016.
Note: ESCS = economic, social, and cultural status; PISA = Program for International Student Assessment.

student achievements between the private and the public sectors (table 1.2) (CERD 2017). For grade 9, the private sector outperformed the public sector by more than 15 percentage points. With more than one out of four (27 percent)[12] grade 9 students in the public sector failing the national examinations, these children face a high risk of exclusion from secondary schooling and other learning opportunities. At the secondary school level,

TABLE O.2 **Student numbers and passing rates in 2017 national examinations**

	STUDENT NUMBERS				PASSING RATES	
	PUBLIC SECTOR		PRIVATE SECTOR		PUBLIC SECTOR	PRIVATE SECTOR
Grade 9 Brevet	17,725	100%	38,409	100%	72.9%	88.0%
Grade 12 Baccalaureate	18,392	100%	21,241	100%	80.7%	81.2%
per field of specialization						
Life sciences	5,415	29%	8,002	38%	77.7%	86.2%
General sciences	2,103	11%	2,955	14%	85.9%	95.6%
Literature and humanities	1,361	7%	556	3%	84.4%	84.7%
Economics and sociology	9,513	52%	9,728	46%	80.7%	72.6%

Source: CERD 2017.
Note: In orange, statistically significant differences between public and private sectors. In blue circles, percentage of students in each academic stream out of all students per education sector (percentages are rounded and might not add up to 100 percent). CERD = Center for Educational Research and Development.

there was no statistical significance between public and private schools when taking into consideration all students passing the grade 12 national examination. However, when looking at each field of specialization, there were significant differences between the two sectors. In the sciences, including both life sciences and general sciences, private sector students outperformed public sector students by 8.5 and 9.7 percentage points, respectively. However, this gap disappeared in the literature and humanities field and was reversed for the social sciences field, where public students outperformed by 8.1 percentage points. These results might explain findings from the public perception survey, conducted under the R4R program, where private school parents expressed that their children faced difficulties in Arabic language instruction, the humanities, and social sciences, while public sector parents expressed this concern for science subjects, math, and foreign languages (which are also the languages used for math and science instruction). These findings were also reflected in the enrollment numbers in each academic stream, with public sector students being significantly less likely to choose science fields compared to private school students: 52 percent of grade 12 students in the private sector were specialized in science fields in 2017 versus only 40 percent of public sector students (table O.2) (CERD 2017).[13] This difference in orientation toward field of specializations between public and private school students perpetuates inequity in life opportunities and career prospects, with significantly fewer public school students pursuing education opportunities and careers in science, technology, engineering, and mathematics (STEM) fields.

In addition to inequity in student learning outcomes, there are large gaps in educational attainment as the poorest children are not reaching higher levels of education. At the secondary and tertiary levels of education, the shares of the 20 percent poorest students decrease to 11 percent and 4 percent, respectively, this indicates that poor households are not fully benefiting from the government's investment in education, particularly at higher grade levels (figure O.16). The socioeconomic inequity in education starts early in the poorest children's lives. As early as the primary school level, the 20 percent poorest children comprise nearly half of all overaged children, indicating high repetition rates for the poorest children at the primary education level.

FIGURE O.16

Composition of each school level by socioeconomic quintile

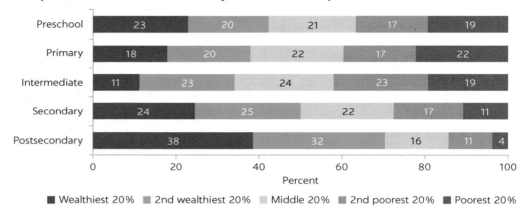

Source: Calculations using CAS (database), Household-based Survey 2011–2012, Central Administration of Statistics, Beirut, http://www.cas.gov.lb/index.php/demographic-and-social-en/householdexpenditure-en.
Note: Wealth quintiles defined by asset index. Levels include corresponding vocational and technical programs. The total for each bar is not equal to 100 percent because percentages have been rounded. CAS = Central Administration of Statistics.

Efficiency

A review of public expenditures in the education sector reveals that there are several areas where gains in efficiency can be made regarding teacher workforce management and deployment. The teacher salaries cost per student in the public sector has seen a dramatic increase in past years (figure O.17). In 2015, the Lebanese government was spending a total of US$1,743 per student on teacher salaries, an increase of 36 percent from the 2011 rate of US$1,277 per student, and an increase of 140 percent from the 2006 rate of US$727 per student.

Over the period 2011–15, increase in teacher salaries cost was on average 3.7 times the inflation rate in Lebanon.[14] Increase in teacher salaries cost has been driven by (a) a salary inflation for civil servants; (b) workload policy; and (c) increased recruitment of contractual teachers. Due to a system of automatic promotion based on seniority, the pay grade of civil servants is skewed toward the higher ranks of the pay scale, even though 40 percent of civil servants did not possess a university degree in 2015. Additionally, teacher workload decreases with years of service for civil servants, and there is no enforcement of nonteaching responsibilities for more experienced teachers. Lebanon has low levels of workload required from teachers, as it averages 431 hours per year compared to 771 hours per year in the OECD countries.[15] Finally, due to a hiring freeze for civil servants and low teacher workload, Lebanon had an increasing trend of recruiting contractual teachers. From 2011–17, the number of contractual teachers in the public sector increased by 123 percent. The hiring of contractual teachers follows much less stringent requirements and can represent a risk for the quality of education service delivery in schools. High per-student teacher salaries cost can put tremendous fiscal pressure on the government; hence the need to develop policies that ensure a clearly laid-out work program for teachers, with a balance between teaching and nonteaching tasks to effectively translate substantial investment in teachers into actual student learning.

FIGURE O.17

Total cost of teacher salaries per student in the public sector

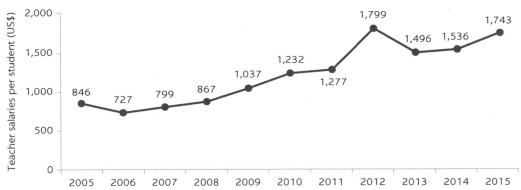

Sources: Teacher salaries expenditures based on data provided from the Ministry of Finance in 2016; enrollment numbers based on CERD statistical yearbooks, Beirut, https://www.crdp.org/statistics?la=en.
Note: Government increased civil servants' wages in 2012. In 2013, number of non-Lebanese children in public schools nearly doubled, bringing down teacher salaries cost per student. Note that these calculations include total enrollment but exclude second-shift students and teachers. They also exclude "supplemental teachers" financed by donors and hired to teach Syrian students. CERD = Center for Educational Research and Development.

FIGURE O.18

Number of public schools by ownership over time

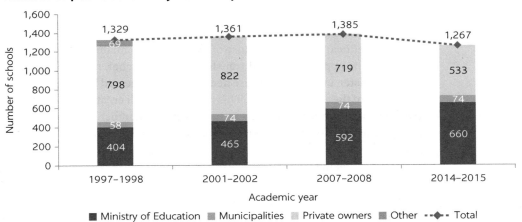

Sources: CERD statistical yearbooks, Beirut, https://www.crdp.org/statistics?la=en; and data provided by the MEHE and CDR in 2016.
Note: CDR = Council for Development and Reconstruction; CERD = Center for Educational Research and Development; MEHE = Ministry of Education and Higher Education.

In addition to significant investments in teacher salaries, the government undertook major school construction efforts during the last 15 years. School construction aimed to expand the reach of public schools in the regions and decrease reliance on renting of schools from private owners. With these efforts, the government was able to decrease the total number of schools by 7 percent over the period 2001–15 through consolidation of small schools (figure O.18). This is an indication that there are efficiency gains to be made in the system in terms of school distribution.

WHY IS THE SYSTEM NOT REACHING ITS FULL POTENTIAL?

Political economy of education

The education system in Lebanon presents both strong assets and major challenges for the effective and efficient promotion of student learning. It is rooted in a national philosophy, culture, and legislation that extend social services and build on active community dynamics. It is a source of national pride and receives full support from all levels of the societal and political spectrums. Moreover, the diversity in the education provision model can be an asset for the country and can provide a healthy environment for building coalitions, collaboration, and competitiveness to enhance education success. However, the system also has significant challenges related to political instability, consensual decision making, conflict of interest, and organizational efficiency.

The education sector is characterized by many actors, who often have misaligned and contradictory interests impeding the achievement of education outcomes for all children. The absence of objective, precise, and transparent standards, criteria, and procedures in many aspects of education sector management, and the lack of accountability mechanisms for the application of existing standards, criteria, and procedures, leave space for interference by politicians and special interest groups. Processes of patronage politics and rent-seeking interfere with decision-making and divert focus from learning and results. Politicians use the education sector to provide services to their constituents, for example, through the recruitment and deployment of teachers.

Centralization of decision-making power is a salient characteristic of the Lebanese education system. Most of the decisions made by the ministry, including the appointment and transfer of every teacher, must be approved by the minister, even though these decisions are processed by at least four or five layers of the administration. This modus operandi creates an administrative burden in public institutions by increasing the number of transactions in the system, delaying decision making, or even resulting in no decisions being made.

Decision making, planning, and execution processes showed high fragmentation and a lack of coordination between different entities in the system. This is observed in areas such as teacher professional development, the management and use of education data, and the assessment of student learning. The advancement of the education system in Lebanon could have been faster and more effective if a "systems approach" had been used when planning for reforms, along with structured and well-institutionalized processes. The absence of an integrated, aligned, and holistic approach in implementation processes have made it hard to achieve a reasonable consensus, collegial cooperation, and a high sense of drive—all of which are required in a functioning education system.

Public-private partnerships

Education subsidization programs typically aim to decrease inequity in access to a high-quality education. In Lebanon, the government has a system for subsidizing private schools through both school allowances for civil servants and direct

FIGURE O.19

Student composition of each type of school by wealth quintile

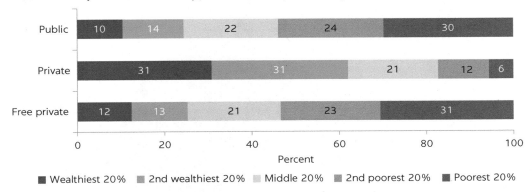

Source: CAS (database), Household-based Survey 2011–2012, Central Administration of Statistics, Beirut, http://www.cas.gov.lb/index.php/demographic-and-social-en/householdexpenditure-en.
Note: Wealth quintiles defined by asset index. The total for each bar is not equal to 100 percent because percentages have been rounded. CAS = Central Administration of Statistics.

subsidies for "free-private" schools—schools that cannot charge tuition above 150 percent of the monthly minimum wage and in return get direct fund transfers from the government for every student enrolled. By examining the student composition of each type of school using data from the Central Administration of Statistics (CAS) 2011–2012 survey[16] (figure O.19), it is revealed that students in public and free-private schools had a similar socioeconomic background. However, even though more than one-fifth of education public expenditures are spent on school allowances for civil servants to enroll their children in paid private schools, these schools had low enrollment from the poorest households—the poorest 40 percent of children constituted only 18 percent of students at private, fee-charging schools. Consequently, the school allowance subsidization program has not been effective in expanding equitable access to the poorest Lebanese.

In fact, the current subsidy system does not properly target the poorest households. On the contrary, an analysis based on CAS 2011–2012 household survey data revealed that the poorest two quintiles (40 percent) received only 16 percent of education allowances provided by the government. Conversely, the wealthiest quintile received nearly half (47 percent) of total education allowances provided by the government (figure O.20). In fact, for the subsidy system to be equitable and focus on learning, it should support the two poorest quintiles.

SUMMING UP THE SYSTEM AND FRAMING THE DRIVERS AND INTERCONNECTIONS

The scope and scale of the system analysis that was done for this volume provided an opportunity to draw a summative framing of the overarching elements of the education system in Lebanon around six macro and intermediate dimensions that constitute the foundations of an education system and form an enabling environment for education service delivery: (a) standards and norms; (b) resources and expertise; (c) delivery of instruction, school and teaching

FIGURE O.20

Distribution of government education allowances by wealth quintile

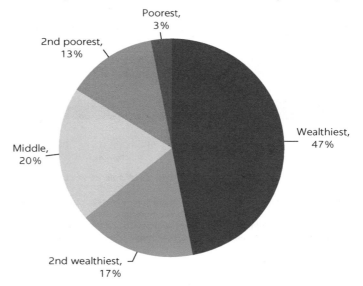

Source: Calculations using CAS (database), Household-based Survey 2011–2012, Central Administration of Statistics, Beirut, http://www.cas.gov.lb/index.php/demographic-and-social-en /householdexpenditure-en.
Note: CAS = Central Administration of Statistics.

services, and school management relationships; (d) governance and leadership; (e) information, evidence, and feedback; and (f) accountability and quality assurance. At the center of the education system, links and connectors across the system represent the enabling functionalities for stronger alignment, connection, and integration. Figure O.21 illustrates the key findings from the system diagnostic methodology, including strengths and weaknesses across the system and between the various elements and levers that comprise the Lebanese education system.

The diagnostic, which was done along the six dimensions of the education system, led to the following:

1. **Standards, vision, and norms:** Overall, there are solid foundations for a renewed functionable and operational strategy in terms of policy framework, culture of choice, expectations and demand for high quality education, and direction for the curriculum. However, the current education system is guided by an old vision, and there is a need for a modernized and strategic focus to move the system forward and achieve growth in human capital. This new strategic focus should methodically tackle the issue of equity at all levels of the system, including in the allocation of education resources.
2. **Resources and expertise:** Generally, investment in inputs is adequate in Lebanon, but requires strengthening in terms of efficiency and efficacy. The current infrastructure is covering the sector needs and has been improving well over time. Budgeting is an issue in all sectors in Lebanon, including education. Human resources have promising capacity but are underutilized and inefficiently managed throughout the system. Data systems have been consuming significant resources but have not yet been properly established.

FIGURE O.21

The Lebanon education system's foundations: Diagnostic results

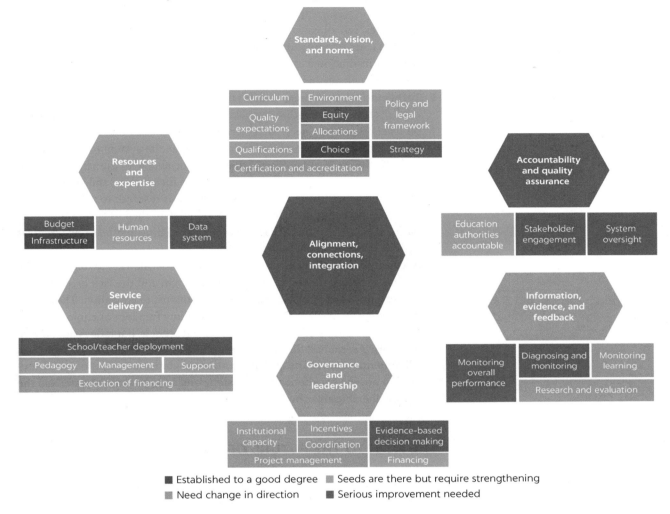

3. **Service delivery, including instruction and management at the school level:** While this area has solid foundations in its promotion of good pedagogy, support services, and strong management at the central and local levels, there is significant space for strengthening the system for better efficiency and higher learning outcomes. Major issues in relation to teacher deployment and ensuring compliance with teaching and working loads persist, and human resources reform is needed to ensure top qualifications, full utilization, and efficient distribution and deployment of teachers and school staffs. Another delivery issue is with the execution of school financing, as the delay in disbursement to schools affects the whole teaching and learning process; one such example is the delay in the procurement of textbooks by schools for all their students.

4. **Governance and leadership:** While there are financing policies and clear budget commitments to the education sector, there is a need to strengthen the institutional capacity, the management of reforms and projects, and the coordination between major players in the education system, especially in critical

areas related to teachers, data, and curriculum. One major weakness of the system is its ability for evidence-based decision making in relation to investment in the sector, especially in matters related to teacher recruitment and incentives, school construction and rehabilitation, and the improvement of teaching and learning methods. Another major area of development is the need for institutional capacity building based on a theory of change, tackling national challenges and the need for sustainable growth.

5. **Information, evidence, and feedback:** The system could benefit from explicit strategies targeting diagnostics and the monitoring of performance at all levels. Strategies need to be accompanied by clear and specific mechanisms for monitoring and evaluation to enable the system to measure and quantify the areas and processes that are associated with the achievement or nonachievement of goals. Also, the support to the teaching and learning process could benefit from evaluation and rigorous research to promote better teaching and end results. Norms need to be established to ensure that feedback loops are institutionalized to improve teaching and learning practices and the management of schools.

6. **Accountability and quality assurance:** This dimension is the weakest in the system, especially in terms of external oversight and the lack of systematic and sustained stakeholder engagement in support of education. The education system in Lebanon is well crafted to allow freedom of choice and the offering of a variety of options to parents and schools, but it does not do well in ensuring accountability and returns on investment in terms of learning.

7. **Alignment, connections, and integration:** Alignment, connections, and integration are the backbone of any system; and in Lebanon, they are also the most vulnerable areas in the education system.

THE PATH TO THE FUTURE OF EDUCATION

Previous studies on the factors that affect education outcomes have focused on measures of school inputs, such as school buildings, pupil-teacher ratios, teacher characteristics, and availability of textbooks and learning materials. However, the capacity of the education system to translate these inputs into education outcomes has not been researched thoroughly. A recent system-level analysis conducted at the global level found that countries with well-tied system policies have, on average, better education outcomes, when controlling for their level of education expenditures and GDP per capita (Newman, King, and Abdul-Hamid 2016). Building on this global evidence and on the R4R program's analysis of system-level parameters, this research uncovers the following reform angles, which should constitute a foundation for dialogue to shape the path to the future of the education sector.

Energizing the ecological layers and the political will to strengthen education

The mandates of the education system in Lebanon are based on the support and actions of multiple actors from the government, political parties, society, and local communities. Hence, the norms that guide an education strategy must be derived from an in-depth understanding of the political economy and the interaction between all those actors. The internal contests of organizations involve not just the micropolitics of individuals and departments but also the social groups, interests, and resources of the surrounding context. As a result, for education reform to succeed in reaching the beneficiaries (i.e., children), there must be consideration for the ecology of the system centered on the child; and thus, to move the system forward, political will for education reform needs to be energized at all levels of the system (e.g., parents, teachers, civil society organizations, municipalities, private schools, universities, employers, politicians).

Strengthening governance, institutionalization, and internal organization

There are several institutional areas that need to be strengthened for the education system in Lebanon to operate more effectively. This analysis of the education system revealed issues around how different education entities interact and coordinate with one another. To this end, the government should update and ensure alignment and coherence among key elements, principles, laws, and regulatory frameworks. Clear standards and norms that are followed by practical steps for execution are essential to support the next phase of education reforms; a review of roles and responsibilities is crucial to foster harmony in the management of the system and the execution of services; and strategic alignment that enables different education entities to operate in a collaborative setting can reinforce and scale up some of the crucial initiatives and innovations that these different entities are achieving.

Finally, the system should create feedback loops and foster a culture of evidence. It is crucial for the success of any reform to ensure a shift from running an operation and focusing on inputs to monitoring and achieving results. Good governance will seek to enact (a) open and accessible communication with the public; (b) active participation by citizens (and not only politicians) as much as possible in policy formation; (c) clear accountability apportioned among all relevant entities; and (d) transparency in the assessment and evaluation of effectiveness in achieving results.

Reducing gaps and inequity within and between schools

Monitoring gaps within and between schools and looking for means to systematically reduce them should be a priority for the government. Given the different types of schools and the different institutional frameworks in Lebanon, it is important to track and reduce inequalities between schools in terms of available resources and activities. In all cases, the monitoring of gaps should be part of a national strategy and should be well communicated to ensure compliance and effectiveness in creating a proper climate for learning in all schools. A critical point for reducing gaps between students is the investment in early years, as it has been proven globally to yield better outcomes for children from all socioeconomic backgrounds with stronger benefits for poorer children. Moreover, strengthening school-level capacity in planning and budgeting to be able to plan for results also supports efforts in reducing gaps between schools.

While the government continues to improve public schools, there also remain significant differences in performance (i.e., student learning) between private schools, including free private schools, which are subsidized by the government.

Hence, the MEHE is not the sole responsible authority for reducing gaps, and there is a need for innovations and better networking and collaboration between individual schools, private schools' associations, and the government.

Evaluating and scaling up innovations servicing schools

Many aspects of the current model of education provision are showing positive results in schools, as reflected in the positive public perception of parents, teachers, and school administrators. In this area, there are several activities that stand out as innovations that would need to be scaled up. To do so, it is important that first these activities are rigorously and scientifically assessed and evaluated for their impact and effectiveness, and that they are planned in a systematic, cost-effective, and institutionalized manner while drawing lessons learned from previous experiences in implementation. Examples of activities that show innovations in the system include pedagogical, psychosocial, and health counseling; school grants for school improvement plans; and accelerated and remedial learning programs.

Strengthening the regulatory framework guiding school performance

Freedom of education provision was not meant to transfer the responsibility of accountability to parents. To improve education in Lebanon, both public and private schools must achieve their best performance within a strong oversight and accountability framework. Competition between schools might lead in general to better quality based on well-defined standards and norms. However, competition alone cannot guarantee good quality. The Ministry of Education, in its interaction with private schools, has so far been focused on administrative compliance for issues such as legal requirements, curriculum standards, examinations and certification, and fair tuition and teacher salary scales. However, the MEHE should have a stronger oversight and regulatory role when it comes to the quality of education and learning outcomes.

Establishing a quality assurance system intended to ensure that services delivered meet agreed-upon standards is thus a necessity. Given the variety of providers and stakeholders in education in Lebanon, there is a need for modern and professionally crafted standards, evidence-based practices, and public policies that specify outcomes and lay out processes to ensure quality implementation. The quality oversight is critical and should consist of measurement, comparison of findings to standards, and feedback to practitioners and authorities for reflection and calibration. The framework for quality standards and oversight should be developed in consultation with all stakeholders and implemented by an oversight body under the umbrella of the ministry. It should be designed with a focus on school improvement, by identifying needs for supporting and providing feedback to schools. It should be providing feedback not only to the central administration but also to schools and all service delivery arms. At the central level, the system should be able to monitor student learning across grade levels and school types to measure the effectiveness of the system in yielding better student learning outcomes. There are many examples of such systems in OECD countries that could serve as a reference. Additionally, some private school associations have introduced such systems to monitor and support their own schools; and lessons learned from their experience can be scaled up to cover the whole system.

Strengthening data systems to track budgets, personnel, and infrastructure

Ensuring the fiscal and financial sustainability of the system is crucial. The education system in Lebanon is overstretched financially and sometimes beyond the capacity of the country's economy. The system is in urgent need of systematic public financial management. Data systems to monitor inputs into the education system could help in providing evidence for policy makers to maximize the use of resources using principles of efficiency, effectiveness, economy, and value for money. Adequate financing keeps the system going and allows for innovations. Some of the key functions and data to be monitored are related to (a) school-level expenditures; (b) school asset management and school maintenance and rehabilitation needs; (c) teaching and learning material procurement, including textbooks; and (d) teacher management and deployment, including the management of teacher working load, the distribution and sharing of teachers between schools, and the recruitment of contractual teachers.

Improving institutional capacity

Improving education outcomes on a substantial scale requires the country to engage in bold, holistic, systematic, and sustainable institutional capacity improvement at the central, regional, and school levels. Capacity building should be comprehensive in scope and should directly address the emerging needs of the system. An assessment of capacity needs and a program for capacity building should cover the following areas: (a) leadership and management, (b) strategy and planning, (c) data and technology, (d) equity, (e) teaching and learning, (f) engaging in strategic partnerships with key external stakeholders, (g) aligning the institutional policies and practices, and (h) strengthening research capacity.

POLICY DIALOGUE AND INSTITUTIONALIZATION OF THE RESEARCH UPTAKE

The principal aim of R4R is to facilitate policy dialogue through the generation of essential evidence on the education system. This volume covers the system-level analysis using a political economy approach, and the forthcoming volume will focus on teaching and learning in schools, as well as education for vulnerable and refugee children. The R4R model of engagement includes a series of discussion panels, seminars, and workshops with multiple stakeholders to share and discuss research evidence and generate policy recommendations for improving the sector. At the institutional level, within the MEHE and the CERD, R4R represents an important shift into high-quality research underpinned by good research governance. The program created a strong platform for investing in longer-term research to guide Lebanon's progress toward the 2030 Sustainable Development Goal (SDG) for Quality Education. However, a 3-year research program is short in the life cycle of education sector reform. The role of the CERD, which is the primary institution mandated to lead education research in the country, should be strengthened to set up a full portfolio of high-quality research and rigorous impact evaluations over the coming decade. The CERD should be supported by a network of public and private stakeholders, who can help in raising funds for educational research, guiding priorities for the research agenda, and reinforcing the policy uptake of research findings. The R4R

Steering Committee served as a good example of such a network and could thus be expanded into a Research Governance Committee with leadership from the CERD and MEHE and membership from both the public and private sectors.

NOTES

1. R4R was governed by a Steering Committee chaired by the Ministry of Education and Higher Education (MEHE) and a Technical Committee chaired by the Center for Educational Research and Development (CERD). The program was executed by the World Bank and was financed by the U.K. Department for International Development (DFID), the United States Agency for International Development (USAID), and the World Bank.
2. Ministry of Finance data, 2016. Total expenditures on the education sector averaged around US$1.2 billion annually: around US$900 million on general education, US$225 million on tertiary education, and US$90 million on technical and vocational education and training (TVET).
3. Calculations based on 2015 tuition data of 955 private schools provided by the MEHE. Private schools are mandated to provide tuition data to the MEHE.
4. Lebanon Public Perception Survey, Research for Results (R4R), World Bank 2016–17, conducted for this report.
5. Harmonized Learning Outcomes Dataset, World Bank, Washington, DC.
6. Education Statistics (EdStats) (database), World Bank, Washington, DC, http://datatopics .worldbank.org/education/country/lebanon. Retrieved in April 2018.
7. Thirty points on the PISA scale are nearly equivalent to 1 year of schooling; which means that students in Lebanon were 3 years of schooling behind students in OECD countries in math, 3.5 years of schooling behind in science, and 5 years of schooling behind in reading.
8. In Lebanon, the reading section was either in English or in French, depending on the language of instruction of the school.
9. As of the date of writing, benchmarks set for reading fluency were still preliminary, and thus figures might be subject to change.
10. Education Statistics (EdStats) (database), World Bank, Washington, DC, http://datatopics .worldbank.org/education/country/lebanon. Retrieved in April 2018.
11. QITABI 2017, financed by USAID.
12. According to the "CERD Statistical Bulletin 2016–2017" (CERD 2017), the passing rate for public school students who failed the first round of the grade 9 national examination and who attempted the second round was only 18.6 percent at the second round.
13. The split of science students between life sciences and general sciences was the same across both the public sector and the private sector, with the ratio of life sciences students to general sciences students being 7–3 in both sectors.
14. Inflation rates are estimations from the World Bank.
15. OECD 2015; working hours for Lebanon were calculated by the author using the CERD statistical yearbooks, Beirut, https://www.crdp.org/statistics?la=en.
16. CAS (database), Household-based Survey 2011–2012, Central Administration of Statistics, Beirut, http://www.cas.gov.lb/index.php/demographic-and-social-en/household expenditure-en.

REFERENCES

Altinok, N., N. Angrist, and H. A. Patrinos. 2018. "Global Data Set on Education Quality (1965–2015)." Policy Research Working Paper 8314, World Bank, Washington, DC. https:// openknowledge.worldbank.org/handle/10986/29281.

CERD (Center for Educational Research and Development). 2017. "CERD Statistical Bulletin 2016–2017" (in Arabic). CERD, Beirut. https://www.crdp.org/files/201712220733131.pdf (accessed May 2018).

———. 2018a. "PISA 2015 National Report. Program for International Student Assessment." CERD, Beirut. https://www.crdp.org/pdf/uploads/PISA_Report_18-1.pdf.

———. 2018b. "TIMSS 2015 – Grade 8 National Report. Program for International Student Assessment." CERD, Beirut. https://www.crdp.org/files/201811210625183.pdf.

Gallup. 2015. "Satisfaction With K-12 Education." World Poll 2015. https://wpr.gallup.com/.

LocaLiban (Centre de ressources sur le développement local au Liban). 2015. "Private Schools in Lebanon: Religiously Affiliated Schools in Lebanon." November 27. https://www.localiban.org/article5190.html (accessed April 8, 2018).

Newman, J. L., E. M. King, and H. Abdul-Hamid. 2016. "The Quality of Education Systems and Education Outcomes." Background Paper, *The Learning Generation: Investing in Education for a Changing World,* International Commission on Financing Global Education Opportunity, New York.

OECD (Organisation for Economic Co-operation and Development). 2015. *Education at a Glance 2015: OECD Indicators. Paris:* OECD Publishing.

———. 2018. "PISA 2015 Results in Focus." PISA in Focus 67, OECD Publishing, Paris. https://www.oecd.org/pisa/pisa-2015-results-in-focus.pdf.

———. 2019a. Public spending on education (indicator), database, OECD, Paris. https://data.oecd.org/eduresource/public-spending-on-education.htm.

———. 2019b. Private spending on education (indicator), database, OECD, Paris. https://data.oecd.org/eduresource/private-spending-on-education.htm.

QITABI (Quality Instruction towards Access and Basic Education Improvement). 2017. "EGRA Combined Baseline Report." Unpublished Paper, QITABI, Beirut.

World Bank. 2016. "Lebanon—Program for International Student Assessment 2015 (English)." PISA Education Brief. World Bank, Washington, DC. http://documents.worldbank.org/curated/en/301971483073044618/Lebanon-Program-for-international-student-assessment-2015.

———. 2018. "Key Messages from PISA for Middle East and North Africa." Unpublished Paper, World Bank, Washington, DC.

1 Background, Methodology, Research, and Evidence

MAIN MESSAGES

1. This volume surveys and assesses the foundations of the education system in Lebanon using a political economy approach. The areas covered in this chapter include the Research for Results (R4R) program, the methodology for the research, and a review of the education literature that has been produced so far in Lebanon.

2. The system-level analysis presented in this volume uses a mixed-method approach. Qualitative and quantitative analyses were conducted based on a review and analysis of more than 1,900 research papers/articles/books, laws and policies, expenditures, and enrollment and outcomes indicators data. In addition to this, rigorous primary data collection was conducted using tools such as focus groups, interviews, and opinion and perception surveys. All data collection and research were done in a structured manner while complying with strict standard operating procedures.

3. The purpose of this research is to support Lebanon to engage in evidence-informed decision making and to institutionalize this type of research for future policy decisions in the education sector. The program aimed to generate new evidence on the education system structure, successes and challenges, and student and teacher performance across school types to create policy recommendations meant to strengthen the efficiency and quality of education services by public and nonstate providers.

4. The R4R program is an umbrella to foster this type of research. While universities and other institutions are covering quite a few areas of education research in their work, there are still areas which are relevant and critical for education service delivery that need to be tackled. These areas of study would greatly benefit from having the Ministry of Education and Higher Education (MEHE) and the Center for Educational Research and Development (CERD) play a more active role in driving and steering education research in the country. Hence, it is important for the MEHE—and particularly the CERD, which has a mandate for education research delivery—to take up more ownership of designing and

institutionalizing a robust research process while building partnerships with universities and research institutions. This approach is expected to align actors and build coalitions around a structured and systematic mechanism for improving education research and service delivery in Lebanon.

5. The governance of the research program was led by the MEHE and the CERD with support from two committees—the Steering Committee and the Technical Committee. The Steering Committee, chaired by the MEHE, endorsed the work plan, including activities, and reviewed research results; the Technical Committee, chaired by the CERD, provided technical advice on the research activities at all stages to ensure that the research undertaken under this program was conducted in a technically and ethically sound manner.

6. The comprehensive literature review conducted under R4R revealed that the education research output in Lebanon nearly doubled from 2000–15, mainly driven by the large contribution of university graduate students through master's theses and doctoral dissertations. While a large variety of themes were covered, there was scarcity in the use of certain methodological elements, such as random representative sampling, measurement using tools with good psychometric properties, the use of control groups and random assignment in experimental studies, control for confounding variables, and the use of rigorous protocols and evaluation criteria in qualitative research methods. Furthermore, few studies have samples on a national scale, thus limiting the benefit of generalizable findings for policy making at the national level.

7. Under R4R, a full bibliography was developed with a list of 1,906 research pieces, including abstracts, keywords, and links to the publications when available. The list is accessible to the public on the CERD website and is an attempt for strengthening documentation of education research in the country and for fostering future research.

8. Although considerable research has been done on a variety of topics, further insights are needed to better understand the educational landscape and to inform future policy reform. Lebanon has made great strides in this area, but the research agenda needs to be followed rigorously and incorporated in every area of decision making to come up with data-driven policies which are more grounded in evidence and allow for realistic, effective, and efficient policy decisions.

INTRODUCTION

This volume uses a political economy approach to study the drivers and factors that guide education operations to produce and utilize education outcomes. This includes the study of context, stakeholders, and processes that shape education policies, institutions, and activities. It also aims to identify enablers and constraints for policy change, policy implementation, and results achievement. In this context, the analysis encompasses how education policies are developed; how education consumables—such as curricula, textbooks, and learning materials—are produced, distributed, and used by learners; how education services are delivered and monitored; and how achieved results are measured in terms of fulfilling learners' and society's needs and aspirations. It includes the identification of the most influential actors in the education arena, as well as their vested interests. It also examines unfavorable frameworks of action that are likely to block the adoption of reforms and delay or derail their implementation through missteps at various levels of the implementation processes, thus undermining efforts to deliver education services in an equitable, efficient, and effective manner.

This volume covers the macro and the intermediate dimensions of the system in terms of policies and structures that constitute the foundations of an education system and form an enabling environment for education service delivery: (1) standards and norms; (2) resources and expertise; (3) delivery of instruction, school and teaching services, and school management relationships; (4) governance and leadership; (5) information, evidence, and feedback; and (6) accountability and quality assurance; in addition to the connections, alignment, and integration that enable the functionalities of the system across all dimensions (figure 1.1).

FIGURE 1.1
Framework for system diagnostic

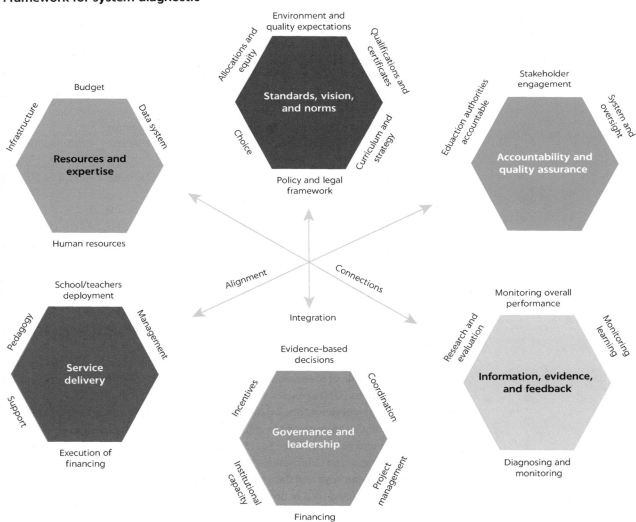

METHODOLOGY

The research presented in this volume used a mixed-method approach: qualitative and quantitative analyses were conducted based on primary and secondary data sources.

Sources of information

Information was collected using literature reviews, focus groups and interviews, opinion surveys, and data analysis of primary and secondary sources. All data collection and research were done in a rigorous manner while complying with strict standard operating procedures.

1. **Literature review:** The research started with a thorough literature review of education research that has been conducted in Lebanon since 2000. The comprehensive review and analysis included more than 1,900 research papers, articles, books, trends, expenditures, enrollment and outcomes data, and laws and policies.
2. **Focus groups and interviews:** The research included focus groups with different education stakeholders, along with structured interviews with government officials (current and former) at different stages of the research, including initiation, execution, and reflection on initial findings. The initial focus groups consisted of 12 stakeholder groups and were conducted in January 2016, followed by a series of semistructured interviews conducted between September 19, 2016, and March 3, 2017. A total of 44 interviews with 65 individuals were conducted, including the:
   - Former Ministers of Education and Higher Education;
   - The President and Secretary of the Parliamentary Commission for Education and Culture;
   - The Director General of Education and the Director General of Higher Education at MEHE;
   - The President of the CERD and former CERD presidents;
   - Present and former staff in key positions at the MEHE and the CERD;
   - A sample of experts and personnel from various bodies who were involved in previous or present reforms;
   - A sample of prominent stakeholders from private education establishments;
   - A sample of members of teachers' unions and associations;
   - A sample of school principals who were involved in previous or present reforms;
   - A sample of local community members engaged in the education sector; and
   - A sample of professionals and experts from the donor community, United Nations (UN) agencies, and civil society organizations (CSOs).

   The interviews focused on (1) the constitutional foundations; (2) the government's commitment to reform; (3) steps undertaken for sector development and achievements; (4) factors affecting sector reform; and (5) events, challenges, and externalities affecting the sector.
3. **Opinion surveys and data analysis:** A public perception survey was designed and conducted on a nationally representative sample of 1,500 households. In addition to primary data sources, secondary data sources—such as enrollment data, expenditure data, and learning outcomes data from national and international assessments—were compiled and analyzed within the scope of the study.

Research teams

The World Bank team conducted the initial focus group interviews, the review of expenditures, and the compilation and analysis of major secondary data sources. Other data collection was conducted by firms that were procured using a rigorous international competitive bidding process, following the World Bank's standard procurement procedures. The Lebanese Association for Educational Studies (LAES) conducted the education literature review under the leadership of Dr. Adnan El Amine; and the Consultation and Research Institute (CRI) conducted the public perception study. Political economy interviews were mainly conducted by Dr. Ramzi Salame, of Saint Joseph University and a member of LAES, while the last round of interviews with key stakeholders was completed by the World Bank's R4R research team.

Research protocol

The research followed the protocol defined in the R4R operations manual and was in accordance with the MEHE's and CERD's guidelines. A set of guiding principles and ethical standards was established to serve education researchers' professional responsibilities and conduct while working on the R4R program. The guiding principles included professional competence, integrity, respect for people's rights, dignity, diversity, and social responsibility. The ethical standards included informed consent, confidentiality, data sharing and anonymity of information, conflict of interest, and authorship and quality standards.

The terms of reference for each of the studies were reviewed, discussed, and approved by the R4R's Steering and Technical Committees. Outputs were also reviewed and discussed by members of the two committees. Two rounds of reviews for each of the studies were conducted to ensure that the highest quality standards were met.

THE R4R PROGRAM

The R4R program was launched in 2016 in response to a request from the MEHE to the World Bank identifying the need for evidence-based policy recommendations to strengthen the efficiency and quality of education services by public, private, and free-private providers. The request from the MEHE was met with great interest from the U.K. Department for International Development (DFID) and from the U.S. Agency for International Development (USAID) to provide generous funding to carry out the research program. The program intended to analyze system challenges in governance, service delivery, accountability, standards, and information management resources. The research program included system-level analysis and stakeholder outreach to create and share new information about education services for uptake by policy makers and system stakeholders. The primary objective was to generate new evidence on student and teacher performance across school types and to create policy recommendations to strengthen the efficiency and quality of education services by public, private, and nonstate providers. This research program was intended to contribute to decision making in the education sector for years to come, and to look at both service delivery in schools and system-wide dynamics.

The "Systems Analysis and Communications" arm covered the political economy of education policy reform, system governance analysis, and impact and communications activities for policy uptake. These activities included the development of an overall communication and outreach impact plan for the research program and the assessment of the current education status in Lebanon using system analysis and perception surveys. The proposed activities covering the "Service Delivery" arm included classroom observation, student learning assessments, school management and learning environment surveys, and parent and teacher surveys. The R4R team consulted with teacher unions, education nongovernmental organizations (NGOs), parent associations, and other stakeholders to gather input and engage in research activities to inform the education reform agenda.

To ensure good governance of the research program, the process was led by the MEHE and the CERD with support from two committees: the Steering Committee and the Technical Committee. The Steering Committee included the Director General of General Education (Chair), the Director General of Higher Education, the President of CERD, the Dean of the Faculty of Education at the Lebanese University, the World Bank, DFID, USAID, and a minister-appointed representative of private universities. The Technical Committee was chaired by the CERD and included one member representing the MEHE, one faculty of education member of a public university, one faculty of education member of a private university, two representatives from the private school system, a research community member, and the World Bank. The Steering Committee endorsed the work plan—including the studies, the activities, and the timetable—and reviewed research results, whereas the Technical Committee provided technical advice on the research activities at all stages and guidance to ensure that the research undertaken for this program was conducted in a technically and ethically sound manner.

BUILDING ON PREVIOUS EDUCATION RESEARCH IN LEBANON

There has been considerable progress in terms of education research conducted and published over the past few years in Lebanon. The education research output nearly doubled from 2000–15. The R4R literature review recorded 151 education research pieces produced in 2015, compared with 76 in 2000. This steady increase has been mainly driven by a large contribution from university graduate students producing master's theses and doctoral dissertations. These constituted approximately two-thirds of research products in education in Lebanon, while journal articles were less than 6 percent of research outputs. The Lebanese University, the American University of Beirut (AUB), the Lebanese American University (LAU), and the Saint Joseph University (USJ) have been among the largest producers of education research. In addition to universities, a few local NGOs and CSOs have also conducted research on specific education topics related to public interest.

Since 2000, it is estimated that more than 2,000 research pieces covering education topics have been published, including studies by the MEHE and the CERD, scholarly papers, academic books, doctoral dissertations, and master's theses at various universities, and papers and reports published by local associations or international organizations.

Nearly half of the education publications since 2000 have been in Arabic, 37 percent in English, and 13 percent in French. However, the share of publications written in English and French has been steadily increasing, while publication output in Arabic has been relatively constant across the years. Since 2011, the number of publications in English has reached and slightly surpassed the number of Arabic publications.

What has been covered in research?

The research studies undertaken so far have identified several challenges for education policy and practices in Lebanon in relation to the political system and its effect on education decisions. Table 1.1 shows which education themes or topics were the most or least common in education research in Lebanon.

While a large variety of themes were covered by the education research in Lebanon, there was scarcity in the use of certain methodological approaches. For example, many elements that are essential for high-quality empirical quantitative research, such as random representative sampling and measurement using tools with good psychometric properties, were rarely used. Experimental studies sometimes did not include a control group, and in other times, there was no random assignment of participants or researchers failed to control for confounding variables. When qualitative research methods were used, researchers rarely followed specific and rigorous protocols, norms, and criteria for evaluating data. This was partly due to the low share of peer-reviewed journal papers in the Lebanese education research output and the reliance of the Lebanese research community on student theses completed within the scope of a degree program or course. Furthermore, while the use of case studies was common, there were few studies that had a sample at a national scale, thus limiting the benefit of generalizable findings for policy making at the national level. In addition to the challenges related to research methodology, the literature review identified a need for strengthening research documentation practices in the country, including the use and update of online databases by universities and the CERD, and the standardization of abstract writing and use of keywords. Under R4R, a full bibliography was developed with a list of 1,906 research pieces, including abstracts, keywords, and links to the publications when available. The list was made accessible to the public on the CERD website and thus constituted a first attempt for strengthening documentation of education research in-country and for fostering future research.

The rest of the chapter includes a survey of main findings for major themes of education research in Lebanon while also noting some of the limitations in methodology and scope. The references for all themes surveyed in the annotated bibliography under the R4R program are listed in appendix A.

TABLE 1.1 **Most and least common education research themes in Lebanon**

MOST COMMON EDUCATION RESEARCH THEMES OR TOPICS	LEAST COMMON EDUCATION RESEARCH THEMES OR TOPICS
• Curricula and textbooks	• Access and equity in education
• Teaching methods	• Refugee/vulnerable children education
• Science and math education	• Social sciences education
• English language education	• Humanities education
• Learning difficulties	• Arts and sports education
• Teachers' preparation and training	• Teachers' work conditions/incentives
• School management	• History and systems of education
• Information and communication technology (ICT) in education	• Socioeconomic and political aspects of education

Source: Based on Lebanon Education Literature Review (unpublished) conducted for this report.

Literature review

Education policy

- Most research on education policy in Lebanon has been descriptive and historical as compared to empirical studies. They are largely focused on the Lebanese education policy, with very few papers looking at the topic from a comparative lens with other countries.
- Main findings on the topic were centered around the role of the sectarian and political system in Lebanon in defining education policy and the need for political solutions first and foremost for comprehensive education policy to succeed.
- The literature pointed to the lack of evidence showing success of one of the objectives set forth in the 1994 education plan, which is to build a sense of national identity. Recommendations from researchers included the need for a stronger focus on specific subject areas, such as Arabic language, history, civics, and teaching about religions in an inclusive manner.
- Researchers advocated for more decentralization in the decision-making processes at the Ministry of Education and for strengthening the CERD's role in delivering research and policy recommendations.

Curriculum

- Research on curriculum in Lebanon highlighted the importance of a participatory approach to curricula reform. Studies documented the need for engaging school-level actors, mainly school principals and teachers, in the design and implementation processes of curricula reform.
- The literature emphasized the need for shifting the curricula design process from an approach based on separate subject matters to an interdisciplinary framework. Knowledge integration across subjects was one of the main recommendations of research on curriculum.
- Some studies explored the need for integrating into the Lebanese curriculum relevant topics such as financial and economic skills, the role of women in society, health education, and environmental education.
- For citizen education, the literature emphasized embedding and blending a series of knowledge, values, and skills across all subject matters within the national curriculum.

Student achievement and learning

- Most studies on student achievement, specifically for sciences, were conducted at the intermediate or secondary level. The need for more research on student learning in early grades and in primary schools is evident.
- Studies explored how different instructional methods affected student learning. One of the findings included a positive correlation between the use of concept mapping and students' cognitive skills and achievement. The research showed that a demonstration-based approach seemed to improve students' achievement more than a lecture-based approach to teaching.
- It is important to note, however, that research on the topic of student learning in Lebanon had several methodology limitations, including nonrepresentative sampling, which limits generalizability; the researcher being the teacher implementing the intervention, which introduces researcher bias; little time assigned for the intervention (in many cases less than 4 months), which limits the ability to measure improvement in student learning; and a lack of evidence for the validity and reliability of the assessment instruments.

Arabic language teaching

- For teaching Arabic, studies emphasized the need for collaboration between the school, teachers, and parents to improve students' learning of the Arabic language. Additionally, cooperation among learners appeared to enrich their skills in formal Arabic.
- An area of recommendation from the literature was to focus on improving the content of Arabic texts used for instruction and ensuring their relevance to students' lives.
- More research is needed in the areas of improving parents' and learners' perception of the Arabic language and its importance.
- At the macro level, research recommended a holistic linguistic strategy for the state to improve Arabic language teaching, in addition to the establishment of benchmarks for assessing Arabic language ability.

Information and communication technology in education

- The majority of information and communication technology (ICT) in education research in Lebanon has been focused on the teaching of sciences. Many followed quasi-experimental designs with a treatment and a control group.
- Studies found positive effects on student engagement and student learning when ICT was introduced with a change in teaching methods toward greater active participation of students in the classroom.
- Teachers appeared to show interest in training on technology. It seemed that the more teachers had skills in technology, the more they wanted to apply these skills in their teaching. It also appeared that classroom management was positively affected when teachers used technology in their teaching.
- Research also surveyed perceptions of ICT among school administrators, teachers, parents, and learners, with a majority of stakeholders holding favorable views toward using ICT in the classroom.
- There is need for more research at the macro level of education policy to understand how best to design and implement policies of ICT integration.

Teachers' classroom practices

- There were many limitations in methodology used by researchers when looking at what happens inside the classroom. Most publications used quantitative methods; however, there was little evidence on how the instruments used to collect data were constructed, with measures of validity and reliability for these tools being completely absent. When qualitative methods were used, there was no clear protocol nor norms or criteria for evaluating data.
- Most studies focused on the classroom management skills of teachers, with fewer studies looking at the emotional support role that teachers play or at specific instructional and pedagogical skills, such as fostering analysis and inquiry or providing feedback to learners.
- Teachers in Lebanon appeared to require support to improve their skills in creating a positive classroom atmosphere, establishing classroom norms and routines, redirecting student misbehavior, and improving student-teacher interactions.
- Teachers with higher self-efficacy had students with increased motivation, stronger social skills, and better learning outcomes.
- Most of the studies were teacher-centric, and thus there is need for more studies to look at the topic from the students' perspective.

Additionally, more research is needed to study the links between classroom practices and other factors, such as socioeconomic variables, teacher background, and school climate, among others.

Teachers' preparation, recruitment, and in-service training

- With regard to teacher preparation, comparative studies identified gaps in teacher preparation programs in Lebanon compared with international benchmarks. There also seemed to be a misalignment in theoretical frameworks, professional practices and ethics, and scope of programs between different institutions providing teacher preservice training in Lebanon. Additionally, research indicated that there seemed to be a weak connection between current teacher preparation programs and what was expected from them to deliver in schools.
- While several studies focused on teachers' preparation in Lebanese universities by analyzing the content and organization of programs and the eligibility criteria for admission and successful completion, a limited number appeared to focus on understanding the attitudes of teachers, students, and supervisors toward these programs.
- The literature recommended that a standardization of teacher preparation programs be completed, along with the establishment of a quality assurance system for higher education institutions. Furthermore, the legal framework on teacher recruitment would need to be strengthened to limit recruitment of teachers to holders of teacher certification degrees from accredited higher education institutions.
- The issue of contractual teachers was raised in the literature as having a negative effect on the education system. Sectarian and political considerations, as opposed to competence, were credited for the recruitment of many contractual teachers. As a result, these teachers had not received sufficient preparation in the teaching profession and also have fewer incentives and opportunities for professional development.
- With regard to in-service training, teachers trained in methods to cope with the uncertainties and challenges arising in a classroom appeared to be more effective in adopting diverse strategies for ensuring a positive classroom environment, stronger student-teacher interactions, and improved classroom management techniques. Moreover, coaching and mentoring seemed to support teachers' performance and their levels of satisfaction.
- It appeared from the literature that the quality of training materials and resources available to teachers, as well as the incentive structure for professional development, could be improved for teacher training to be more effective.

School management and education administration

- Research on this topic focused largely on educational leadership and the practices of school principals. The topic was frequently addressed from the micro level rather than a macro level, and it was rare for researchers to study how school administration was affected by regional or central education policy making.
- The literature documented the need for setting and complying with specific criteria for assigning school principals of public schools. It also suggested that preservice and in-service training was effective in improving school leaders'

skills in planning, management, and fostering teacher professional development.

- Using case studies, the literature generally indicated that several school principals in Lebanon followed a democratic approach to school management by including school staff and other stakeholders in the administration of the school.

Institutional assessment and evaluation

- There is growing interest from public and private schools' stakeholders in assessment at all levels of the education system, from student learning assessment, to teachers' assessment, and to assessment of the education system as a whole.
- On student assessments, the literature highlighted the need for a revision of official examinations and assessment methods to ensure alignment with competency-based curricular objectives and with international benchmarks.
- It appeared that periodic and ongoing follow-up on school assessments—with the participation of various education stakeholders and a focus on diagnostic and formative, rather than high-stakes, assessments—was more effective in improving school performance and outcomes.
- Research also emphasized the importance of self-assessment by establishing adequate standards for the institution or by adopting international standards. Self-assessment helped institutions in understanding the gold standards that they needed to achieve and to incorporate the needs identified in the development and improvement process.
- Findings on institutional assessment highlighted that the longer teachers have been in the education system, the more value they attribute to institutional evaluation. However, it appeared that teachers had a different understanding of institutional evaluation than school administrators. A recommendation from the literature was to revise teacher preparation programs to ensure that assessment concepts are an integral part of those programs.

Parents' engagement with schools

- The research found that parents in Lebanon were generally engaged in the scholastic lives of their children, monitoring closely their academic progress and achievement. The only area where studies found parents to be relatively disengaged was sexual education.
- Parents' engagement seemed to be greater in private education than in public schools. It was also higher in some subject areas to which they attributed higher importance such as math and English language. Parents with younger children and children with special needs were more engaged in their children's scholastic lives compared to other parents.
- Parents' engagement in schools had a positive impact on the relationship between parents and children when it was based on increased communication and interaction. However, this engagement had no impact in the case of directly assisting the children in completing their homework or in the case of providing private lessons to children.
- The establishment of parents' associations at schools was not sufficient to strengthen parents' engagement. Additionally, many school-parent

interactions were led by schools lecturing parents on school requirements rather than collecting feedback from parents and requesting active participation.

Although considerable research has been done on a variety of topics, further insights are needed to better understand the educational landscape and to inform future policy reform. Lebanon has made great strides in this area, but the research agenda needs to be followed rigorously and incorporated in every area of decision making to come up with data-driven policies which are more grounded in evidence and allow for realistic, effective, and efficient policy decisions.

2 A Historical Perspective on Education in Lebanon

MAIN MESSAGES

1. The education sector has been shaped by multiple episodes and events that marked Lebanon's history. The main historical milestones that defined the sector included the drafting of the Constitution in 1926, the postindependence reforms from 1943–75, the post–civil war reconstruction efforts, and the recent Syrian refugee crisis from 2012.

2. The foundational provision for education was set in the 1926 Constitution, where Article 10 put emphasis on the freedom of education service providers, most notably on the right of religious institutions and communities to establish their own schools. This emphasis reflected the strong presence of the private sector led by religious institutions and foreign missionaries before Lebanon's independence. It also protected the private sector and allowed its development and expansion. As a result, as of 2018, private schools provided education services to 71 percent of all Lebanese students, compared with 29 percent for public schools. Moreover, for Lebanese students, enrollment trends in the past 15 years showed a steady increase in the share of private schools at the expense of public schools.

3. The 1926 Constitution also defined the relationship between the private education sector and the Lebanese state by enshrining the state's role in regulating education in both public and private schools. However, further legislation and government decrees did not establish a comprehensive and detailed monitoring and regulation framework for the private sector. Furthermore, Lebanon, since before independence, has allowed the use of foreign curricula and foreign languages of instruction in both public and private schools, and in 1950, the government started subsidizing a segment of private schools, mainly those affiliated with religious institutions.

4. The postindependence period witnessed the setup of the organizational and management structure of the education sector, with the establishment of the Directorate General of Education (DGE) in 1953 and the CERD in 1971. Much of the legislation and many of the decrees governing the bureaucracy and management of the sector were passed in 1959 and are still unchanged in the present day.

5. After a 15-year destructive sectarian civil war, the Taef reconciliation agreement sought to leverage education as a medium for building a unified national identity and social cohesion among all Lebanese citizens. The 1994 Plan for Education Reform and the 1997 curriculum, developed in line with the aspirations of the Taef agreement, are still in effect in the present day.

6. The 1997 curriculum aimed at building a national identity, improving children's sense of belonging to the Lebanese nation, and modernizing the objectives and content of the curriculum to be aligned with the development needs of the country. On the first objective, while the goal of unifying the civics textbook was reached, the unification of the history textbook was not accomplished and remains to date a suspended issue. On the second objective, the curriculum sought to align curricular objectives with the country's labor market needs by introducing four different tracks in secondary education leading into tertiary education. However, there have been no major updates in the curriculum for more than 22 years, despite tremendous changes in the labor market and in the country's economic development needs.

7. The beginning of the 21st century was marked with attempts at sector-wide reforms; however, the politically unstable period that followed the assassination of the former prime minister in 2005 and the Syrian refugee crisis that started in 2012 introduced serious difficulty for achieving long-term sector development reforms. Nevertheless, one of the main achievements was the expansion of free and compulsory education to cover the entire basic education period (nine years of schooling) and the expansion of public provision of early childhood education to three years starting at age three.

8. The Syrian refugee crisis had a significant effect on the public education sector, since, as of 2018, the number of non-Lebanese students nearly reached the number of Lebanese students in public schools. The expansion of formal education to Syrian refugees was made possible through the establishment of second shifts in public schools, where 70 percent of non-Lebanese students were enrolled in 2018.

9. The MEHE was cognizant of the specific academic, psychological, social, and emotional needs of refugee children and has initiated many innovations in the sector to support their integration into formal schooling and recognize their education achievements. Some of these innovations included the deployment of psychosocial and health counselors to schools and the development of non-formal education (NFE) programs, including accelerated programs, to support out-of-school children in acquiring necessary skills and help them transition into formal schooling. These innovations, while introduced initially as part of the response to the Syrian refugee crisis, could have great benefits for the whole system, especially in the areas of educational equity, inclusive education, and socioemotional learning.

10. With the Syrian crisis becoming a protracted crisis, the MEHE sought to combine its humanitarian response with a longer-term vision and plan for sector development. It was essential that the humanitarian activities for supporting Syrian refugees did not overshadow the necessity of sector-wide reforms that would benefit both Lebanese and non-Lebanese children. Within this scope, the MEHE initiated in 2018 the development of its Education 2030 Plan, which would support Lebanon in reaching the Sustainable Development Goals (SDGs) and meeting the aspirations of the Lebanese people.

INTRODUCTION

The Lebanese education sector has been shaped and directed by the multiple milestones and events that have marked Lebanon's history, starting with the adoption of the Constitution in 1926 and continuing until the present day. This rich history included a series of complex geopolitical and socioeconomic events, such as the French mandate, the country's independence and postindependence reforms, the Palestinian refugees' influxes in 1948 and 1967, a 15-year civil war, post–civil war reconstruction efforts, the political instability following the assassination of a prominent former prime minister, and the recent Syrian refugee crisis. Table 2.1 draws on the main historical milestones in Lebanon and identifies major reform attempts that have characterized the education sector.

THE CONSTITUTION: SETTING THE FREEDOM OF PRIVATE EDUCATION PROVIDERS

The foundational provision concerned with the delivery of education services was set in Article 10 of the 1926 Constitution, which was drafted during the French mandate. The article puts an emphasis on the freedom of education service providers, most notably on the right of religious institutions and communities to establish their own schools. The article also highlights the role of the state in regulating education service delivery in both public and private schools:

> *Education shall be free insofar as it is not contrary to public order and morals and does not affect the dignity of any of the religions or sects. There shall be no violation of the right of religious communities to have their own schools provided they follow the general rules issued by the state regulating public instruction.* Article 10, Lebanese Constitution, 1926.

This emphasis in Article 10 reflected the status of education before Lebanese independence, with a strong presence of the private sector led by religious institutions and foreign missionaries. The Constitution drafted under the French mandate protected the private sector and allowed its development and expansion. As a result, and despite significant expansion of the public education sector since independence in 1943 (figure 2.1), the private sector in Lebanon still

TABLE 2.1 **Timeline of historical milestones and reform attempts of general education in Lebanon**

DATES	REFORM ATTEMPTS	HISTORICAL MILESTONE
1926	The Constitution	French mandate
1943–75	Postindependence reforms establishing the DGE and the CERD	Postindependence
1989	Provision of the Taef Agreement	Post–civil war reconstruction efforts
1994	Plan for Education Reform in Lebanon	
1997	Curriculum reform	
2003	Education for All (EFA) Plan of Action	Contemporary sector development reforms
2010	Education Sector Development Plan (ESDP)	
2014	Reaching all Children with Education (RACE)	Response to the Syrian refugee crisis
2016	Reaching all Children with Education 2 (RACE 2)	

Source: Based on Lebanon Political Economy Study (unpublished) conducted for this report.
Note: CERD = Center for Educational Research and Development; DGE = Directorate General of Education.

dominates education service delivery in terms of number of schools and number of students. While most of the private sector is financed through tuition paid by households, there is a segment of the private sector, mainly affiliated with religious institutions, which since 1950 has been subsidized by the government. These schools are known as "free private schools" as they use subsidies from the government to dramatically reduce tuition paid by parents.

Private schools, in 2018, provided education services to 71 percent of all Lebanese students (57 percent in paid schools and 14 percent in free private schools), whereas public schools served 29 percent of all Lebanese students (figure 2.2). Moreover, for Lebanese students, enrollment trends in the past 15 years have shown a steady increase in the share of private schools at the expense of public schools (figure 2.3).

The largest networks of private schools are religiously affiliated. In 2015, an estimated 41 percent of all private schools were officially affiliated with religious establishments. They enrolled 58 percent of private school students (both paid and subsidized) and 34 percent of all students in Lebanon (LocaLiban 2015).

FIGURE 2.1

Number of private and public schools, 1943–2018

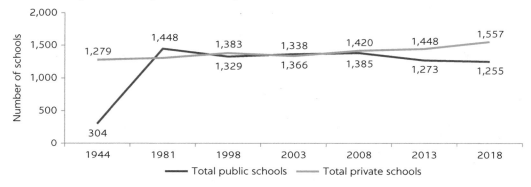

Sources: Data for 1944, 1981, and 1998 based on Kobeissi 2012; data for 2003 and later years based on CERD statistical yearbooks, Beirut, https://www.crdp.org/statistics?la=en.
Note: The number of total private schools between 1944–98 is estimated. CERD = Center for Educational Research and Development.

FIGURE 2.2

Distribution of Lebanese students by education sector, 2018

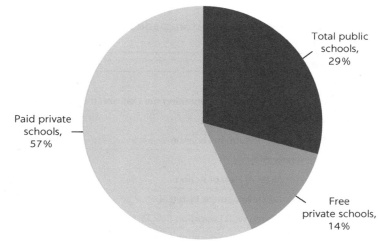

Source: CERD statistical yearbook 2017–18, Beirut, https://www.crdp.org/files/201908271242061.pdf (retrieved April 8, 2018).
Note: CERD = Center for Educational Research and Development.

Since before independence, Lebanon allowed the use of foreign curricula and foreign languages of instruction in both public and private schools. The French mandate introduced the French Baccalaureate as a secondary school examination, which until the present day is equivalent to and can thus substitute for the Lebanese Baccalaureate. The French mandate also instilled French as a language of instruction in schools (Ghait and Shabaan 1996), in line with declaring French as an official language in Article 11 of the 1926 Constitution. While Article 11 was amended by a constitutional law after independence in November 1943 (Lebanese Constitution 1995), the effect on the policy of language of instruction is still present to date. Foreign languages (French and English) are used by both public and private schools as languages of instruction, especially for scientific subjects (biology, chemistry, physics) and math. Box 2.1 takes a deeper look at the foreign language and foreign curriculum policy of the country.

FIGURE 2.3

Number of Lebanese students by education sector

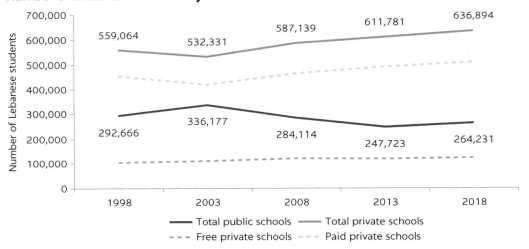

Sources: CERD statistical yearbooks, Beirut, https://www.crdp.org/statistics?la=en.
Note: Number of Lebanese students for 1998 and 2003 were estimated from the total number of students in those years based on the distribution of Lebanese and non-Lebanese students in 2005.
CERD = Center for Educational Research and Development.

BOX 2.1

Foreign curriculum and foreign language policy in Lebanon

The history of foreign curriculum and language of instruction policy dates back from the 17th century with the influx of foreign missionaries and their opening of schools across the country (Bacha and Bahous 2011). The French, the British, the Americans, and others were active during the Ottoman period in opening private schools and forging bonds with local communities. With the French mandate starting after World War I, the French curriculum and language for instruction became dominant, and the Constitution of 1926 has set French as an official language in the country and as a language of instruction in schools (Shaaban and Gaith 1999). English, as a language of

continued

Box 2.1, *continued*

instruction, started to gain prominence in the 1970s with the rise of the language as a global means for communication.

Language of Instruction Policy

The current Lebanese curriculum, approved in 1997 based on the 1994 Plan for Education Reform in Lebanon, gives an equal number of hours of instruction (6 hours per week) to the Arabic language and one foreign language (French or English). A second foreign language ought to be taught in schools, with 2 hours per week dedicated to its instruction. The first foreign language is used for the instruction of math and the sciences (including biology, physics, and chemistry), at least from grade 7 until grade 12. While Arabic could be used for the teaching of math and science for grades 1–6, in practice, it is rarely used, with textbooks being largely published in French or English (BouJaoude and Ghaith 2006). A household survey conducted under R4R and covering a nationally representative sample of 1,507 households found that out of 1,805 children enrolled in schools, 96 percent were being taught sciences and math in French or English (see chapter 3).

In recent years, there has been a significant shift in the distribution of students by language of instruction, with a notable increase in the proportion of students enrolled in schools where English is the language of instruction at the expense of schools where French is the language of instruction (figure B2.1.1).

Foreign curriculum policy

Several foreign curricula are taught in Lebanon, in parallel with the Lebanese curriculum. The French curriculum which leads to the French Baccalaureate has been used since the French mandate and is equivalent to the Lebanese Baccalaureate. Any student in Lebanon can enroll in a French curriculum school as long as the school has been approved by the French Ministry of Education. In 2017, there were 41 schools in Lebanon in agreements with French authorities, offering the French curriculum, with more than 58,000 children enrolled in those schools (French Embassy 2018). In 2017, 3,048 out of a total of 43,668

grade 12 students in Lebanon (7 percent of students) completed only the French Baccalaureate and received an equivalence certificate from the Lebanese MEHE (MEHE, Equivalence Department, May 2018 data). A significant number of students also completed both the French and Lebanese baccalaureates in the same year.

In addition to the French Baccalaureate, the Lebanese Parliament in 2017 approved the use of the International Baccalaureate and the British General Certificate of Secondary Education (GCSE) to be equivalent to the Lebanese Baccalaureate. Thus, Lebanese students can opt for those two education tracks rather than sitting for the Lebanese secondary national examination. For all other curricula taught in Lebanon (such as the German curriculum), students must also complete the Lebanese curriculum in tandem.

The main requirements mandated by the Lebanese government for schools offering one of the three equivalent foreign curricula (French, International Baccalaureate, or British) are that Lebanese students should pass the grade 9 national examinations "Brevet" and should be offered Arabic language courses to allow for the recognition of their foreign accreditation to be equivalent to Lebanese accreditation, unless students are exempted by having a second citizenship and/or by studying abroad for multiple years.

FIGURE B2.1.1

Proportion of students by language of instruction

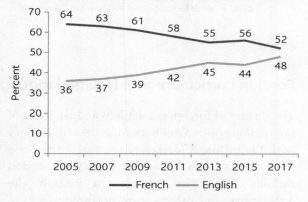

Sources: CERD statistical yearbooks, Beirut, https://www.crdp.org/statistics?la=en (retrieved April 8, 2018).
Note: CERD = Center for Educational Research and Development.

POSTINDEPENDENCE REFORMS: SETTING THE ORGANIZATION OF THE EDUCATION SECTOR

The postindependence era was marked by a significant commitment of the Lebanese government in the public education system. The number of public schools increased significantly, from 304 schools in 1943 to 1,354 in 1973, and the number kept increasing, even during the civil war, as it reached 1,448 in 1981 (figure 1.22). A large number of those schools were established in remote areas across the country to ensure education opportunities for all citizens. The expansion of public schools was accompanied by several changes and reforms, including in the curriculum (1946 and 1968–71) and in the organizational and management structure of the sector.

Directorate General of Education (DGE)

The most noticeable action took place in 1953, when the ministry, inherited from the French mandate, was reorganized with the establishment of a DGE, encompassing several services and units. The Director General of Education (DG) currently holds the highest ranked administrative position responsible for the management of general education. In 1959, a series of laws and decrees adopted by the government shaped the entire management of governmental affairs, established the supervisory bodies, and defined the bureaucracy of the education sector. Many of the organizational features established by these texts were left unchanged and still define the organizational structure and bureaucratic processes of the present day.

Center for Educational Research and Development

In 1971, Lebanon passed a law establishing the CERD. The CERD is a public institution with financial and administrative autonomy, under the custodianship authority of the Minister of Education. The major functions of the CERD are to inter alia (a) conduct education research, disseminate results, and undertake documentation of education publications; (b) advise on, review, and prepare educational plans; (c) study curricula, produce textbooks and educational resources, and approve types of national examinations; (d) train teachers, school principals, and education staff; and (e) propose norms, specifications, and conditions for school buildings and equipment.

POST-CIVIL WAR REFORMS: TOWARD BUILDING NATIONAL IDENTITY AND SOCIAL COHESION

From 1975–90, Lebanon witnessed a destructive sectarian civil war that caused political, social, and military turmoil across the country. The education sector, like all other sectors, was affected by the war with the destruction of schools and the loss in human capital due to deaths, injury, or forced displacement. The adoption of the Taef Agreement by the Lebanese Parliament in 1989 put an end to the conflict and sought to build national unity.

The Taef Agreement

The Taef Agreement is essential for understanding the general postconflict political climate surrounding education. Education was indeed considered essential from an equity standpoint for providing equal opportunities to all regions and all communities in the country and for building a common national identity for future generations. Two constitutional provisions stated below codified the guarantee for equality of opportunity in all areas of life, including education and equal treatment for all:

> *The even development among regions on the educational, social, and economic levels shall be a basic pillar of the unity of the state and the stability of the system.* Preamble of the constitutional law of September 21, 1990 (Paragraph G).

> *There shall be no segregation of the people based on any type of belonging.* Preamble of the constitutional law of September 21, 1990 (Paragraph I).

The Taef Agreement reinforced the freedom of private and religious education providers with a call for strengthening the regulatory role of the state. The agreement also called for a revision of the national curriculum to improve social integration and cohesion and encourage cultural and religious openness. The specific need for unifying the civics and history textbooks was mentioned. In fact, the Taef Agreement would be the basis of several major post–civil war education reforms which constitute the present-day foundations of the sector, including the 1994 Plan for Education Reform and the 1997 curriculum reform.

The 1994 Plan for Education Reform in Lebanon

Following the Taef Agreement, the Council of Ministers adopted, in 1994, the "Plan for Education Reform in Lebanon." The plan was drafted by the CERD, in concertation with the MEHE, and constitutes the basis for the current education landscape.

The main goals of the 1994 plan were to (a) build a national identity by rethinking the curriculum, (b) improve pre-tertiary education, (c) hone academic knowledge and required competencies, (d) align education with labor markets' needs, (e) achieve an enrollment balance between academic and vocational tracks, and (f) advance in the sciences and technology.

The 1997 curriculum reform

As stipulated by the Taef Agreement and planned under the 1994 plan for education reform, the national curriculum for general education was revised in 1997. The new curriculum aimed at achieving the goals set forth in the 1994 plan with a focus on building a national identity and improving children's sense of belonging to the Lebanese nation; and modernizing the objectives and content of the curriculum to be aligned with the development needs of the country.

Under the first goal of building a national identity and improving social cohesion, the 1997 reform unified the civic education textbook to be used by all schools, including both private and public schools. However, the unification of the history textbook was not accomplished and remains to date a suspended issue.

Under the second goal of aligning curricular objectives with the country's development and labor market needs, the curriculum introduced four tracks in secondary education—general sciences, life sciences, humanities, and economic and social sciences—to improve the alignment between secondary and tertiary education.

Finally, the curriculum introduced changes to the educational ladders by reorganizing the academic cycles, and most importantly, expanding Early Childhood Education (ECE) to 4-year-olds. As of 2017, the 1997 curriculum was still in effect, with no major changes to its content, despite tremendous changes in the labor market and the country's economic development needs.

CONTEMPORARY SECTOR DEVELOPMENT REFORMS: TOWARD ACHIEVING THE MILLENNIUM DEVELOPMENT GOALS

With the implementation of the 1997 curriculum reform, Lebanon moved toward developing long-term sector development plans for expanding quality Education for All (EFA) and working toward achieving, by 2015, the Millennium Development Goals (MDGs) adopted in 2000 at the United Nations General Assembly (UNGA).

Education for All Plan of Action

In 2003, the EFA Plan of Action was drafted by the MEHE and supported by a large national consultative body composed of governmental and nongovernmental stakeholders. The main action points identified as reform priorities were (a) expanding public preschool education to 3-year-olds; (b) implementing compulsory education and expanding it to include 15-year-olds, including combating dropping out; (c) expanding inclusive education to students with special needs; (d) professionalizing the teaching force and improving teacher management; (e) improving school curricula; (f) improving and rationalizing the use of school premises; and (g) improving educational and school management.

Education Sector Development Plan (ESDP)

In 2010, the Council of Ministers approved the ESDP. The plan encompassed the following programs of actions for general education: (a) increasing enrollment of children ages 3–5 in public kindergarten; (b) improving retention and achievement; (c) developing infrastructure to ensure the adequate and equitable distribution of school facilities in all regions; (d) professionalizing the teaching force; (e) modernizing school management; (f) developing a curriculum which is consistent with national needs and global trends; (g) strengthening citizenship education; (h) promoting the use of ICT in the education system; (i) determining the necessary qualifications for education-related professions; and (j) building institutional development (work flow effectiveness, management information system, performance-based budgeting, and so on). These programs of action were further detailed into 58 specific projects with performance indicators and plans for achievement by 2015.

Expanding free and compulsory education

A key aspect of contemporary reforms in general education was the expansion of free and compulsory education, notably to include ECE and intermediate education. Table 2.2 illustrates the changes in the structure of the education cycles across the years and the expansion of free and mandatory education in Lebanon.

TABLE 2.2 **Structure of education cycles and expansion of free and compulsory education in Lebanon**

	GOVERNMENT / MINISTRY OF EDUCATION PLAN	LEGISLATION ENACTED	AGE														
			3	4	5	6	7	8	9	10	11	12	13	14	15	16	17
REFORM YEAR	1946	1959			KG	Primary						Intermediate			Secondary		
	1994	1998		KG		Primary						Intermediate			Secondary		
	2003	2011	KG			Primary						Intermediate			Secondary		

◼ Free ◼ Compulsory free ◼ Noncompulsory

Source: Based on Lebanon Political Economy Study (unpublished) conducted for this report.
Note: Intermediate = intermediate school; KG = kindergarten; Primary = primary school; Secondary = secondary school.

Starting in 1959,[1] legislation was passed to assert that primary education should be provided free of charge and is a right to every Lebanese citizen. At the time, primary education was composed of five years of schooling, as established in the decrees issued by the government in 1946 organizing the education cycles.

In 1998,[2] another law was passed, following the 1994 plan approved by the Cabinet of Ministers, to reorganize primary education to six years of schooling and making it compulsory and free of charge. Public ECE was also expanded to two years.

In 2011,[3] the legislation expanded compulsory and free education to include the intermediate cycle for a total of nine years of schooling (basic education) and expanded public ECE to three years starting from age 3.

As of 2018, the MEHE started the review of the legal framework for compulsory education with the aim of expanding it from the current age range of 6–15 to an age range of 3–18. The DGE has especially set ECE as a priority with a target of reaching universal enrollment.[4]

Teachers' rights and working conditions

Lebanon has also enacted several laws and decrees concerning teachers' employment conditions and access to social benefits, including medical insurance, family allowances, and retirement benefits. The teachers' wage scale is regulated and set by the government. It is also shared across all education sectors (private and public), ensuring equal treatment of all teachers. Nevertheless, private schools are allowed and sometimes do provide additional compensation for their teachers.

RESPONSE TO THE SYRIAN REFUGEE CRISIS: REACHING ALL CHILDREN WITH EDUCATION (RACE)

Contemporary sector development reforms set up in 2003 and 2010 were accompanied with instability in the geopolitical scene in Lebanon. As early as 2005, the assassination of former Prime Minister Rafic Hariri brought upheaval in the political landscape of Lebanon. This was followed by the 2006 Israel-Lebanon war, the civil unrest in 2008, and a frequent change in governments. With the onset of the war in the Syrian Arab Republic in 2011, Lebanon started hosting a large number of Syrian refugees, of which nearly half a million were school-age children requiring education services.

To respond to the refugee crisis, the Lebanese government, with support from the international community, approved the RACE strategy in 2014. The initiative was first developed for three years (2014–16), and in 2017, the second

phase (RACE 2) was launched for five years. RACE 2 focuses on three compo-
nents/pillars: (a) expansion of access to public schools to all children in Lebanon,
(b) improvement of the quality of education in public schools, and (c) strengthening education systems to be more resilient to shocks.

As of 2018, the MEHE succeeded in integrating 220,498 non-Lebanese children
into public schools (figure 2.4), a significant accomplishment, given that the public
education system had to increase its capacity by approximately 77 percent in six
years, with non-Lebanese students comprising 45 percent of total students in the
public system in 2018. The expansion in formal education to Syrian refugees was
made possible through the establishment of second shifts in public schools (figure
2.5). In fact, in 2018, 70 percent of non-Lebanese students were enrolled in second
shifts, which were uniquely dedicated to their instruction, while the remaining
30 percent were going to schools with their Lebanese peers during the first shift.

FIGURE 2.4

Number of Lebanese and non-Lebanese children, ages 3–18, in public schools

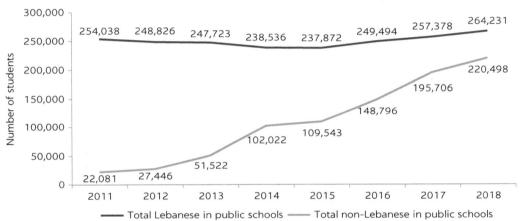

Sources: Data for Lebanese students: CERD statistical yearbooks, Beirut, https://www.crdp.org/
statistics?la=en; data for non-Lebanese students: RACE PMU (February 1, 2018).
Note: CERD = Center for Educational Research and Development; PMU = Program Management Unit;
RACE = Reaching All Children With Education.

FIGURE 2.5

Distribution of non-Lebanese students across first and second shifts

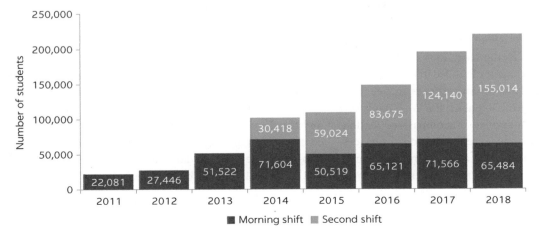

Source: Data provided by RACE PMU (February 1, 2018).
Note: PMU = Program Management Unit; RACE = Reaching All Children With Education.

In addition to enrolling refugee children in schools, the MEHE has recognized their specific psychological and emotional needs resulting from forced displacement and has deployed psychosocial and health counselors from their School Guidance and Counseling Department (Direction d'Orientation Pédagogique et Scolaire, DOPS). The counselors visit schools and provide support to administrators, teachers, and students to foster their physical and mental well-being.

One of the main objectives of the MEHE was to ensure that Syrian children receive formal certification and recognition for their education achievements. For that purpose, the MEHE delivered Accelerated Learning Programs (ALPs) to Syrian out-of-school children to facilitate their transition into formal schooling. The ALPs were designed by the CERD based on the national Lebanese curriculum and thus consisted of condensed versions of each grade level. Syrian children would then follow one or several programs depending on their competency level and would then be integrated into formal schooling once they achieved the proper level. Furthermore, the MEHE sought to regulate NFE provided by CSOs and NGOs, which had been active since the beginning of the crisis. The NFE programs targeting a particular age level or competency were designed by the MEHE and the CERD. CSOs and NGOs would then get trained by the MEHE to deliver these programs. The goal of the MEHE was to chart clear NFE pathways for Syrian children that would lead to formal education and certification.

Foreign students were always a component of the Lebanese education system. Before the Syrian crisis, in the academic year 2010–11, 21,642 were Syrian students enrolled in schools in Lebanon.[5] The country also faced several waves of refugees in its history, including the influx of Palestinian refugees in 1948 and 1967 and Iraqi refugees since the 2003 Iraq war. Palestinian children are the third-largest group of students in the education sector (after Lebanese and Syrian children). As of 2018, 48,269 Palestinian students were enrolled in schools in Lebanon.[6] However, most Palestinian children (67 percent, or 32,376 students, as of 2018) go to schools dedicated to them, operated by the United Nations Relief and Works Agency (UNRWA). This system of schools operates separately from the Lebanese system. Box 2.2 takes a closer look at the UNRWA school system.

BOX 2.2

Educating Palestinian refugees: The UNRWA school system in Lebanon

The United Nations Relief and Works Agency for Palestine Refugees in the Near East (UNRWA) is a United Nations (UN) agency founded in 1949 to provide social services to Palestinian refugees in Lebanon, Jordan, the Syrian Arab Republic, the West Bank, and Gaza. The agency's services encompass education, health care, microfinance, relief and social services, camp infrastructure and improvement, and emergency assistance. UNRWA's model is external to the host country's education system and is donor financed on a voluntary basis. UNRWA's 2016 budget was US$668 million, with over half (54 percent) of it earmarked for education (UNRWA 2018a) and funded by donor countries. Up until 2018, the United States and the European Union were the largest financial contributors to the agency (UNRWA 2018b). However, as of 2018, the United States cut all its contributions to UNRWA. In more than 60 years, UNRWA has

continued

Box 2.2, *continued*

educated three generations of refugees, or around 4 million children in the region (Cahill 2010).

UNRWA in the region

Today, approximately 500,000 children study in 689 UNRWA schools in the region. The agency relies on the recruitment of Palestinian refugees as teachers, with a network of 17,246 teachers and 587 vocational training instructors across all five territories where it operates. In Gaza, almost 90 percent of the school-age refugee population attends UNRWA schools. Moreover, student learning outcomes in UNRWA schools, as measured by TIMSS and PISA scores, have been high relative to the income levels of the student's families (Abdul-Hamid et al. 2015). These achievements have been possible despite high reliance on unpredictable donor funding and repeated funding shortfalls. Chronic underfunding has undermined UNRWA's capacity to expand the supply of education services and has pushed it to resort to overcrowded classrooms, reaching an average of 45 students per classroom (UN 2004) in Gaza and to multiple shifts per day, with 70 percent of schools operating a second shift and a smaller number operating triple shifts (UNRWA 2017a). Additionally, underfunding has

hindered UNRWA's ability to upgrade school premises which are in dire need of rehabilitation.

UNRWA in Lebanon

In Lebanon, as of 2018, there were 32,376 Palestinian students (67 percent of all Palestinian students) enrolled in general education in 68 UNRWA schools across the country.[a] Additionally, UNRWA operates one vocational training center for 1,143 students (UNRWA 2017b). With the Syrian crisis, many Palestinian refugees initially settled in Syria had to resettle to Lebanon and UNRWA has seen an increase in its student enrollment at the start of the refugee crisis (figure B2.1.1). UNRWA's curriculum follows the Lebanese curriculum, allowing Palestinian refugee students to participate in the official national examinations at the end of basic education in grade 9 ("Brevet") and at the end of secondary education in grade 12 (Baccalaureate) (UNRWA 2016). Nevertheless, UNRWA complements the Lebanese curriculum with its own set of learning and teaching materials, with a stronger focus on specific cross-cutting values and skills such as life skills, communication skills, conflict resolution, and the promotion of human rights (UNRWA 2015).

FIGURE B2.2.1

Number of students in UNRWA schools

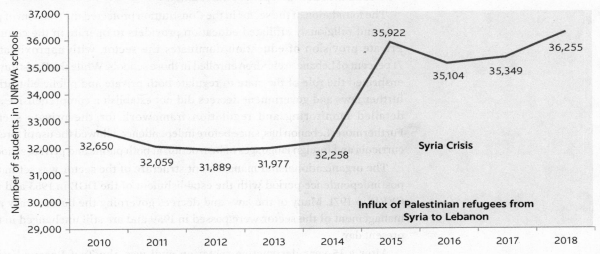

Sources: CERD statistical yearbooks, Beirut, https://www.crdp.org/statistics?la=en.
Note: CERD = Center for Educational Research and Development; UNRWA = United Nations Relief and Works Agency.

a. CERD statistical yearbooks, Beirut, https://www.crdp.org/statistics?la=en.

EDUCATION 2030: TOWARD ACHIEVING THE SUSTAINABLE DEVELOPMENT GOALS

With the Syrian crisis becoming a protracted one, the MEHE sought to combine its humanitarian response with a longer-term vision and plan for sector development. It was essential that the humanitarian activities supporting Syrian refugees did not overshadow the necessity of sector-wide reforms that would benefit both Lebanese and non-Lebanese children. Within this scope, the MEHE initiated in 2018 the development of its Education 2030 plan. The strategy would support Lebanon in reaching the SDGs adopted in 2015 at the UNGA, while tackling essential reforms in the sector.

Some of the major reforms planned under the program include (a) a greater focus on ECE as Lebanon moves toward universal enrollment in ECE, (b) a focus on reducing inequity and dropout rates for the most vulnerable and children with special needs, (c) a comprehensive revision of the 1997 curriculum, (d) the professionalization of the teacher workforce and improvement of teacher professional development programs, (e) strengthening the assessment systems for monitoring student learning, (f) strengthening the use of data and research in policy making, and (g) investment in school infrastructure and equipment.

Lebanon's commitment to achieving the SDGs is the latest milestone in a long history of international commitments that Lebanon has participated in to support the global education agenda. Box 2.3 takes a closer look at the main normative instruments and education provisions that Lebanon has committed to since independence.

CONCLUSION

Lebanon's education journey has been shaped by dynamic historical episodes and several constitutional laws and decrees. These texts have informed the vision and the education path of the country.

The foundation of the sector in the Constitution protected the freedom of private and religiously affiliated education providers to operate in the country. Private provision of education dominates the sector, with approximately 71 percent of Lebanese children enrolled in those schools. While the Constitution enshrined the role of the state to regulate both private and public education, further laws and government decrees did not establish a comprehensive and detailed monitoring and regulation framework for the private sector. Furthermore, Lebanon has, since before independence, allowed the use of foreign curricula and foreign languages of instruction at both public and private schools.

The organizational and management structure of the sector was set in the postindependence period with the establishment of the DGE in 1953 and the CERD in 1971. Many of the laws and decrees governing the bureaucracy and management of the sector were passed in 1959 and are still unchanged in the present day.

After a 15-year destructive sectarian civil war, the Taef Reconciliation Agreement sought to leverage education as a medium for building a unified national identity and social cohesion among all Lebanese citizens. The 1994 Plan for Education Reform and the 1997 curriculum, developed in line with the aspirations of the Taef Agreement, are still in effect in the present day.

BOX 2.3

Alignment with the international and global education agendas

Lebanon was one of the founders of the UN and has been committed to the education provisions of the normative instruments and education provisions adopted by the United Nations General Assembly (UNGA) and the United Nations Educational, Scientific, and Cultural Organization (UNESCO) General Conference. The main international commitments with regard to general education are presented in table B2.3.1.

TABLE B2.3.1 **International normative instruments/articles and provisions related to general education**

INSTRUMENT/ARTICLES	PROVISIONS
Article 26 of the Universal Declaration of Human Rights adopted by the UNGA in 1948	• Everyone has the right to education. • Education shall be free, at least at the elementary and fundamental stages. • Elementary education shall be compulsory. • Parents have a prior right to choose the kind of education that shall be given to their children.
The Convention against Discrimination in Education adopted by the General Conference of the UNESCO in 1960	• All articles are relevant to the provision of education services based on equality of opportunity and treatment.
Article 13 of the International Covenant on Economic, Social, and Cultural Rights, adopted by the UNGA in 1966	• Recognition of the right of education for everyone. • Primary education shall be compulsory and free for all.
Article 28 of the Convention on the Rights of the Child, adopted by the UNGA in 1990	• Recognition of the right of the child to education. • They shall make primary education compulsory and free for all.
The World Declaration on Education for All, adopted by the World Conference on Education for All in 1990	• All articles are relevant to the provision of quality education services based on equality of opportunity and treatment.
The Salamanca Statement and Framework for Action on Special Needs Education, adopted by the World Conference on Special Needs Education in 1994	• All articles are relevant to the provision of education services to children with special needs based on inclusion.
Goal 2 of the MDGs, adopted by the Millennium Summit in 2000	• Achieve universal primary education by 2015.
Goal 4 of the SDGs, Article 25 of the 2030 Agenda for Sustainable Development, adopted by the UN General Assembly in 2015	• Ensure inclusive and quality education for all and promote lifelong learning.

Note: MDG = Millennium Development Goal; SDG = Sustainable Development Goal; UN = United Nations; UNESCO = United Nations Educations, Scientific, and Cultural Organization; UNGA = United Nations General Assembly.

The beginning of the 21st century was marked by attempts at sector-wide reform; however, the politically unstable period that followed the assassination of the former prime minister in 2005, and the Syrian refugee crisis that started in 2012 introduced serious difficulty for achieving long-term sector development reforms. The Syrian refugee crisis had a significant effect on the public education sector; particularly, after 2018, the number of non-Lebanese students nearly reached the number of Lebanese students in public schools.

Despite the geopolitical and socioeconomic constraints, the historical perspective given in this chapter has shown that the Lebanese people, across the years, kept a forward-looking vision for the sector. The Education 2030 agenda, in development as of 2018, is the most recent example of the aspirations for education in Lebanon.

NOTES

1. Article 49 of the legislative decree No. 134, dated 12/6/1959: "Education is free of charge at the first primary level, and it is a right to every Lebanese citizen who is in the age bracket of primary education."
2. Law No. 686: "Education is free of charge and compulsory at the first primary level, and it is a right to every Lebanese citizen who is in the age bracket of primary education. . . . The conditions and organization of this free of charge and compulsory education shall be determined by a decree adopted by the Council of Ministers."
3. Law No. 150, dated 8/17/2011: "Education is compulsory at the basic education level; it is made available free of charge at the public schools; and it is a right to every Lebanese citizen who is in the age bracket of this level of education" . . . The conditions and organization of this free of charge and compulsory education shall be determined by a decree adopted by the Council of Ministers."
4. MEHE Annual Work Plan 2018 for Support to RACE 2 Program.
5. Between 2003 and 2008, the total number of Syrian children enrolled in schools in Lebanon was around 15,000. After that, it rose to 19,655 students in 2009, and then to 21,642 students in 2010 (CERD statistical yearbooks, https://www.crdp.org/statistics?la=en).
6. CERD statistical yearbooks, https://www.crdp.org/statistics?la=en.

REFERENCES

Abdul-Hamid, H., H. A. Patrinos, J. Reyes, J. Kelcey, and A. D. Varela. 2015. *Learning in the Face of Adversity: The UNRWA Education Program for Palestine Refugees*. Washington, DC: World Bank.

Bacha, N. N., and R. Bahous. 2011. "Foreign Language Education in Lebanon: A Context of Cultural and Curricular Complexities." *Journal of Language Teaching and Research* 2 (6): 1320–28.

BouJaoude, S., and G. Ghaith. 2006. "Educational Reform at a Time of Change: The Case of Lebanon." In *Education Reform in Societes in Transition: International Perspectives*, edited by J. Earnest and D. Tragust, 193–210. Rotterdam: Sense Publishers.

Cahill, K. M., ed. 2010. *Even in Chaos: Education in Times of Emergency*. New York: Center for International Humanitarian Cooperation.

French Embassy. 2018. "Network of Schools Operating the French Program in Lebanon" (in French). https://lb.ambafrance.org/Reseau-des-etablissements-a-programmes-francais-au-Liban.

Ghait, G. M., and K. A. Shabaan. 1996. "Language-in-Education Policy and Planning: The Case of Lebanon." *Mediterranean Journal of Educational Studies* 1 (2): 95–105.

Kobeissi, H. 2012. "History of Private Schools in Lebanon." International Research Seminar, "Policies and Politics and Teaching Religion", Byblos, November.

Lebanese Constitution. 1995. *The Lebanese Constitution Promulgated May 23, 1926, with its Amendments*. Retrievable from: The World Intellectual Property Organization, Geneva, http://www.wipo.int/edocs/lexdocs/laws/en/lb/lb018en.pdf.

LocaLiban (Centre de ressources sur le développement local au Liban). 2015. "Private Schools in Lebanon: Religiously Affiliated Schools in Lebanon." November 27. https://www.localiban.org/article5190.html (accessed April 8, 2018).

Shaaban, K., and G. Gaith. 1999. "Lebanon's Language-in-Education Policies: From Bilingualism to Trilingualism." *Language Problems and Language Planning* 23 (1): 1–16.

UN (United Nations). 2004. *Report of the Commissioner-General of the United Nations Relief and Works Agency for Palestine Refugees in the Near East: 1 July 2003–30 June 2004*. New York: United Nations.

UNRWA (United Nations Relief and Works Agency for Palestine Refugees in the Near East). 2015. "UNRWA Education Reform Strategy 2011–2015." UNRWA, Amman. https://www.unrwa.org/userfiles/2012042913344.pdf.

———. 2016. "Schools in Lebanon Open Their Doors to Palestine Refugees." September 1, UNRWA, Amman. https://www.unrwa.org/newsroom/press-releases/unrwa-schools-lebanon-open-their-doors-palestine-refugees.

———. 2017a. "Program Budget 2016–2017." Report of the Commissioner-General of the United Nations Relief and Works Agency for Palestine Refugees in the Near East, UNRWA, Amman, http://www.unrwa.org/sites/default/files/2016_2017_programme_budget_blue_book.pdf.

———. 2017b. "Education in Lebanon." UNRWA, Amman. https://www.unrwa.org/activity/education-lebanon.

———. 2018a. "How We Spend Funds." UNRWA, Amman. https://www.unrwa.org/how-you-can-help/how-we-spend-funds.

———. 2018b. "How We Are Funded." UNRWA, Amman. https://www.unrwa.org/how-you-can-help/how-we-are-funded.

3 Public Perception of Education versus Reality

MAIN MESSAGES

1. Education is a major priority for Lebanese households and is considered a central pillar of the Lebanese economy and society. It is thus not surprising that the public perception study conducted under the R4R program found that Lebanese households held a positive opinion about the quality of education in Lebanon, an opinion they have consistently expressed over the years. However, the reality on the ground in terms of learning outcomes reveals that Lebanon is facing a learning crisis, with overall low levels of learning and high levels of inequity. Moreover, contrary to the general perception of households that education quality was improving, student learning outcomes have been in a declining trend since 2007, with Lebanon performing poorly compared with countries at a similar level of socioeconomic development.

2. In addition to low levels of learning, Lebanon has high levels of inequity, with the gap in learning outcomes between the top and bottom economic, social, and cultural status (ESCS) quintiles being the largest in the Middle East and North Africa region. Lebanon has also a gender gap in math skills in favor of boys and a reverse gender gap in reading skills in favor of girls at all grade levels.

3. Despite the generally positive perception of education quality, the study revealed disparities in parent satisfaction between public and private schools, notably in their perception of pedagogy and curriculum content, teachers' skills, school management, and school infrastructure. The gap in education quality between public and private schools was perceived to be the largest in the early grades, and the quality of public education was perceived as improving as children progressed to higher levels of general education. Nevertheless, the gap in perception of education quality between public and private schools remained significant at the secondary level.

4. In terms of curriculum content and instruction, public school parents reported the most challenges in the instruction of science, math, and foreign languages, while private school parents perceived more challenges in Arabic language instruction, the humanities, and the social sciences.

These difficulties were then reflected in the students' choice of academic stream in secondary school: public sector students were significantly less likely than private sector students to specialize in the sciences; and once they chose the sciences, they were also less likely to succeed in the national examinations and obtain certifications that would facilitate their access to higher education in science, technology, engineering, and mathematics (STEM). In addition to reinforcing STEM fields in the public sector, public school parents were twice more likely to report the need for reinforcing the arts and sports at school. In fact, arts and sports came in the first position among subjects which parents requested to have more time allocated to them in both public and private schools. This finding reflected parents' awareness of the importance of arts and sports education in the holistic development of their children.

5. With regard to teachers' skills, Lebanese households tended to perceive Arabic and social sciences teachers to be the least skilled in both public and private schools. Parents also reported that memorization was a common teaching technique, mostly prevalent for the instruction of languages and social sciences, but also for math and sciences, and across all subjects in public schools. This finding might explain why Lebanese students, in international assessments, performed better on subject knowledge questions, which might have been acquired through rote learning and memorization as compared to application or reasoning questions that required the use of specific concepts to solve problems.

6. In public schools, parents reported low satisfaction rates with the assessment methods used to monitor and measure their children's learning. Additionally, one in five public school parents admitted to never attending meetings with teachers or school management. These combined measures indicate that public school parents do not have the means and tools to follow up and support their children's learning journey. While this might be due to specific characteristics of public school parents, such as low educational attainment, there remains an opportunity for public schools to play a larger role in facilitating parents' involvement and engagement, given their importance in decreasing education inequity among students.

7. Incidence of verbal and physical violence in Lebanese schools was higher than the international average and was confirmed through international assessments to have a negative effect on student learning outcomes. Not only were Lebanese students more likely to face and report cases of physical and verbal violence compared to the international average, but where these cases existed, Lebanese students were also more likely to report a higher frequency of occurrence of violence. These findings necessitate actions on several levels of the system, including at the teachers' and school management levels, to reinforce the use of positive behavior and nonviolent disciplinary methods when interacting with students; and at the students' level, by providing psychosocial support, reinforcing positive behavior, and improving the socioemotional skills of children.

8. With regard to infrastructure, the opinion survey revealed that infrastructure issues did not seem far-reaching, given an acceptable average satisfaction rate by the general public. Nevertheless, there were stark

disparities in the quality of school buildings, access to facilities and amenities, and availability of learning and teaching materials and equipment between regions and between schools. Infrastructure gaps existed mostly in public schools, especially in rural and peripheral areas. Given these findings, large investments in school infrastructure might therefore not be a priority concern for the education system, and the Lebanese government should focus on targeted infrastructure upgrades for schools that have the highest needs.

9. With regard to the impact of the Syrian refugee crisis, Lebanese households asserted that it had negative effects on the education sector in Lebanon. Nonetheless, respondents who were more likely to express negative impacts of the Syrian refugee crisis on education were from households which did not have children currently or recently enrolled in schools and were thus the least likely to be affected by the influx of Syrian refugees. Lebanese households also expressed their preference for the provision of education services to Syrian children through CSOs or second-shift public schools. Conversely, Syrian households expressed strong preference for the integration of Syrian children in daytime public schools, with only a small fraction preferring second-shift schools or provision of education through CSOs.

10. Moving forward, the perception study gauged what areas for reform in the sector were considered as priorities for the Lebanese public. Households prioritized reforms, targeting accountability and quality control systems for schools and teachers for both the private and public sectors. This was an indication that while households generally expressed a positive opinion about the quality of education in Lebanon, they admitted that there was a need for a stronger regulatory framework which holds schools accountable for delivering quality education. Also among the top priority reforms of households were improvements in competencies and skills of teachers and school principals, implying strong support for reforms in the preservice training and in-service professional development of school teachers and administrators. Finally, there was growing support for grouping and consolidating schools; this priority area was specifically voiced by households in rural and peripheral areas, where the prevalence of small and sparsely occupied schools was high.

INTRODUCTION

In Lebanon, more than half of all households in 2013 had at least one child and hence were invested in the cause of education.[1] Education is highly valued by the Lebanese population and is ranked high on their list of priorities, as reflected by the significant amount of household income spent on education services. The 2013 World Values Survey (Inglehart et al. 2014) revealed that 59 percent of households were concerned about their ability to give their children a good education. Hence, the general public and its opinion of education can represent a potential driving force for improving the sector. To identify the priority areas for sector reform that are most valued by Lebanese households, perception surveys can be used to understand stakeholders' perspectives and priorities, gather feedback and suggestions from recipients of education services, and involve citizens in setting the education agenda.

For this purpose, a public perception study, led by the World Bank and implemented by the Consultation and Research Institute (CRI), was conducted in November 2016. Researchers administered a structured questionnaire to a random sample of 1,507 households, including 232 Syrian refugee households living in Lebanon (15 percent of the sample). Out of the total number of households, 731 (49 percent) had at least one child enrolled or recently enrolled in school, out of which 115 were Syrian households (16 percent of households with enrolled children). The sample was representative of the population residing in Lebanon at the regional level and was based on the sampling frame of CAS. The details of the methodology can be found in appendix B.

HOW TO READ PERCEPTION SURVEYS

When reading perception survey results, it is essential to keep in mind their limitations (OECD 2012). While they can serve as an indication of beneficiaries' awareness, engagement, confidence, and satisfaction with certain reforms, one cannot rely on them completely to evaluate the effectiveness of these reforms. Survey participants are often asked to render judgments on complex topics on which they might not have all necessary information, and their responses can be influenced by myriad external factors, including their own attitudes about and interests in the subject. Moreover, participants can in some cases exhibit different types of response biases and might have different criteria and reasons for making judgments about education quality issues; perception surveys are not sufficient to uncover those reasons. Bearing these limitations in mind, perception surveys can be used effectively to understand beneficiaries' priorities, needs, and areas of concerns.

PERCEPTION OF EDUCATION QUALITY

The overall perception of education quality was positive, with 76 percent of respondents rating education quality as "good" or "excellent," and more than half of them stating that the quality of education has been improving (figure 3.1). These perceptions did not vary significantly across respondents' characteristics (e.g., education attainment, enrollment status of children, and so on). This finding was also in line with other public opinion surveys on education in Lebanon; for example, in Gallup surveys of 1,000–2,000 respondents, the satisfaction rate was 72 percent in 2015 (figure 3.2) (Gallup 2015).

Furthermore, the majority (53 percent of surveyed households) seemed to believe that spending on their children's schooling was commensurate with the quality of their children's educational experiences. This judgment did not seem to vary with the income level of the household, but households with children currently or recently enrolled in school were significantly more likely to hold this opinion (62 percent versus 45 percent among households with no currently or recently enrolled children). This might explain why more households have been enrolling their children in private schools and might stem from parents' desire to believe that they are giving their children the best education they can provide by incurring significantly higher expenses.

With regard to the difference in quality between Lebanese private and public schools, the majority of households (85 percent) perceived that the quality of private education was good at all levels—kindergarten, primary, intermediate,

FIGURE 3.1

Households' views on education quality and trend (*N* = 1,507)

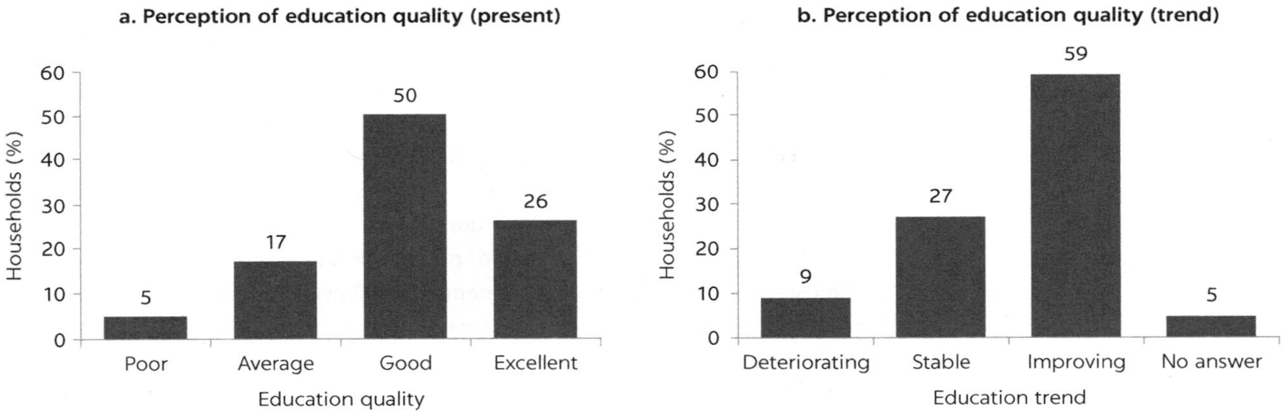

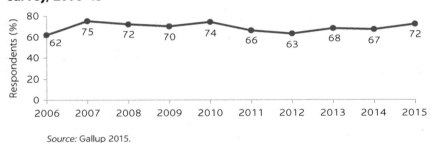

a. Perception of education quality (present)

b. Perception of education quality (trend)

Source: Data based on the Public Perception Survey (unpublished) conducted for this report.
Note: N = number of respondents.

FIGURE 3.2

Percentage of Lebanese respondents satisfied with education: Gallup survey, 2006–15

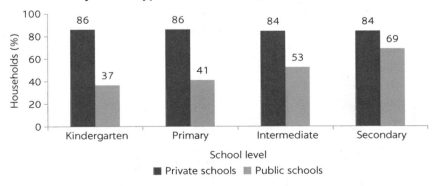

Source: Gallup 2015.

FIGURE 3.3

Percentage of households rating education quality as "good" or "excellent" by school type and level (*N* = 1,505)

Source: Data based on the Public Perception Survey (unpublished) conducted for this report.
Note: N = number of respondents.

and secondary—while the quality of public education was perceived as improving as children progressed to higher levels of general education (figure 3.3). Particularly, more than half of Lebanese households perceived a strong need to improve quality at the kindergarten and primary levels in public schools.

PERCEPTION OF TEACHERS, TEACHING METHODS, AND STUDENT ASSESSMENTS

Among households with children enrolled in schools, overall satisfaction levels with teachers' skills varied significantly between private and public schools (figure 3.4). While 71 percent of private school parents were "fully satisfied" with their children's teachers' skills, only 38 percent of public school parents expressed the same level of satisfaction. These findings were similar across all grade levels but varied significantly across school subjects.

Both public and private school parents perceived math teachers to be the most skilled. Both types of respondents also believed that Arabic and humanities/social sciences teachers were the least skilled at their schools, while the sciences and foreign languages teachers in the private sector were perceived to be significantly more skilled than their counterparts in the public sector.

In terms of grade levels, primary school teachers were portrayed by respondents to be the least effective, with slightly less than half of respondents (49 percent) being satisfied with their skills. Satisfaction with kindergarten teachers was slightly higher, at 55 percent. Intermediate- and secondary-level teachers were perceived to be the most effective, with 60 percent and 65 percent of respondents expressing satisfaction with their skills, respectively.

Moreover, respondents' level of satisfaction with teachers' skills seemed to increase with the age of the respondents. The percentage of respondents who reported full satisfaction with teachers' skills increased from 48 percent among those who are under age 25 to 64 percent among those age 55–64 (figure 3.5), indicating a clear generation gap in the perception of teachers and teaching methods, with parents from newer generations expressing higher levels of dissatisfaction with teachers' skills in Lebanese schools.

In terms of teaching methods, memorization appeared to be used as a common teaching strategy in the social sciences (history, geography, civic education, economics, and so on), as perceived by approximately half of the surveyed households (figure 3.6). For math, the sciences, and foreign languages,

FIGURE 3.4

Households' satisfaction with teachers' skills by school type and subject (N = 731)

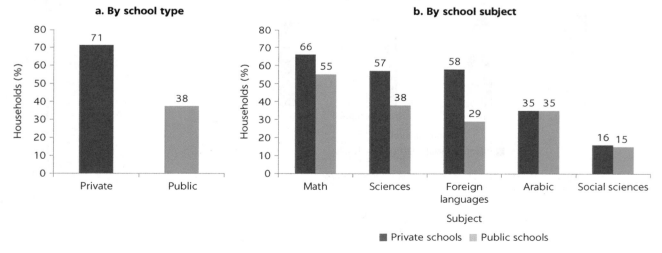

Source: Data based on the Public Perception Survey (unpublished) conducted for this report.
Note: N = number of respondents.

FIGURE 3.5

Satisfaction level with teachers' skills by age group (N = 731)

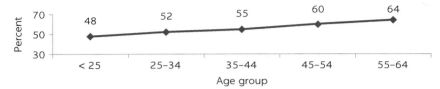

Source: Data based on the Public Perception Survey (unpublished) conducted for this report.
Note: N = number of respondents.

FIGURE 3.6

Percentage of households reporting "memorization" as the prevalent teaching technique used at school by school type and subject (N = 731)

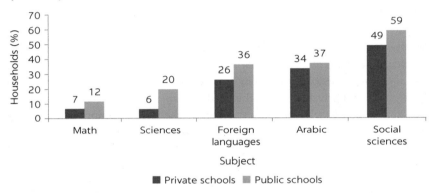

Source: Data based on the Public Perception Survey (unpublished) conducted for this report.
Note: N = number of respondents.

more public school households reported the use of memorization as a teaching strategy than private school households. The use of memorization as a teaching strategy in sciences and math might be one of the reasons explaining Lebanon's performance on the 2015 TIMSS, where Lebanese grade 8 students performed better on subject knowledge questions, which might have been acquired through rote learning and memorization compared to application or reasoning questions that required the use of specific concepts to solve problems.[2]

With regard to methods used for student assessments, satisfaction levels were significantly higher in private schools, with 71 percent of households being "fully satisfied" with their children's school assessment methods, compared to only 35 percent of public school parents expressing the same level of satisfaction (figure 3.7). These findings were similar across all grade levels, and indicate a perception by public school parents of the need to reform how student learning is measured and assessed in the public sector. Nevertheless, the majority of all surveyed households (86 percent) believed that schools effectively prepared their children for the national examinations. Only 4 percent of private school parents and 15 percent of public school parents thought that their children were not adequately prepared to take the official examinations.

FIGURE 3.7

Percentage of households fully satisfied with school assessment by school type (*N* = 731)

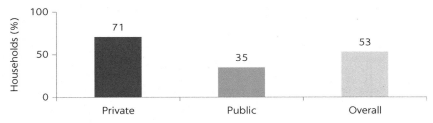

Source: Data based on the Public Perception Survey (unpublished) conducted for this report.
Note: N = number of respondents.

PERCEPTION OF SCHOOL CURRICULA AND TEXTBOOKS

The perception study identified some key areas of improvement in school curricula, particularly the need for strengthening teaching and learning in the social sciences (history, geography, civic education, economics, and so on) in both public and private schools, the need for expanding arts and sports education, and in public schools, more specifically, the need for improving teaching and learning of math, the sciences, and foreign languages.

With regard to time allocated in schools for each subject, arts and sports came in the first position among subjects which needed to have more time allocated to them in both public and private schools (figure 3.8). This finding reflected an awareness among parents of the importance of arts and sports education in the holistic development of their children and the role of the school in fostering these subjects. When comparing public and private school parents, public school parents were twice more likely to report the need for more weekly periods for arts, foreign languages, the sciences, and math—an indication of the need to reinforce those subjects in public schools.

When asked to assess the difficulty of various school subjects, public school households were most likely to find math, foreign languages, and sciences to be difficult subjects, while Arabic language instruction and the social sciences were perceived to be much easier (figure 3.9). This trend was not detected for private school households. Despite finding difficulty in foreign language instruction, public school households seemed to continue to be supportive of the use of foreign language of instruction (English and French) for the teaching of math and the sciences, with 79 percent of them classifying it as beneficial for their children. That percentage was significantly higher for private school households, at 88 percent.

In terms of the appeal of school subjects, public school parents were significantly less likely to find the sciences, math, and foreign languages to be interesting/appealing, a finding correlated with public school parents' perception of the difficulty of these subjects. These findings have significant equity implications, as they suggest that according to parents' perceptions, public school students were more likely to find STEM subjects to be difficult and less appealing compared to private school students, thus decreasing the share of public school students who choose to pursue higher education and careers in STEM.

FIGURE 3.8

Percentage of households reporting a need for more weekly periods by subjects and school type (*N* = 731)

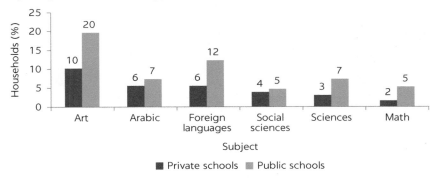

Source: Data based on the Public Perception Survey (unpublished) conducted for this report.
Note: N = number of respondents.

FIGURE 3.9

Percentage of households reporting that a subject is difficult by school type (*N* = 731)

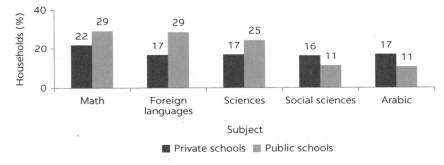

Source: Data based on the Public Perception Survey (unpublished) conducted for this report.
Note: N = number of respondents.

Furthermore, the social sciences were perceived to be the least interesting/ appealing and the least beneficial subject by both private and public school parents (figure 3.10). This finding was positively correlated with the income level of the household, with 8 percent of low-income households, 17 percent of middle-income households, and 27 percent of high-income households finding the social sciences to be nonbeneficial. There might be different reasons behind this perception, but this finding indicates a clear need for improving teaching and learning of the social sciences across both the public and private sectors to reinforce its importance in building essential and transversal skills of children.

With regard to textbooks, the social sciences textbooks received the highest dissatisfaction rates from all respondents. Additionally, public school parents expressed higher dissatisfaction with foreign language instruction textbooks (French and English) compared with private school parents (figure 3.11). This finding could be attributed to the reliance of private schools on textbooks issued by private publishers, especially for the teaching of foreign languages, rather than the use of official Lebanese textbooks.

FIGURE 3.10

Percentage of households finding a subject appealing (*N* = 731)

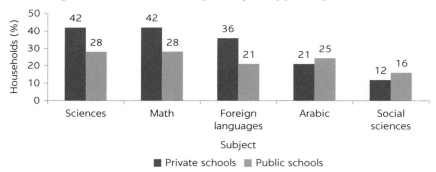

Source: Data based on the Public Perception Survey (unpublished) conducted for this report.
Note: N = number of respondents.

FIGURE 3.11

Percentage of households dissatisfied with textbooks (*N* = 731)

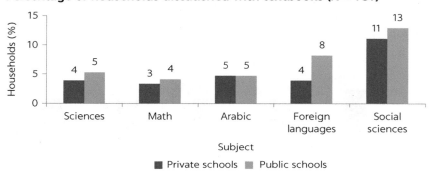

Source: Data based on the Public Perception Survey (unpublished) conducted for this report.
Note: N = number of respondents.

Dissatisfaction with foreign language and social science textbooks seemed to be positively correlated with the age of the student (figure 3.12), with higher dissatisfaction rates for textbooks at higher grade levels, partly explained by a potential increase in the interest of parents in the social sciences and foreign languages as their children approach the transition to tertiary education and the job market.

PERCEPTION OF SCHOOL MANAGEMENT AND PARENTS' ENGAGEMENT

Perception of school management and school principals' leadership skills followed a pattern similar to the perception of teachers' skills, with 72 percent of private school households being "fully satisfied" with school management and only 39 percent of public school households expressing the same level of satisfaction.

With regard to parents' engagement with schools, while most households (60 percent in public schools and 70 percent in private schools) highlighted the importance of parent committees, only 37 percent of private school households

FIGURE 3.12

Percentage of households dissatisfied with foreign language and social science textbooks (*N* = 731)

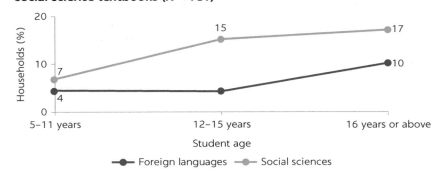

Source: Data based on the Public Perception Survey (unpublished) conducted for this report.
Note: N = number of respondents.

FIGURE 3.13

Percentage of households by frequency of parent-teacher meetings (*N* = 731)

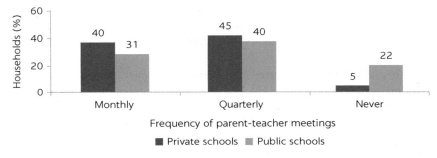

Source: Data based on the Public Perception Survey (unpublished) conducted for this report.
Note: N = number of respondents.

and 16 percent of public school households found them to be effective. Consequently, and according to parents, the current legal mandate of parents' committees has not constituted an effective way of engaging parents in the school's improvement and decision-making processes. Moreover, more than one in five parents (22 percent) of children in public schools admitted that they never meet with their children's teachers (figure 3.13), raising concerns about the ability of public school parents to support their children's learning. Some of these concerns are due to the characteristics of these parents—for example, private school parents were four times more likely than public school parents to have completed secondary education (46 percent versus 13 percent), and five times more likely to have completed higher education (21 percent versus 4.5 percent). Despite these challenges, there remains an opportunity for public schools to play a larger role in facilitating parents' involvement and engagement, given their importance in decreasing education inequity among students.

PERCEPTION OF SCHOOL CLIMATE AND VIOLENCE

Concerning school climate, households were asked whether they were aware of cases of physical or nonphysical (e.g., verbal abuse, bullying, and so on) violence at their children's schools. Reporting from parents indicated a relatively high incidence of violence (whether physical or verbal) in Lebanese schools, especially in public schools. These findings were comparable to reports by students in the 2015 TIMSS survey (TIMSS 2015a) for grade 8 math students, which showed that students in Lebanon, when compared to the international average, were more likely to face and report cases of physical and verbal violence (figure 3.14); and where these cases existed, Lebanese students were also more likely to report a higher frequency of occurrence of violence. Only half of the Lebanese students (52 percent) reported that they were almost never a victim of verbal or physical violence, which is significantly lower than the international average of 63 percent. Moreover, nearly one in five (19 percent) Lebanese students reported being a victim of verbal or physical violence on a weekly basis, compared to 8 percent of students internationally. The same survey (TIMSS 2015b) triangulated reports of violence by children with school principals' reports and found that 20 percent of students in Lebanon, compared with 11 percent internationally, go to schools with moderate to severe disciplinary problems (including absenteeism, classroom disturbance, cheating, profanity, bullying, vandalism, theft, verbal abuse, and physical injury). These findings have significant implications on students' well-being and learning achievement. In fact, the average grade 8 math TIMSS score for students who have never been a victim of violence in school in Lebanon was 456, compared to 412 for students who reported being a victim of violence on a weekly basis.

Public school parents reported higher levels of violence in schools, compared with private schools (figure 3.15). Not only were the rates higher for violence among students, with 28 percent of public school households reporting cases of verbal violence and 18 percent reporting physical violence in schools, but these rates were also significantly higher for teacher-to-student violence, with 15 percent of public school parents reporting verbal abuse from teachers to students, and 9 percent admitting to cases of physical violence perpetrated by teachers on students.

FIGURE 3.14

Distribution of students by frequency of verbal and physical violence

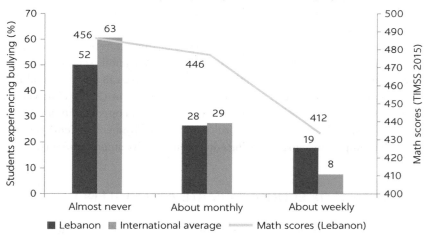

Source: TIMSS 2015a.
Note: TIMSS = Trends in International Mathematics and Science Study.

FIGURE 3.15

Percentage of households reporting cases of physical and nonphysical violence at school (*N* = 731)

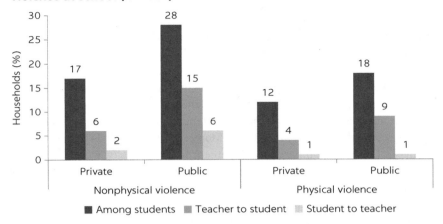

Source: Data based on the Public Perception Survey (unpublished) conducted for this report.
Note: N = number of respondents.

FIGURE 3.16

Percentage of households reporting cases of violence in public schools by children's age group (*N* = 341)

Source: Data based on the Public Perception Survey (unpublished) conducted for this report.
Note: N = number of respondents.

Incidence of violence was even higher when disaggregating by age groups of children, with violence seeming to peak in the 12–15 age category, which corresponds to the intermediate school cycle in Lebanon (figure 3.16). These findings necessitate actions on several levels of the system, including at the teachers' and school management levels, to reinforce the use of positive behavior and nonviolent disciplinary methods when interacting with students; and at the students' level, by providing psychosocial support, reinforcing positive behavior, and improving the socioemotional skills of children.

Health and counseling services are critical for addressing challenges such as bullying and violence. However, according to the surveyed households, access to such services in Lebanese schools was considered to be low, with only 27 percent of schools offering health services (36 percent in private schools and 17 percent in public schools) and 15 percent offering counseling services (21 percent in private schools and 9 percent in public schools). When these services were available, 78 percent of private school households were "fully satisfied" with these services, while 53 percent of public school households expressed the same level of satisfaction.

PERCEPTION OF SCHOOL INFRASTRUCTURE AND FACILITIES

Surveyed households did not appear to find major issues in school buildings and basic infrastructure, with 94 percent expressing satisfaction with the quality of school buildings. These findings were shared by both public and private school parents. They were also aligned with reporting from teachers in the TIMSS survey of 2015, which showed that, in general, math and science teachers in Lebanon could not identify major concerns or problems in the condition of their school infrastructure and resources (school maintenance, repair, cleanliness, adequate workspace, and so on) (TIMSS 2015c). More specifically, only 14 percent of students in Lebanon, compared to 23 percent internationally, were enrolled in schools where science teachers reported moderate to severe problems in school condition and resources. This percentage was similar to the ones reported by science teachers in Bahrain, Oman, Japan, Norway, the United Kingdom, and the United States, among others. Nevertheless, the TIMSS results showed a clear positive correlation between the condition of school buildings and learning outcomes, with grade 8 learning outcomes in math and science being significantly lower in schools with major infrastructure problems compared with schools with minor or no issues in school infrastructure. It is thus essential for Lebanon to address major issues in school infrastructure where they are present. However, the relatively low percentage of students enrolled in schools where teachers have reported moderate to serious issues in school conditions and the high satisfaction rates expressed by parents through the public perception survey indicate that school infrastructure is not a far-reaching problem in Lebanon and that large investments in school infrastructure might therefore not be a priority concern for the education system.

While the perception survey found overall satisfaction with school infrastructure and buildings, there were some areas of concern identified, warranting additional attention and follow-up, notably some inconsistencies in the availability of basic needs such as good-quality water, good toilet hygiene, and cooling and heating amenities or the availability of certain educational facilities and resources.

The issue of water quality was quite salient in public schools, where nearly one in five respondents (18 percent) rated water quality as bad, three times higher than in private schools (6 percent). The governorates of South Lebanon and North Lebanon had the highest number of complaints about water quality: 33 percent and 20 percent, respectively. Similar to water quality, dissatisfaction with toilet hygiene was more than three times higher in public schools than in private schools, with 38 percent of public school households rating the cleanliness of school toilets as either "bad" or "very bad." Toilet hygiene and bad water quality could have seriously negative effects on children's health. It is essential for education and government officials to ensure that cases of bad water quality are properly diagnosed and addressed on time.

The availability of heating and cooling was not consistent or homogeneous across the country. While climate differences between coastal and mountainous areas could be one factor explaining those differences, the survey identified significant contrasts between private and public schools in the same geographical areas (figure 3.17). Across Lebanon, it appeared that in schools, cooling amenities were less prevalent than heating amenities. South Lebanon and Beirut were two out of the top three governorates where both cooling

FIGURE 3.17

Percentage of households reporting that schools lacked cooling or heating (*N* = 731)

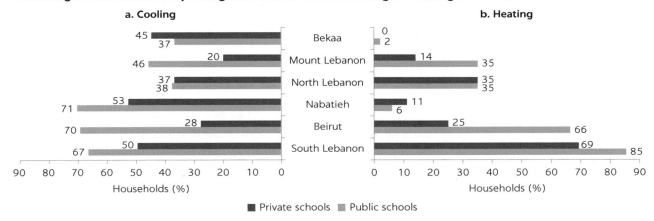

Source: Data based on the Public Perception Survey (unpublished) conducted for this report.
Note: N = number of respondents.

FIGURE 3.18

Percentage of households reporting a lack of school facilities (*N* = 731)

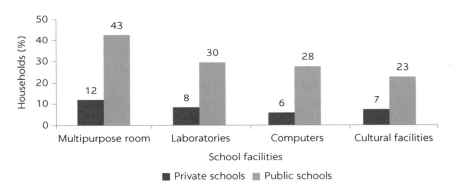

Source: Data based on the Public Perception Survey (unpublished) conducted for this report.
Note: N = number of respondents.

and heating amenities were not available. Nabatieh had also high unavailability of cooling amenities, with 71 percent in public schools and 53 percent in private schools.

Concerning the availability and quality of school facilities and equipment necessary to implement the school curriculum effectively, a large share of households with children in public schools reported that these facilities were absent in their children's schools, compared with private school households (figure 3.18). About 43 percent of parents of children enrolled in public schools stated that there were no multipurpose rooms at school, and around a quarter of parents (25 percent) noted a lack of art and cultural facilities (theater, music room, and so on). Moreover, a significant share of public school households reported an absence of laboratories (30 percent) and computer equipment (28 percent). Shortages of laboratory and computer facilities could lead to limited opportunities for applied learning in STEM and could thus increase inequity between students in public and private schools. According to the TIMSS 2015 survey (TIMSS 2015d), school principals reported that approximately

85–86 percent of students in Lebanon, compared to 72 percent internationally, were enrolled in schools where science and math instruction were negatively affected by shortages in instructional and educational resources, including technology.

PERCEPTION OF ACCESS TO EDUCATION

In terms of access to schools, children from low-income-level households were more likely to be enrolled in public schools, while middle-income and high-income families were more likely to have their children enrolled in private schools (figure 3.19), confirming a public perception that public schools were catering to the most vulnerable and socioeconomically disadvantaged children in Lebanon.[3] More importantly, among 1,805 children included in the survey, 10 percent had to transfer from a private to a public school due to cost issues, and an additional 6 percent due to other reasons, including quality of education and distance of school; most of the transfers occurred at the basic education stage (primary and intermediate levels). A much lower percentage (2 percent) of children transferred from a public to a private school, mostly for the quality of education or for other personal reasons; these transfers occurred predominantly at the kindergarten and primary education levels.

Most of the interviewed households appeared to perceive that some school-age children faced inequity in accessing educational opportunities in Lebanon; specifically, 54 percent of the interviewed households believed that there were school-age children who lacked access to education. That figure went up to 67 percent among Syrian respondents. In terms of geographic differences, perceptions of lack of access were more prevalent in the following districts (*caza*): Baabda (74 percent), Aley (73 percent), Tripoli (70 percent), Beirut (67 percent), and Saida (63 percent), indicating that inequity in access was most visible in major urban areas. Additionally, the perception of equity in access was correlated with the income level of the respondent, with more vulnerable households perceiving higher levels of inequity than high-income households.

When looking at the cost of education, there was a significant difference in education expenditures between public and private schools across all cost components (table 3.1). On average, private school households declared spending 8.5 times more than public school households on education—a cost

FIGURE 3.19

Enrollment by sector type, income level, and reason for selecting school (*N* = 731)

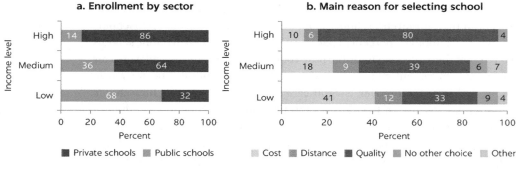

Source: Data based on the Public Perception Survey (unpublished) conducted for this report.
Note: N = number of respondents.

TABLE 3.1 **Average education expenditures (*N* = 731)**

	TUITION (US$/ SCHOOL YEAR)	TEXTBOOKS/ STATIONARY (US$/ SCHOOL YEAR)	TRANSPORTATION (US$/SCHOOL YEAR)	OTHERS (US$/ SCHOOL YEAR)	TOTAL COST OF EDUCATION FOR PARENTS (US$/SCHOOL YEAR)
Public schools	120	60	130	26	336
Private schools	2,250	300	240	92	2,882

Source: Data based on the Public Perception Survey (unpublished) conducted for this report.
Note: N = number of respondents.

FIGURE 3.20

Yearly transportation cost per governorate (*N* = 731)

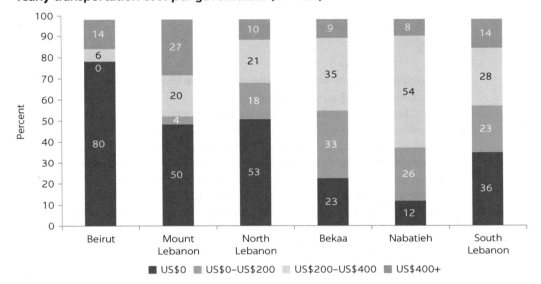

Source: Data based on the Public Perception Survey (unpublished) conducted for this report.
Note: N = number of respondents.

difference largely driven by tuition but also by all other cost components. For public school parents, transportation represented the largest cost component, with up to 40 percent of total education costs. However, there were significant variations across governorates, with households in Nabatieh and Bekaa paying the highest transportation bill (figure 3.20).

When asked about the distance between homes and schools, around one-quarter of the households reported that their children's school was far from their home, a share that increased to 46 percent in the Bekaa region, where population density is low, and decreased to 17 percent in Beirut, where population density is high. As a result, 58 percent of Beirut's households stated that their children walked to schools, compared to only 15 percent in Bekaa. While buses remained the preferred mode of transportation for both public and private school students, a larger share of private school households reported the use of formal school buses, compared with public school households, where the use of informal private buses is more prevalent. Additionally, private cars were the second most used mode of transportation for private school students, while walking was the second-most-used mode of transportation for public school students (figure 3.21). The average school trip is

FIGURE 3.21

Percentage of households by means of transportation (*N* = 731)

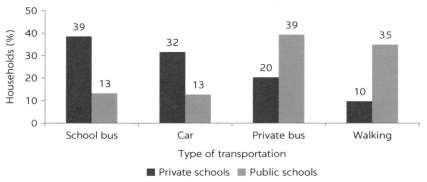

Source: Data based on the Public Perception Survey (unpublished) conducted for this report.
Note: N = number of respondents.

estimated to be 17 minutes, ranging between 15.5 minutes for public school students and 18.5 minutes for private school students.

Class size is generally used as one indicator of education access and quality. Teachers working wit /SCHOOL YEAR h a smaller group of students can more readily and easily utilize active and participatory approaches of learning with their students, in addition to providing more individual attention to each student, while overcrowded classrooms have been associated with higher levels of aggression among students and lower levels of classroom engagement, in turn leading to decreased opportunities for learning.[4] The average number of students per classroom in Lebanon based on households' reports was around 24, with almost no difference between public (24) and private schools (23) and between cycles: primary (25), intermediate (24), and secondary (23). Nearly a quarter of households (23 percent) perceived their children's schools to be crowded, with significantly more public school parents (28 percent) reporting crowdedness compared to private school parents (17 percent).

PERCEPTION OF THE IMPACT OF THE SYRIAN REFUGEE CRISIS ON THE EDUCATION SYSTEM

Overall, more than half of Lebanese households (56 percent) attributed negative effects to the Syrian refugee crisis on the quality of teaching and learning, school facilities and equipment, and relationships among students. The negative attribution seemed to increase with the age of the respondent, as the percentage of households reporting a negative effect of the Syrian crisis on the quality of teaching and learning increased from 52 percent among respondents under the age of 25 years to 63 percent among respondents age 65 and above (figure 3.22). Moreover, it is noteworthy that households which did not include a currently or recently enrolled student were significantly more likely to report a negative impact of the Syrian crisis on the education sector (at 60 percent of households), compared to households that included currently or recently enrolled students (at 50 percent of households). This finding could be an indication that efforts—led by the Ministry of Education, CSOs, and other education stakeholders—to

FIGURE 3.22

Percentage of Lebanese households reporting a negative impact of the Syrian crisis on the quality of teaching and learning (N = 1,221)

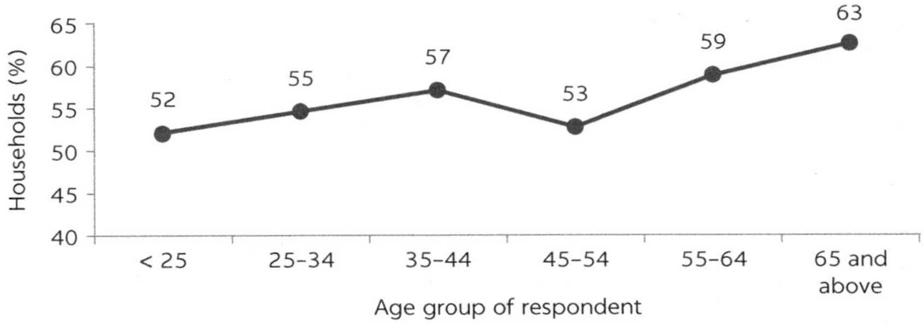

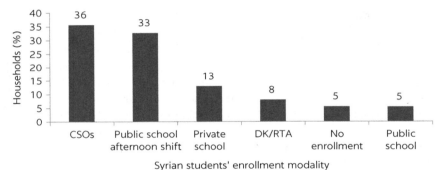

Source: Data based on the Public Perception Survey (unpublished) conducted for this report.
Note: N = number of respondents.

FIGURE 3.23

Percentage of Lebanese households by preferred refugee education provision modality (N = 1,221)

Source: Data based on the Public Perception Survey (unpublished) conducted for this report.
Note: CSO = civil society organization; DK/RTA = don't know or refuse to answer;
N = number of respondents.

mitigate the effects of the Syrian crisis on schools were starting to bear fruit, given that households with children in schools were the least likely to consider the influx of Syrian refugee children as detrimental to the education sector.

With regard to providing access to education for all refugee children in Lebanon, a large majority of surveyed Lebanese households supported this effort. The most favored position was the provision of education services through CSOs, with 36 percent of households advocating for this approach. Lebanese parents with currently or recently enrolled students were significantly more in favor of this approach, with 38 percent of those households expressing this view, compared with 31 percent of households with no currently or recently enrolled student. The second-most favored approach for refugee education provision, as expressed by 33 percent of respondents, was the establishment of second-shift schools, which are public schools operating afternoon shifts exclusively for Syrian students (figure 3.23). Nevertheless, half of Lebanese households surveyed perceived the introduction of a second shift for Syrian refugees in public schools as having major negative effects on the school infrastructure, given the increase in frequency of use of school buildings, equipment, and furniture. Only 5 percent of Lebanese households preferred the integration of Syrian refugees in first shifts of Lebanese public schools, even though, in academic year 2016–17, a total of 70,000 Syrian refugee children were enrolled in first-shift public schools and refugee children represented 22 percent of first-shift students in basic education (grades 1–9) and 33 percent in kindergarten (KG1, KG2, KG3) (CERD 2017). These findings indicate that while Lebanese households were supportive of refugee children's education in Lebanon, they were also concerned about the integration of Syrian children with Lebanese children in the same classroom or school.

PERCEPTION OF THE EDUCATION EXPERIENCE BY THE SYRIAN REFUGEE POPULATION

In general, Syrian households perceived education in Lebanon to be of good or excellent quality (figure 3.24), with 82 percent expressing these views. Moreover, around half of Syrian households (46 percent) had the impression that the quality of education was improving in Lebanon, while 32 percent believed that it was stable over time. These views on education quality mirror the views of Lebanese households regarding education quality.

However, as opposed to what most Lebanese believe, most Syrian households did not attribute any negative impact of the Syrian refugee crisis to the education system in Lebanon (figure 3.25). Less than a third of Syrian households perceived a negative impact of the Syrian crisis on the quality of teaching and learning in Lebanese public schools, and 73 percent and 65 percent of Syrian respondents asserted that the refugee crisis had no impact on the infrastructure of schools and on student relations, respectively. Even when asked about the effect of introducing a second shift in a school, only 14 percent of the Syrian households perceived a negative impact on school infrastructure, compared with 50 percent of Lebanese households.

With regard to access to education, the majority of surveyed Syrian parents (54 percent) seemed to prefer regular daytime public schools and private schools for their children, as opposed to 17 percent of Syrian parents, who preferred second-shift schooling or educational opportunities provided by CSOs (figure 3.26), a finding clearly at odds with the preferred options for refugee

FIGURE 3.24

Syrian refugees' views on education quality (N = 228)

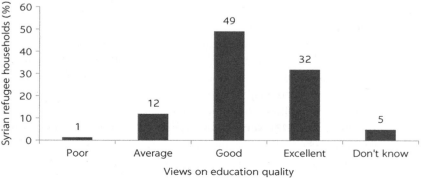

Source: Data based on the Public Perception Survey (unpublished) conducted for this report.
Note: N = number of respondents.

FIGURE 3.25

Syrian refugees' views on the impact of the Syrian crisis on various aspects of education (N = 228)

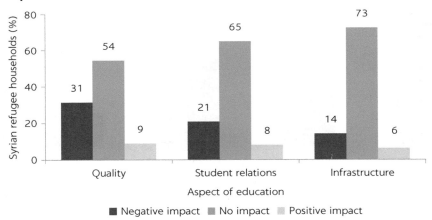

Source: Data based on the Public Perception Survey (unpublished) conducted for this report.
Note: N = number of respondents.

FIGURE 3.26

Syrian refugees' preferred enrollment modality for Syrian students (N = 228)

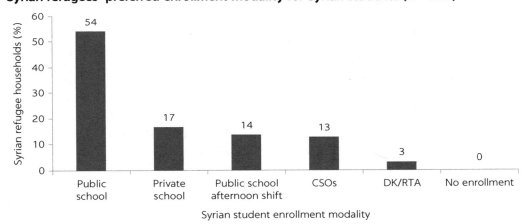

Source: Data based on the Public Perception Survey (unpublished) conducted for this report.
Note: CSO = civil society organization; DK/RTA = don't know or refuse to answer; N = number of respondents.

children's schooling proposed by Lebanese parents. An interesting finding was that in the Governorate of North Lebanon, more Syrian households appeared to prefer private schooling (54 percent) to public schooling (23 percent), which might be due to both push factors from public schools, including crowdedness and potential student relation issues between Lebanese and Syrian children, and pull factors of private schools in the region that might offer affordable education and Syrian-adapted curricula.

Regarding school climate, Syrian households were more likely to report instances of verbal and physical violence than their Lebanese counterparts, including both in terms of student-to-student and teacher-to-student violence (figure 3.27). For example, the reported incidence rate of student-to-student

FIGURE 3.27

Households reporting incidence of violence (*N* = 1,507)

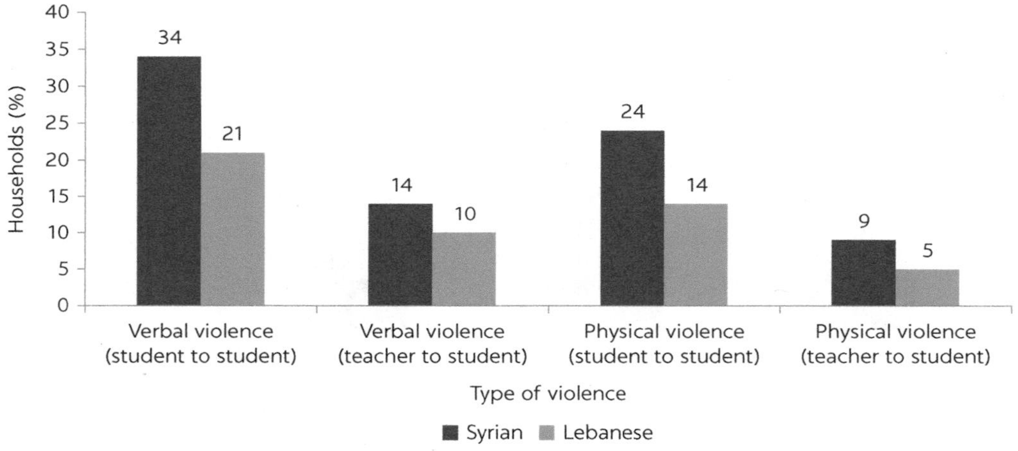

Source: Data based on the Public Perception Survey (unpublished) conducted for this report.
Note: N = number of respondents.

verbal and physical violence is 22 percent for Syrian households compared to 15 percent for Lebanese households.

In terms of their ability to adapt to the Lebanese curriculum, Syrian parents seemed to report that their children faced significant difficulties with foreign language learning, given the transition of language of instruction from Arabic in Syrian schools to a foreign language (French or English) in Lebanon. About 47 percent of Syrian parents found foreign language subjects to be difficult, compared to 29 percent of public school Lebanese parents and 17 percent of private school Lebanese parents. Moreover, only 27 percent of Syrian parents found the sciences to be appealing, compared to a higher share of Lebanese parents (37 percent). The opposite can be said about the interest in Arabic language instruction, as 36 percent of Syrian parents found it appealing, compared to a lower share of 20 percent for Lebanese parents. Finally, more Syrian households (19 percent) reported that they felt their children were not sufficiently prepared for exams than Lebanese households (7 percent).

PERCEPTION OF EDUCATION REFORMS AND PRIORITIES

While the majority of households (53 percent) seemed to believe that spending on their children's schooling is commensurate with the quality of their children's educational experiences, nearly all surveyed households supported investments in the public education sector in Lebanon, so that public schools are able to compete with private schools. In line with this support for public school reform, 88 percent of households supported expanding the number of public kindergartens in the country, indicating potential awareness of the importance of early childhood education among the Lebanese population. Furthermore, the two other key reform priorities for households in Lebanon were an improvement in Arabic language teaching, supported by 90 percent of households, and the reform of the curriculum to reduce its heavy content focus, supported by 79 percent of households (figure 3.28).

FIGURE 3.28

Percentage of households supporting proposed educational reforms (*N* = 1,507)

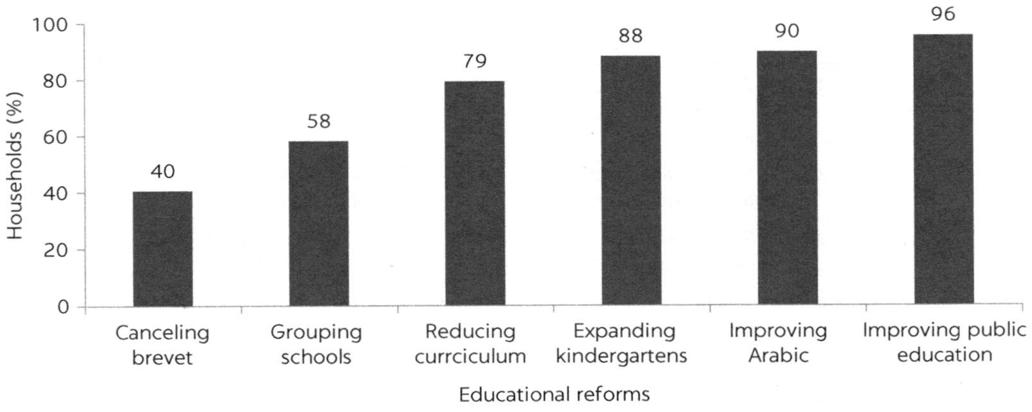

Source: Data based on the Public Perception Survey (unpublished) conducted for this report.
Note: N = number of respondents.

While school consolidation was supported by 58 percent of households overall, support for this reform increased significantly in rural/peripheral areas where there is a high prevalence of small and sparsely occupied schools. Thus, support for this reform was 100 percent in Marjayoun, 95 percent in Akkar, and 90 percent in Minieh-Dennieh. The only urban area with high support for school consolidation was Tripoli (80 percent), which has a relatively high number of schools housed in substandard buildings in the city. Public school parents were also more likely to support schools' consolidation (60 percent, compared to 53 percent among private school parents).

With regard to national examinations, there was no large support for canceling the grade 9 national exam ("brevet"), a reform commonly proposed by Lebanese members of Parliament and politicians; and responses on this topic did not seem to vary significantly between public and private school households. One of the reasons behind households' reluctance to support such a reform could be their need for a certification of their children's educational attainment, in addition to their need for a measure of their children's learning. As stated earlier, for public schools, only 35 percent were satisfied by the assessment mechanism in schools; thus, it seemed reasonable that they would be seeking a national mechanism for assessment of their children's learning.

Households also identified key reform areas for either public or private schools (table 3.2). From this list, reforms targeting accountability and quality control systems for schools and teachers were among the top priorities for both the private and public sectors. Particularly, the strengthening of school accountability and quality control mechanisms was the top priority for private schools and the second one for public schools, with, respectively, 42 percent and 41 percent of respondents identifying this reform as important. This was an indication that while households generally expressed positive opinions about the quality of education in Lebanon, they admitted that there was a need for a stronger regulatory framework which holds schools accountable for delivering high-quality education.

TABLE 3.2 **List of key priority reforms by sector, as identified by households in Lebanon (N = 1,507)**

RANK	PUBLIC SCHOOLS' PRIORITY REFORMS	RESPONDENTS (%)	PRIVATE SCHOOLS' PRIORITY REFORMS	RESPONDENTS (%)
1	Teachers' competencies and skills	44	Schools' accountability and quality control	42
2	Schools' accountability and quality control	41	School management and leadership	35
3	School buildings and equipment	39	Teachers' competencies and skills	32
4	Teachers' accountability and incentives	38	Teachers' accountability and incentives	32
5	School management and leadership	32	Principals' recruitment and deployment	31
6	Teachers' recruitment and deployment	31	Teachers' recruitment and deployment	29
7	Principals' recruitment and deployment	28	Schools' community engagement	18
8	Schools' community engagement	10	School buildings and equipment	7

Source: Data based on the Public Perception Survey (unpublished) conducted for this report.
Note: N = number of respondents.

Also among the top priority reforms of households were improvements in the competencies and skills of teachers and school principals, implying strong support for reforms in the preservice training and in-service professional development of school teachers and administrators. This perception was substantiated by the role in education reform that households attributed to key teacher preparation or teacher support institutions (figure 3.29). Hence, the CERD, which provides in-service teacher training, was perceived to be on the list of major players in education reform by 64 percent of households, and 61 percent of households indicated that education faculties at universities, which provide preservice training for teachers, played a major role in education reform. Teachers' unions were also seen as a major player in reform by 61 percent of respondents, given that teachers' accountability and incentives were the fourth priority area for both private and public schools.

Nonetheless, the main actor for education reform was largely perceived to be the MEHE by 93 percent of respondents, a clear vote of confidence from the public in the MEHE's role to drive the sector for both public and private schools. Conversely, households found little role for parents and the community in improving the sector; less than half of the respondents (41 percent) included parent committees on the list of major players in education reform, and only 23 percent of households included CSOs. Schools' community engagement was not seen as a priority reform issue because only 10 percent in public schools and 18 percent in private schools sought to see an improvement in this area. Consequently, one can conclude that despite households' push for a stronger school accountability and quality control mechanism, their expectations were that they would not be playing a major role in that mechanism and that the MEHE would be the one playing that role to guarantee high-quality education for their children.

FIGURE 3.29

List of stakeholders identified as major players in education reform by a given percentage of households (*N* = 1,507)

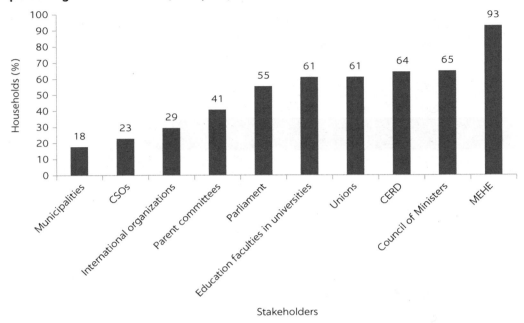

Source: Data based on the Public Perception Survey (unpublished) conducted for this report.
Note: CERD = Center for Educational Research and Development; CSO = civil society organization; MEHE = Ministry of Education and Higher Education; *N* = number of respondents.

PERCEPTION VERSUS REALITY

The perception of quality of education has been consistently positive over the years; and these findings have been replicated numerous times by different opinion surveys. The study for this chapter, conducted in 2016, recorded a satisfaction rate of 76 percent, and the Gallup 2015 survey reported a satisfaction rate of 72 percent (Gallup 2015). A recent survey by the World Economic Forum (WEF) within the 2018 Global Competitiveness Index placed Lebanon 18th globally (out of 137 countries) for perception of overall education quality and 4th globally (out of 137 countries) for perception of quality of math and science education (WEF 2018). Nevertheless, these rankings and perception surveys do not reflect the reality of the sector in Lebanon, as measured by learning outcomes. When considering harmonized learning outcomes (HLO) (Altinok, Angrist, and Patrinos 2018), Lebanon had an average score of 401 in 2015, based on learning assessments in reading, math, and science conducted in both public and private schools at different grade levels. This placed Lebanon approximately at the 35th percentile globally in terms of learning outcomes (ranking 92 out of 141 countries)[5] (World Bank 2018a). In contrast, using the Gallup surveys for cross-country comparison of satisfaction rates, Lebanon was approximately at the 75th percentile globally in terms of perception of education quality (ranking 37 out of 141 countries) (Gallup 2015). This large discrepancy between perception and reality of education quality is illustrated in figure 3.30.

FIGURE 3.30

Perception of education quality versus learning outcomes in Lebanon and comparator countries

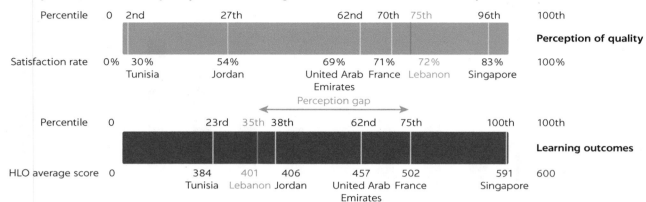

Sources: HLO scores from Education Statistics (EdStats) (database), World Bank, Washington, DC, https://datatopics.worldbank.org/education/country /lebanon; perception scores from Gallup (2015).
Note: HLO = harmonized learning outcomes.

LEARNING OUTCOMES

Student performance in Lebanon has been significantly lower than the international average, with a declining trend as measured by international learning assessments.

Results from TIMSS, a large-scale standardized assessment administered globally and in Lebanon in both private and public schools, indicated that learning outcomes in math and science for grade 8 students have been decreasing since 2007 (figure 3.31).[6] In math, while Lebanon's average performance was at the international average in 2007, by 2015, Lebanon's performance had significantly decreased below the international average. In science, Lebanon has been consistently performing significantly below the international average, and the gap between Lebanon and the international average has been widening. Comparatively, the average performance in the Middle East and North Africa (MENA) region has been consistently improving since 2007. In 2007, Lebanon's learning outcomes were significantly higher than the MENA average, but by 2015, the MENA average scores had reached or exceeded the Lebanon scores in both math and science.

Lebanon's low performance compared to the international average was also demonstrated through the PISA 2015 results. PISA, which measures learning outcomes for 15-year-olds in math, science and reading, showed that Lebanese students were on average approximately 4 years of schooling behind students in the OECD countries (figure 3.32) (World Bank 2016).[7] In Reading,[8] Lebanon was the worst performer among all 70 participating countries (OECD 2018).

While private schools performed better than public schools, results were significantly low for both sectors. For example, in science, private school students outperformed public school students by 64 points (CERD 2018a), which is equivalent to 2 years of schooling (figure 3.33).

FIGURE 3.31

TIMSS scores in math and science, 2003–15

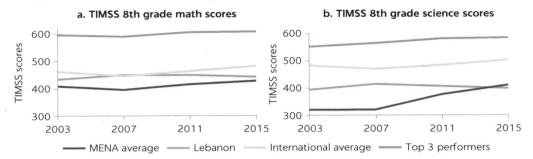

Source: Education Statistics (EdStats) (database), World Bank, Washington, DC, https://datatopics.worldbank.org /education/country/lebanon.

Note: MENA = Middle East and North Africa; TIMSS = Trends in International Mathematics and Science Study.

FIGURE 3.32

PISA 2015 scores in reading, math, and science

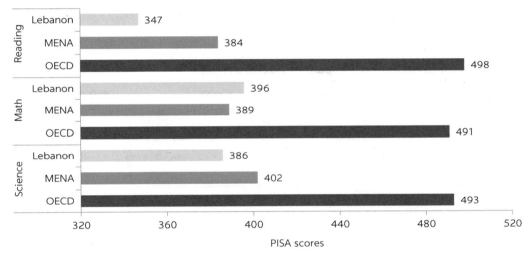

Source: World Bank 2016.

Note: MENA = Middle East and North Africa; OECD = Organisation for Economic Co-operation and Development; PISA = Program for International Student Assessment.

However, Lebanese private school students still fell behind students in OECD countries by 75 points, equivalent to 2.5 years of schooling. Table 3.3 illustrates the difference in performance in PISA 2015 between the Lebanese public and private education sectors.

It is important to note that in TIMSS 2015, there were no statistically significant differences in performance between public and private schools (CERD 2018b). In other words, grade 8 public and private school students had similar scores in math and science in TIMSS. A possible explanation for the absence of the private sector's lead in TIMSS compared to PISA is the different focus that each assessment has. TIMSS puts a greater focus on curriculum and requires certain content to have been covered by the nominated grade; PISA, on the other hand, focuses less on curriculum content and more on skills and knowledge applications to real-life situations.

FIGURE 3.33

Lebanon PISA 2015 scores in science by school profile

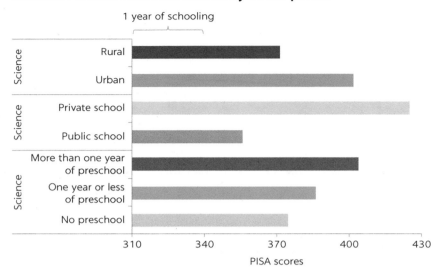

Source: World Bank 2016.
Note: PISA = Program for International Student Assessment.

TABLE 3.3 **PISA 2015 results by sector of education compared to OECD average**

SUBJECT	LEBANON—PUBLIC SCHOOLS (PISA SCORES)		LEBANON—PRIVATE SCHOOLS (PISA SCORES)		OECD AVERAGE (PISA SCORES)
Reading (English)	329	+50	379	+119	498
Reading (French)	293	+99	392	+106	498
Math	361	+69	430	+61	491
Science	354	+64	418	+75	493

Source: Disaggregation by sector of education was retrieved from CERD 2018a.
Note: CERD = Center for Educational Research and Development; OECD = Organisation for Economic Co-operation and Development; OECD AVERAGE = average score for OECD countries; PISA = Program for International Student Assessment.

FIGURE 3.34

Lebanon PISA 2015 proficiency levels in reading, math, and science

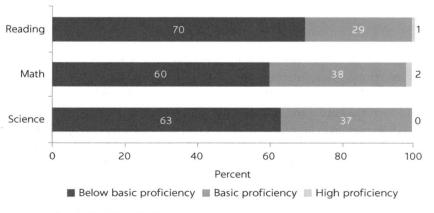

Source: World Bank 2016.
Note: PISA = Program for International Student Assessment.

The low PISA 2015 scores for Lebanon also highlighted alarmingly low levels of proficiency in math, science, and reading, among Lebanese students. Using the PISA 2015 proficiency benchmarks, the results showed that 60 percent of

Lebanese students did not achieve basic proficiency in math, 63 percent in science, and 70 percent in reading (figure 3.34).

Compared to countries at a similar level of economic development (that is, similar GDP per capita PPP), Lebanon's performance was significantly low. For example, in science, at Lebanon's GDP per capita PPP, Lebanon's average score was 46 points below the expected score for a country with an equal GDP per capita PPP (figure 3.35) (World Bank 2016); this is equivalent to approximately 1.5 years of schooling (World Bank 2018).

These figures point to a learning crisis in Lebanon, with nearly two-thirds of students at age 15 not reaching basic proficiency in reading, math, and science, placing them at a risk of exclusion from secondary school. Low proficiency in foundational skills has also been measured in Lebanon as early as in grades 2 and 3. In 2016, a nationally representative Early Grade Reading Assessment (EGRA) found that more than 83 percent of students in grades 2 and 3 performed at the lowest benchmark set by the Lebanese government education institutions.[9] In grade 2, 10 percent of children were not able to read a single word, and a total of 37 percent were not able to read more than 10 words (QITABI EGRA 2017).

FIGURE 3.35

PISA 2015 scores in science as a function of GDP per capita PPP

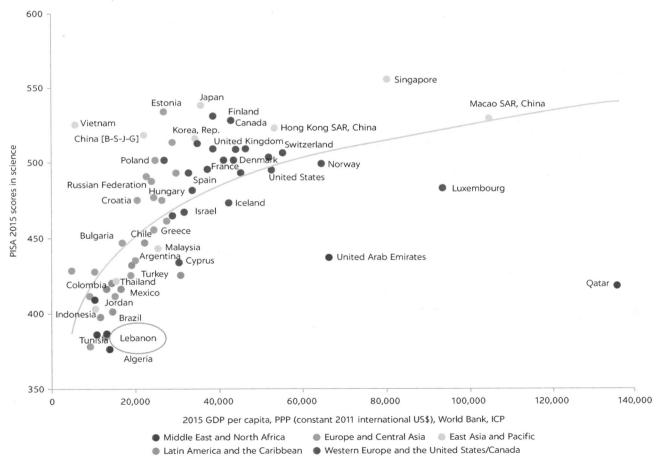

Sources: World Bank 2016; ICP (database), World Bank, Washington, DC, https://databank.worldbank.org/reports.aspx?source=international-comparison-program-(icp)-2011.

Note: B-S-J-G = Beijing-Shanghai-Jiangsu-Guangdong; GDP = gross domestic product; ICP = International Comparison Program; PISA = Program for International Student Assessment; PPP = public-private partnership.

EQUITY

In addition to low mean scores in reading, math, and science, Lebanon had a high dispersion rate. Dispersion rates measure the difference in scores between the top and bottom performers, and thus countries with high dispersion rates are countries where inequity is high, and there are large gaps in learning achievements between schools and between individual students. Figure 3.36 illustrates the low mean score and high dispersion for TIMSS grade 8 science scores as an example.[10]

Economic, social, and cultural status (ESCS) is a key factor driving inequity in learning achievement in Lebanon. In fact, in the Middle East and North Africa region, Lebanon has the highest gap in student performance between the top and bottom ESCS quintiles. As an example, PISA 2015 science scores showed a difference of approximately 2.8 years of schooling between the top and bottom ESCS quintiles (figure 3.37) (World Bank 2018).

The large inequity in education outcomes between children from high and low ESCS could be in part explained by inequalities in the allocation of resources (material and staff) to schools. Using the PISA 2015 questionnaire data, Lebanon had some of the highest differences in resources availability between advantaged and disadvantaged schools (figure 3.38) (IMF 2018), including both public and private schools. Advantaged schools are those where the average ESCS of students is high. The model in figure 3.38 indicates that in Lebanon, this stark difference in staff and material resources between schools explains the low learning outcomes obtained in the PISA 2015 science assessment (that is, the values for Lebanon are well fitted on the regression line for PISA 2015 science scores as a function of the difference between advantaged and disadvantaged schools).

FIGURE 3.36

TIMSS grade 8 science: Mean scores and score dispersion rates

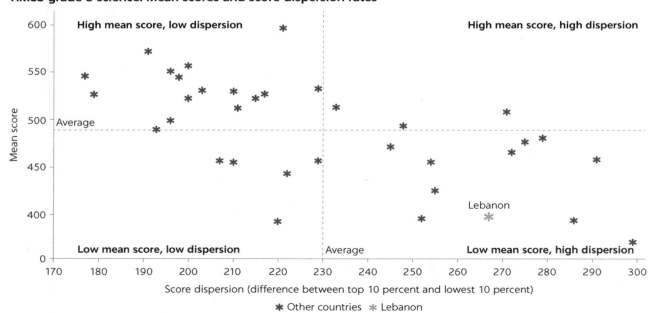

Sources: Education Statistics (EdStats) (database), World Bank, Washington, DC, https://datatopics.worldbank.org/education/country/lebanon.

FIGURE 3.37

PISA 2015 science scores by top and bottom ESCS quintile in the Middle East and North Africa

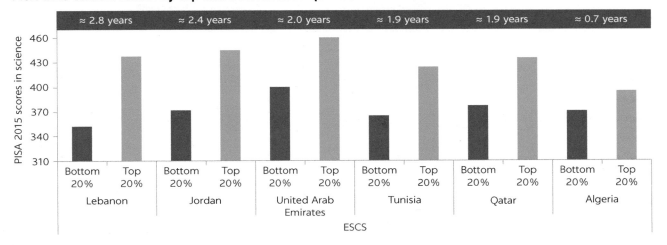

Source: World Bank 2016.
Note: ESCS = economic, social, and cultural status; PISA = Program for International Student Assessment.

FIGURE 3.38

Difference in material resources between advantaged and disadvantaged schools and average PISA science score

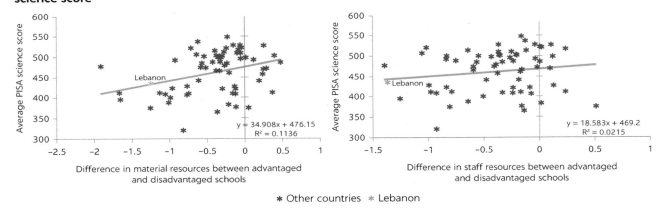

Source: Adapted from IMF 2018.
Note: Negative values mean disadvantaged schools have fewer resources. PISA = Program for International Student Assessment.

In addition to ESCS, Lebanon had a gender gap in reading skills, with girls outperforming boys. This gap is observed at different grade levels, starting with grade 2, as measured by the EGRA in 2016, where girls outperformed boys significantly on all reading subskills (table 3.4).[11] This gender gap continues until secondary school, as measured by PISA for 15-year-olds, with girls scoring 14 points higher than boys (353 for girls versus 339 for boys).[12] Lebanon also has a gender gap in math, with boys outperforming girls. This result was demonstrated in TIMSS 2011 and then in PISA 2015. In the latter, boys significantly outperformed girls, by 22 points (408 for boys versus 386 for girls).[13]

There is also evidence for regional inequity in terms of learning achievement. The EGRA 2016 data demonstrated that grade 2 students in Mount Lebanon performed significantly better in reading fluency than students in all other governorates.[14] The PISA 2015 showed that students in Mount Lebanon and Beirut

TABLE 3.4 EGRA 2016 grade 2 results per reading subtask and gender of student

SUBTASK	RAW SCORE RANGE	RAW SCORE		
		OVERALL	BOYS	GIRLS
Letter name recognition	0–100	13.5	12.7	14.2*
Letter sound knowledge	0–100	9.0	8.5	9.5*
Phoneme isolation	0–10	3.0	2.8	3.2*
Syllable segmentation	0–10	4.0	3.8	4.2*
Familiar words reading	0–50	16.2	14.6	17.8*
Reading vocabulary	0–10	4.3	4.2	4.5*
Oral reading fluency (passage A)	0–75	15.7	14.3	17.1*
Reading comprehension (passage A)	0–6	1.1	1.1	1.1
Reading comprehension (passage B)	0–6	2.5	2.4	2.6*

Source: QITABI 2017.
Note: EGRA = Early Grade Reading Assessment; QITABI = Quality Instruction towards Access and Basic Education Improvement.
* statistically significant difference at $p < 0.05$.

performed significantly better than students in all other governorates (Bekaa, North, South, and Nabatieh) in science, math, and reading (CERD 2018a).

Another equity concern apparent from the study was the difference in education outcomes between public and private schools. Indeed, passing rates for national examinations in 2017 revealed that there are differences in student achievements between the private and the public sectors (table 3.3) (CERD 2017). For grade 9, the private sector outperformed the public sector by more than 15 percentage points. With more than one out of four (27 percent) grade 9 students in the public sector failing the national examinations, these children face a high risk of exclusion from secondary schooling and other learning opportunities.[15] At the secondary school level, there was no statistical significance between public and private schools when taking into consideration all students passing the grade 12 national examination. This finding might be behind the improvement in perception of public school education quality at the secondary level. However, when looking at each field of specialization, there were significant differences between the two sectors. In the sciences, including both life sciences and general sciences, private sector students outperformed public sector students by 8.5 and 9.7 percentage points, respectively. This gap, however, disappeared in the literature and humanities field and was reversed for the social sciences field, where public students outperformed by 8.1 percentage points. These findings confirm the results of the public perception survey, where private school parents expressed that their children faced difficulties in Arabic language instruction, the humanities, and social sciences, while public sector parents expressed this concern for science subjects, math, and foreign languages (which are also the languages used for math and science instruction). These findings were also reflected in the enrollment numbers in each academic stream, with public sector students being significantly less likely to choose science fields compared to private school students: 52 percent of grade 12 students in the private sector were specialized in science fields in 2017 versus only 40 percent of public sector students (table 3.5) (CERD 2017).[16] This difference in orientation toward field of specializations between public and private school students perpetuates inequity in life opportunities and career prospects, with significantly fewer public school students pursuing education opportunities and careers in STEM fields.

TABLE 3.5 **Student numbers and passing rates in 2017 national examinations**

	STUDENT NUMBERS				PASSING RATES	
EXAMINATION	PUBLIC SECTOR		PRIVATE SECTOR		PUBLIC SECTOR	PRIVATE SECTOR
Grade 9 Brevet	17,725	100%	38,409	100%	72.9%	88.0%
Grade 12 Baccalaureate	18,392	100%	21,241	100%	80.7%	81.2%
per field of specialization						
Life sciences	5,415	29%	8,002	38%	77.7%	86.2%
General sciences	2,103	11%	2,955	14%	85.9%	95.6%
Literature and humanities	1,361	7%	556	3%	84.4%	84.7%
Economics and sociology	9,513	52%	9,728	46%	80.7%	72.6%

Source: CERD 2017.
Note: In orange, statistically significant differences between public and private sectors. In blue circles, percentage of students in each academic stream out of all students per education sector (percentages are rounded and might not add up to 100 percent). CERD = Center for Educational Research and Development.

CONCLUSION

The perception survey showed high satisfaction rates of the general public with the education sector in Lebanon, reflecting the belief of Lebanese households in the importance of education as a pillar of the Lebanese economy and society. Nevertheless, there were variations in satisfaction rates between parents with children enrolled in private schools and parents with children enrolled in public schools, specifically in their perception of teachers' skills, pedagogy and curriculum content, school management, and school infrastructure. Particularly, parents in the public education sector found the most challenges in science, math, and foreign language instruction; while parents in the private education sector faced more challenges in Arabic language instruction, the humanities, and the social sciences. These difficulties were then reflected in the students' choices of field of specialization in secondary school, where public sector students were significantly less likely than private sector students to specialize in the sciences. These difficulties were then reflected in the students' choices of academic stream in secondary school: public sector students were significantly less likely than private sector students to specialize in the sciences; and once they chose the sciences, they were also less likely to succeed in the national examinations and obtain certifications that would facilitate their access to higher education in science, technology, engineering, and mathematics (STEM).

Regarding infrastructure, the opinion survey revealed that infrastructure issues did not seem far-reaching, given an acceptable average satisfaction rate by the general public. Nevertheless, there were stark disparities in the quality of school buildings, access to facilities and amenities, and availability of learning and teaching materials and equipment between regions and between schools. Infrastructure gaps existed mostly in public schools, especially in rural and peripheral areas. Given these findings, large investments in school infrastructure might therefore not be a priority concern for the education system. However, the Lebanese government should focus on targeted infrastructure upgrades for schools that have the highest needs. Chapter 4 of this volume presents evidence on the association between high-quality school buildings and higher levels of student achievement.

With regard to the impact of the Syrian refugee crisis, Lebanese households asserted that it had negative effects on the education sector in Lebanon.

Nonetheless, respondents who were more likely to express negative impacts of the Syrian refugee crisis on education were in households which did not have children currently or recently enrolled in schools and were thus the least likely to be affected by the influx of Syrian refugees. Lebanese households also expressed their preference for the provision of education services to Syrian children to be through CSOs or second-shift public schools. Conversely, Syrian households expressed strong preference for the integration of Syrian children in daytime public schools, with only a small fraction preferring second-shift schools or provision of education through CSOs. Syrian parents were more likely to report incidences of verbal and physical violence in schools, even though these reports were also high for Lebanese households compared to international benchmarks.

Households prioritized reforms, targeting accountability and quality control systems for schools and teachers for both the private and public sectors. This was an indication that while households generally expressed positive opinion about the quality of education in Lebanon, they admitted that there was a need for a stronger regulatory framework which holds schools accountable for delivering quality education. Also among the top priority reforms of households were improvements in the competencies and skills of teachers and school principals, implying strong support for reforms in the preservice training and in-service professional development of school teachers and administrators. Finally, there was growing support for grouping and consolidating schools; this priority area was specifically voiced by households in rural and peripheral areas, where the prevalence of small and sparsely occupied schools was high.

Finally, the overall positive perception of education quality in Lebanon was not reflected in the actual learning outcomes and achievements of students. Compared to countries at a similar level of development, Lebanon's results on international assessments have been low and have been decreasing over the years since 2007. This decreasing trend is in stark contrast to the perception that education quality was improving, as highlighted in the opinion survey. Moreover, based on existing evidence from available assessments, proficiency levels were low in Lebanon at all grade levels, starting with the early grades, where more than 83 percent of grade 2 and 3 students were at the lowest benchmark for reading skills, and including 15-year-olds, where between 60 percent and 70 percent of students performed below basic proficiency levels in math, science, and reading. In addition to low levels of learning, Lebanon had high levels of inequity, with the gap in learning outcomes between the top and bottom ESCS quintiles being the largest in the Middle East and North Africa region. Lebanon also had a gender gap in math skills in favor of boys and a reverse gender gap in reading skills in favor of girls at all grade levels. These low levels of learning and high levels of inequity stand in contrast to a strong commitment of the government and private households to invest in education. The next two chapters (chapters 4 and 5) explore this commitment and try to uncover the systemic challenges in efficiency and political economy that are impeding Lebanon's ability to translate this commitment in education into actual learning.

NOTES

1. Children in Lebanon. Central Administration of Statistics (CAS). September 2013.
2. http://timssandpirls.bc.edu/timss2015/international-results/timss-2015/science/achievement-in-content-and-cognitive-domains/achievement-in-science-cognitive-domains/.

3. Households were classified into three income categories based on monthly gross income: low (under 1.5 million Lebanese pounds [LL]), medium (1.5 million LL–4.5 million LL), and high (4.5 million LL or more).

4. http://sites.psu.edu/ceepa/2015/06/07/the-importance-of-school-facilities-in-improving -student-outcomes/.

5. Harmonized Learning Outcomes Dataset, World Bank, Washington, DC.

6. Education Statistics (EdStats) (database), World Bank, Washington, DC, http://datatopics .worldbank.org/education/country/lebanon. Retrieved in April 2018.

7. Thirty points on the PISA scale is nearly equivalent to one year of schooling, which means that students in Lebanon were 3 years of schooling behind students in OECD countries in math, 3.5 years of schooling behind in science, and 5 years of schooling behind in reading.

8. In Lebanon, the reading section was either in English or in French, depending on the language of instruction of the school.

9. As of the date of writing, benchmarks set for reading fluency were still preliminary, and thus figures might be subject to change.

10. Education Statistics (EdStats) (database), World Bank, Washington, DC, http://datatopics .worldbank.org/education/country/lebanon. Retrieved in April 2018.

11. QITABI 2017, financed by USAID.

12. Education Statistics (EdStats) (database), World Bank, Washington, DC, http://datatopics .worldbank.org/education/country/lebanon. Retrieved in April 2018.

13. Education Statistics (EdStats) (database), World Bank, Washington, DC, http://datatopics .worldbank.org/education/country/lebanon. Retrieved in April 2018.

14. QITABI 2017, financed by USAID.

15. According to the "CERD Statistical Bulletin 2016–2017," the passing rate for public school students who failed the first round of the grade 9 national examination and who attempted the second round was only 18.6 percent at the second round.

16. The split of science students between life sciences and general sciences was the same across both the public sector and the private sector, with the ratio of life sciences students to general sciences students being 7 to 3 in both sectors.

REFERENCES

Altinok, N., N. Angrist, and H. A. Patrinos. 2018. "Global Data Set on Education Quality (1965–2015)." Policy Research Working Paper 8314, World Bank, Washington, DC. https://openknowledge.worldbank.org/handle/10986/29281.

CERD (Center for Educational Research and Development). 2017. "CERD Statistical Bulletin 2016–2017" (in Arabic). CERD, Beirut. https://www.crdp.org/files/201712220733131.pdf (accessed May 2018).

——. 2018a. "PISA 2015 National Report. Program for International Student Assessment." CERD, Beirut. https://www.crdp.org/pdf/uploads/PISA_Report_18-1.pdf.

——. 2018b. "TIMSS 2015 – Grade 8 National Report. Program for International Student Assessment." CERD, Beirut. https://www.crdp.org/files/201811210625183.pdf.

Gallup. 2015. "Satisfaction With K-12 Education." World Poll 2015. https://wpr.gallup.com/.

IMF (International Monetary Fund). 2018. "Jordan Public Expenditure Review and Rationalization: Issues and Reform Options." Unpublished Technical Assistance Report, IMF, Washington, DC.

Inglehart, R., C. Haerpfer, A. Moreno, C. Welzel, K. Kizilova, J. Diez-Medrano, M. Lagos, P. Norris, E. Ponarin, B. Puranen, et al. eds. 2014. "World Values Survey: Round Six." Madrid: JD Systems Institute. Country-Pooled Datafile Version, www.worldvaluessurvey .org/WVSDocumentationWV6.jsp.

OECD (Organisation for Economic Co-operation and Development). 2012. *Measuring Regulatory Performance: A Practitioner's Guide to Perception Surveys.* Paris: OECD Publishing. https://www.oecd.org/gov/regulatory-policy/48933826.pdf.

——. 2018. "PISA 2015 Results in Focus." PISA in Focus 67, OECD Publishing, Paris. https://www .oecd.org/pisa/pisa-2015-results-in-focus.pdf.

QITABI (Quality Instruction towards Access and Basic Education Improvement). 2017. "EGRA Combined Baseline Report." Unpublished Paper, QITABI, Beirut.

TIMSS (Trends in International Mathematics and Science Study). 2015a. "Student Bullying." TIMSS 2015 International Reports. http://timssandpirls.bc.edu/timss2015/international -results/timss-2015/mathematics/school-safety/student-bullying/.

——. 2015b. "School Discipline Problems – Principals" Reports." TIMSS 2015 International Reports. http://timssandpirls.bc.edu/timss2015/international-results/timss-2015 /mathematics/school-safety/school-discipline-problems/.

——. 2015c. "Problems with School Conditions and Resources – Teachers' Reports." TIMSS 2015 International Reports. http://timssandpirls.bc.edu/timss2015/international-results /timss-2015/mathematics/school-composition-and-resources/problems-with-school -conditions-and-resources/.

——. 2015d. "Instruction Affected by Science Resource Shortages – Principals' Reports." TIMSS 2015 International Reports. http://timssandpirls.bc.edu/timss2015/international -results/timss-2015/science/school-composition-and-resources/instruction-affected-by -science-resource-shortages/.

WEF (World Economic Forum). 2018. *The Arab World Competitiveness Report 2018*. Geneva: WEF. https://www.weforum.org/reports/arab-world-competitiveness-report-2018.

World Bank. 2016. "Lebanon—Program for International Student Assessment 2015 (English)." PISA Education Brief. World Bank, Washington, DC. http://documents.worldbank .org/curated/en/301971483073044618/Lebanon-Program-for-international-student -assessment-2015.

——. 2018. "Key Messages from PISA for Middle East and North Africa." Unpublished Paper, World Bank, Washington, DC.

4 Government Commitment to Education

MAIN MESSAGES

1. Education is an investment with high returns: Higher educational attainment corresponds to higher earnings in the labor market. In Lebanon, the latest data on poverty from the Central Administration for Statistics (CAS) estimated that, in 2011–12, the poverty rates among the population aged 22 and above were at 34 percent for individuals with primary education only, 16 percent for those with secondary education, and 9 percent for those with university education.

2. Lebanon invests heavily in education. However, this investment is dominated by private households' out-of-pocket costs. Public expenditures on general education have been low compared to international standards—at 1.8 percent of GDP and 5.5 percent of total government expenditures—but they are complemented by significant investments from private households, bringing total expenditures in the sector to approximately 4.5 percent of GDP, a figure which is comparable to other upper-middle-income countries and in the OECD.

3. The private sector dominates education service delivery in the country, with approximately 71 percent of the Lebanese students enrolled in private schools. Despite the high out-of-pocket cost paid by parents to private schools, the government spends significant amounts on subsidies to the private sector, reaching 28 percent of public education expenditures. Subsidies include school allowances to civil servants such as army personnel, internal security forces, and even public school teachers to enroll their children in private schools, as well as direct subsidies to a selected number of private schools, called the "free-private" schools, which are largely run by religious organizations.

4. Despite the significant investment in the entire education sector, education outcomes are low, with poor learning levels as assessed by national and international assessments and lower-than-expected enrollment rates, especially at the secondary education level. There is high inequity in the system, with children from poor households having a high risk of dropping out before secondary education and having significantly lower learning outcomes compared to students from the wealthiest households.

5. The subsidization program used by the Government of Lebanon exacerbates inequity and does not lead to better education quality and higher learning. Based on data from a household survey conducted by CAS in 2011–12,[1] 47 percent of education subsidies went to the wealthiest quintile in the population, while the bottom quintile received only 3 percent of those subsidies. This mechanism creates both high wealth inequity in terms of access to high-quality schools, in addition to high variation in quality between schools. If the poorest students in Lebanon had equal access to both public and private high-quality schools, then the difference in achievement between public and private school students would be significantly decreased (estimated at approximately 16 percentage points). Models for public-private sector partnerships from other countries, such as Belgium and the Netherlands, could be used to improve the Lebanon subsidization program to be more equitable.

6. In the public system, large inefficiencies exist in terms of teachers' recruitment, allocation, remuneration, and workload. The number of contractual teachers increased by 123 percent in 2011–17, and this growth rate does not account for "supplemental teachers" who were recruited to accommodate the increase in enrollment of Syrian refugee students in the first and second shifts. Because the hiring of contractual teachers follows much less stringent requirements, this could represent a risk for the quality of education service delivery in schools. The increase in the number of public school teachers has been faster than the increase in the number of students. The average student-teacher ratio in Lebanon was 10.7 in 2017. This ratio was low compared to other countries in the region (e.g., Jordan had a ratio of 15.8 and Turkey a ratio of 18.3), and to other upper-middle-income countries. The general indication from the student-teacher ratio is that there is a surplus of teachers in the system.

7. Teacher salaries in the public system are inflated, with more than 80 percent of civil servants having a salary grade higher than 25 out of 52; yet 40 percent of teachers have low education qualifications and do not have a university degree. At the same time, teacher workload is extremely low compared to international standards. Teachers in Lebanon on average spend 431 hours per year working, compared to an average of 771 hours per year for teachers in the OECD countries. Significantly low levels of workloads accompanied by high teacher salary cost per student put a tremendous pressure on the expenditure levels of the government. The cost of teacher salaries per student in the public education system reached a total of US$1,743 per student in 2015, an increase of 36 percent from the 2011 rate of US$1,277 per student, and an increase of 140 percent from the 2006 rate of US$727 per student. Compared to the OECD countries, the teacher salaries cost in Lebanon as a function of GDP per capita tended to be higher than average, especially at the secondary education level.

8. To increase internal efficiency with regard to teachers' management, there is a need to rationalize the recruitment and distribution of teachers across public schools, enforce teacher workload policies, and develop policies that ensure a clearly laid out work program for teachers, with a balance between teaching and nonteaching related tasks. It is also important that the government creates incentives to attract teachers to work in hard-to-staff schools or to teach subjects in critical shortage to avoid having the least qualified teachers or contractual teachers with no proper preservice training working in schools serving the most disadvantaged students.

9. In addition to teachers' management, the public sector faces inefficiencies in schools' distribution and allocation. The Government of Lebanon has consistently insisted on the necessity of expanding the reach of public schools in the regions and ensuring coverage in all administrative districts in the country. This policy prompted not only the construction of new schools but also the renting of privately owned premises to house public schools, with rent costs consisting of 3 percent of the 2015 MEHE budget in basic and secondary education. It is important to note that from 2001–15, due to low enrollment in some schools, the MEHE decreased the total number of public schools by 7 percent through consolidation of small schools. This is an indication that there are efficiency gains to be made in terms of school distribution.

10. In Lebanon, an analysis of how school inputs such as teachers and schools' distribution and infrastructure predict student education outcomes and passing rates revealed that the school size (or total number of students per school) was the single most important factor influencing student passing rates in national examinations, with higher levels of performance for bigger schools. The quality of school buildings was another important factor influencing student passing rates. Good-quality buildings usually have improved school resources, which have been shown to positively affect students' performance. The ownership of the school buildings (owned versus rented) did not seem to have any impact on student scores. This means that the focus of the government should not necessarily be on building schools but on improving the quality of resources in existing schools. This was true across all regions. High teacher salaries per student were associated negatively with learning outcomes. Because higher salaries are usually earned by older teachers according to the salary scale, this finding may be related to the reduction in teaching responsibility for staff with seniority and could also be an indication of higher teacher headcount and lower productivity leading to low student outcomes. This calls for government intervention to focus on improving the productivity of teachers, so the burden of teacher inefficiency does not fall on the students and the government's education budget.

11. The Syrian crisis introduced additional challenges to the public education system by exacerbating fiscal stress in the system. Non-Lebanese children reached up to 45 percent of public students in 2018. While some of the cost for enrolling these children has been covered by international donors and partners, a portion of the cost was also borne by the Lebanese government.

12. A results-based commitment model linked to school and system improvement is key to move the system forward and improve learning. The current system uses student headcount, for example, to distribute funding to schools and does not allocate spending according to different types of schools and students. The current financing model should be revisited to ensure that in the future, the allocation of funds is linked to school improvement and student performance, regardless of school size. Policy enhancement should consider four important principles of a school finance system: adequacy, equity, quality, and efficiency. The system should provide adequate resources at all levels of the education system to ensure that all students (irrespective of their socioeconomic background and other characteristics) receive a high-quality education. There needs to be a mechanism to use adjustments in education spending across governorates, districts *(cazas)*, and school sizes to preserve fiscal neutrality, so that available resources allocations are not biased.

INTRODUCTION

Lebanon is an upper-middle-income country with an average GDP per capita of US$14,675 PPP in 2017.[2] In recent years, Lebanon had a slow GDP growth rate not exceeding 2 percent per year.[3] Economic growth has been largely affected by frequent political shocks and upheavals (figure 4.1), including the 2006 war and the 2011 Syrian refugee crisis.

The overall government budget and macroeconomic environment have been unstable, with a widened fiscal and trade deficit and declining consumer confidence. Affected by the civil war, which lasted for more than 15 years, Lebanon's public finances suffered immensely, leading to increased borrowing. High rates of inflation accompanied with devaluation of the currency in the country put tremendous pressure on interest rates, which also increased the debt burden. This financial instability and inflation have affected the education sector, especially in relation to teacher salaries, because higher consumer prices driven by inflation triggered demand for higher salaries.

Low economic growth and high inflation have adversely affected the poverty levels in the country. The latest poverty estimates from the CAS in Lebanon date back from 2011–12 (at the onset of the Syrian refugee crisis) and indicate that 28.6 percent of the population lived below the poverty line and 8 percent were in extreme poverty.[4] With the influx of Syrian refugees since 2011, the poverty rates have likely increased significantly.

Nonetheless, in the face of adversity, education has been a potential driver for prosperity, as poverty rates decreased significantly with higher levels of education. The CAS household survey from 2011–12 estimated that poverty rates among the population aged 22 and above were at 34 percent for individuals with primary education only, and these rates decreased to 9 percent for those with a tertiary (university) education (figure 4.2). In other terms, Lebanese with tertiary education were four times less likely to be poor than Lebanese with only primary education. Moreover, even secondary education decreased the likelihood of poverty by 33 percent compared to individuals with only intermediate education, and by more than 50 percent compared to individuals with only primary education.

In summary, education is a key pillar of socioeconomic mobility and development in Lebanon. This chapter explores the government's and private households'

FIGURE 4.1

Fluctuations in the annual GDP growth rate

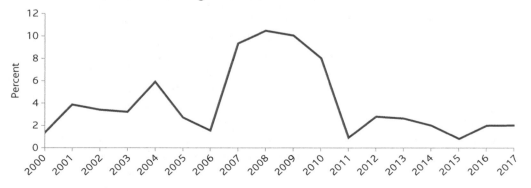

Source: Abdul-Hamid et al. 2018.
Note: GDP = gross domestic product.

FIGURE 4.2

Poverty rate by education level of population age 22 or more

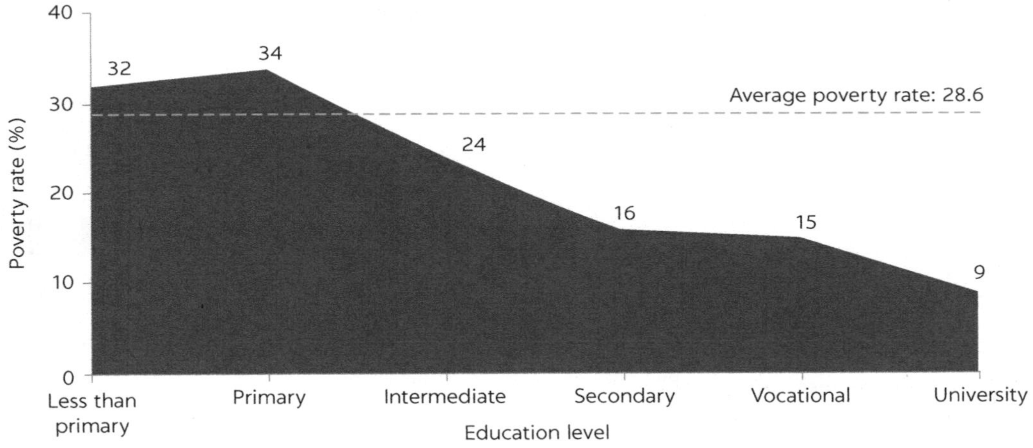

Source: CAS (database), Household-based Survey 2011–2012, Central Administration of Statistics, Beirut, http://www.cas.gov.lb/index.php/demographic-and-social-en/householdexpenditure-en.
Note: CAS = Central Administration of Statistics.

investment in the education sector, while also studying the efficiency of the system. The chapter is based on a comprehensive public expenditure review of education completed by the World Bank in 2017 (Abdul-Hamid et al. 2018).

PUBLIC AND PRIVATE EXPENDITURES ON EDUCATION

The level of public expenditures on education is low in Lebanon compared to international benchmarks, but this is mainly due to high levels of private education provision and private households' out-of-pocket spending. In terms of public expenditures, the government finances education through multiple channels:

1. The MEHE budget for the administration and operation of public schools, including general and vocational education;
2. The CERD budget for teacher training, conducting research, improving curriculum, and other activities in its mandate;
3. The Council for Development and Reconstruction (CDR) budget for school construction;
4. Subsidization to a selected number of private schools based on enrollment figures;
5. Education allowances to civil servants to enroll their children in private schools;
6. Budgets of other ministries and public institutions as needed, such as the education inspectorate.

Data from the Lebanese Ministry of Finance indicate that from 2013–15, actual public expenditures to the general education sector—excluding vocational and tertiary education—were around 1.8 percent of GDP and 5.5 percent of total public expenditures.[5] Public expenditures on general education in those 3 years averaged around US$900 million. While the absolute number has doubled since 2005, the share of education expenditures as a percentage of total expenditures has nearly stayed constant (figure 4.3).

FIGURE 4.3

Public expenditures on general education over time

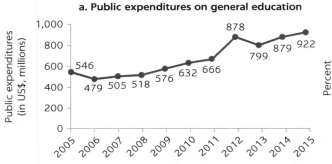

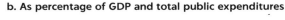

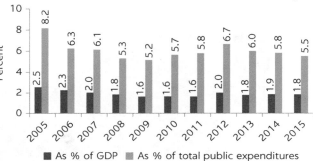

Source: Data provided by the Ministry of Finance, Lebanon, in 2016.
Note: GDP = gross domestic product.

FIGURE 4.4

Breakdown of government expenditures on the general education sector

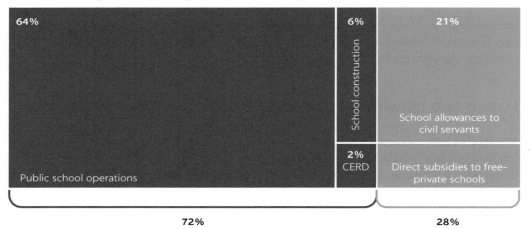

Source: Calculations based on data provided by the Ministry of Finance, Lebanon, in 2016.
Note: CERD = Center for Educational Research and Development.

Figure 4.4 shows an average breakdown of government expenditures on the general education sector. Out of all government expenditures on general education (approximately US$900 million), nearly 28 percent (around US$250 million) were subsidies to the private sector, either through direct subsidies to the "free-private" schools (7 percent) or through education allowances to civil servants (21 percent), to enroll their children in tuition-charging private schools.[6] The remaining 72 percent (around US$650 million) were expenditures on the public education sector, including running public schools through the MEHE (64 percent), investments in public school construction through the CDR (6 percent), and investments in education quality (curriculum, teacher training, research) through the CERD (2 percent).

At 1.8 percent of GDP, public expenditures on general education are considered low compared to other upper-middle-income countries and countries in the Middle East and North Africa region. For example, Tunisia spends approximately 6 percent of GDP on education, while Morocco spends about 4 percent. However, in these countries, education provision is mainly public. In Lebanon, the public share of enrollment in general education is low and is around 29 percent. With 71 percent of students enrolled in private schools, Lebanon is in the top 2 percent of countries and territories in terms of the private sector's share of education enrollment.[7]

Data from the Ministry of Education revealed that in 2015, the average tuition fee for private education was US$2,892 per year,[8] and thus the private general education sector had a market size of US$1.6 billion. The Government of Lebanon covered through education allowances to civil servants around US$200 million of the tuition market, while the rest (US$1.4 billion) was covered by private households' out-of-pocket expenditures. With the dominance of private schools in the country and the unequal level of subsidization from the government, private households' expenditures constitute a major pillar of the education sector's financing in Lebanon; at US$1.4 billion, it is greater than the government's public expenditures. When both public and private education expenditures are combined, Lebanon's total education expenditures reach 4.5 percent of GDP, a figure which is comparable to other upper-middle-income countries and in the OECD (figure 4.5).

Comparing the average per student expenditures between private and public schools shows that there is potential to increase government investment in public schools (table 4.1). Particularly, per student expenditures in primary schools are nearly 15 percent lower than the per student expenditures at the secondary level, and thus increase in government spending should focus on the lower levels of education to ensure a strong head start. Nonetheless, by estimating the per student expenditures in subsidized private schools, it seems that there might be efficiencies to be gained in the public sector and that the tuition-charging private sector might have comparatively inflated tuitions.

While public expenditures might be low, they are largely dominated by salaries. From the MEHE's actual budget, on average over 2013–15, salaries and benefits to both civil servants and contractual teachers and staff constituted more than 82 percent of the annual total expenditures, while rent costs exceeded 3 percent. The breakdown of MEHE expenditures is included in table 4.2.

FIGURE 4.5

Public and private education expenditures as percentage of GDP

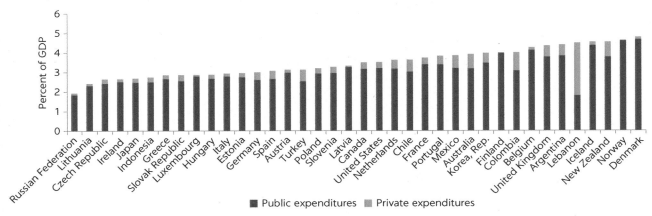

Source: Calculations using data from Public spending on education (database), OECD, Paris, https://data.oecd.org/eduresource /public-spending-on-education.htm.
Note: GDP = gross domestic product.

TABLE 4.1 **Average per student education expenditures by level of education and by sector**

EDUCATION SECTOR	ENROLLMENT NUMBERS IN GENERAL EDUCATION	AVERAGE PER STUDENT EXPENDITURES (US$)
Private	540,942	2,892
Public	284,805	2,022
Subsidized private[a]	140,608	1,240[a] (approx.)
All sectors[b]	966,355	2,395

Sources: Calculations using data provided by the Ministry of Finance, Lebanon; enrollment numbers from CERD 2015.
Note: CERD = Center for Educational Research and Development.
a. Subsidized private schools: The per student cost in the subsidized private sector is an estimation as this sector is mostly run by religious and nonprofit organizations which might have contributions through donations and other means. Subsidized private schools receive a per student subsidy from the government, which amounts to 100 percent of the minimum monthly wage. They also get an additional 25 percent of the minimum monthly wage if 70 percent of the teachers at the school are permanent teachers (noncontractual). Additionally, subsidized private schools can charge parents up to 150 percent of the minimum monthly wage for tuition. In sum, public and private expenditures in the subsidized private sector could amount to 275 percent of the minimum monthly wage. The minimum monthly wage in Lebanon in 2015 was US$450.
Sources: Law for Organizing the Teaching Body in Private Schools (Law 49 published on 27/06/1956) and its amendments Decree 10832 dated 9/10/1962 and Law 32/65 dated 11/6/1965). http://teacherssyndicate.com/law/10/en?type=2.
b. Excludes UNRWA as it caters to Palestinian students only and is funded by donor countries to the UN.

TABLE 4.2 **Annual average MEHE expenditures on general education, 2013–15**

BASIC AND SECONDARY PUBLIC EDUCATION	SHARE (%)	ACTUAL (US$, MILLIONS)
Salaries and benefits	75.0	477.6
Civil servant salary	*62.4*	*397.0*
Contractual worker salary	*8.6*	*54.6*
Transportation allowance	*4.1*	*26.0*
Rent and maintenance of schools	2.7	17.0
Other recurrent costs	1.3	8.0
Subtotal	**79.0**	**502.6**
MEHE general administration		
Civil servant and contractual salaries	3.9	25.0
Transportation and other allowances	3.5	22.0
Rent costs and other recurrent costs	0.5	3.0
Subtotal	**7.9**	**50.0**
Other		
Contributions to the public sector	3.8	24.0
Contributions to nonprofit organizations	9.4	60.0
Grand total	**100.0**	**636.6**

Source: Ministry of Finance, Lebanon.
Note: MEHE = Ministry of Education and Higher Education.

INTERNAL EFFICIENCY IN GOVERNMENT SPENDING

Teacher recruitment and salaries

The Lebanese salary grading system for teachers who are civil servants uses a scale from 0 to 52. In 2015, 80 percent of all civil servant teachers in public schools had a salary grade exceeding 25 (figure 4.6 and table 4.3). Yet 40 percent of them did not possess a university degree (figure 4.7), indicating the possibility

FIGURE 4.6

Distribution of teachers by salary grade, 2014–15

Kernel = epanechnikov, bandwidth = 1.1978

Source: Data provided by the MEHE, Lebanon, 2015.
Note: The salary grade is a predetermined compensation level for a given position. Each teacher has a corresponding salary grade which determines their salary based on Lebanese law. MEHE = Ministry of Education and Higher Education.

TABLE 4.3 **Salary grades of teachers, 2014–15**

SALARY GRADE RANGE	NUMBER OF TEACHERS	SHARE (%)
0–14	589	2.28
15–19	1,725	6.67
20–24	3,032	11.72
25–28	6,004	23.21
29–32	6,177	23.88
33–52	8,336	32.23
Total	25,863	100.00

Source: Data provided by the MEHE, Lebanon, 2015.
Note: The salary grade is a predetermined compensation level for a given position. Each teacher has a corresponding salary grade which determines their salary based on Lebanese law. MEHE = Ministry of Education and Higher Education.

FIGURE 4.7

Distribution of teachers by educational qualifications, 2014–15

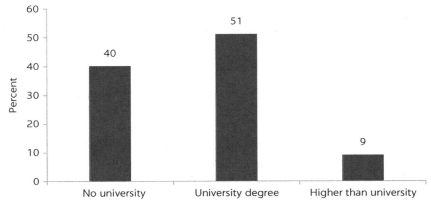

Source: CERD 2015.

of grade inflation in teacher recruitment. Moreover, public school teachers seemed to be relatively older than teachers in the private sector (figure 4.8), and because pay increases are linked to seniority, this explains the significant weight that teacher salaries have on the MEHE budget.

FIGURE 4.8

Age distribution of teachers, 2014–15

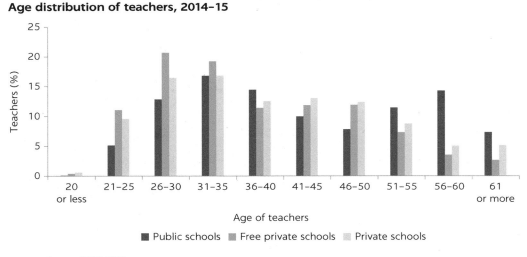

Source: CERD 2015.
Note: CERD = Center for Educational Research and Development.

FIGURE 4.9

Number of teachers in public schools by employment type

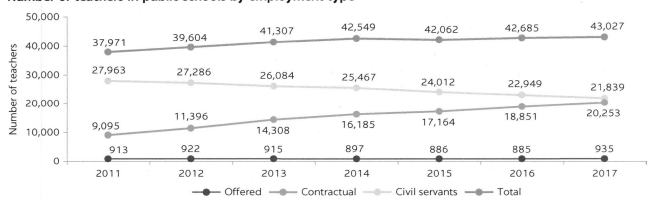

Source: CERD 2017.
Note: Numbers do not include "supplemental teachers" financed by donors and hired to teach Syrian students (see the section on the impact of the Syrian refugee crisis at the end of this chapter). "Offered" teachers are teachers financed by organizations outside of the MEHE, such as municipalities or nongovernmental actors. CERD = Center for Educational Research and Development; MEHE = Ministry of Education and Higher Education.

The recent hiring freeze for civil servants in the public sector, combined with a system of automatic promotion based on seniority, has produced this concentration of teachers in the higher grades. Aligning the hiring process with evolving demand (for example, replacing retiring teachers) is important. Regular, rather than one-time, hiring rounds, would improve distribution across grades with more entry-level teachers.

In addition to civil servants' salary inflation, Lebanon has an increasing trend of recruitment of contractual teachers. In 2011–17, the number of contractual teachers in the public sector increased by 123 percent (figure 4.9), while the number of civil servants decreased by 22 percent over the same period. This heavy reliance on contractual teachers led to a majority of public schools having more contractual teachers than permanent staff: in academic year 2014–15, 64 percent of public schools (810 schools) had more contractual teachers than civil servant (permanent) teachers. The hiring of contractual teachers follows much less stringent requirements and can represent a risk for the quality of education service delivery in schools.

Both civil servants' salary inflation and the tremendous increase in the number of contractual teachers have driven up the teacher salaries cost per student in the public sector (figure 4.10). As a result, in 2015, the Lebanese government was spending a total of US$1,743 per student on teacher salaries, an increase of 36 percent from the 2011 rate of US$1,277 per student, and an increase of 140 percent from the 2006 rate of US$727 per student. Over the period 2011–15, increase in teacher salaries cost was on average 3.7 times the inflation rate in Lebanon.[9]

Breaking down the cost of teacher per student per education level, the salary cost of teachers per student at the primary education level was at US$1,506, but it was significantly higher at the secondary education level, where it reached US$2,745. While the teacher salary costs per student were lower than the OECD average (table 4.4), they were still higher than comparator countries, such as Chile, Estonia, Hungary, the Slovak Republic, Turkey, and Mexico.

In terms of the adequacy of teacher pay, a full-time teacher's starting salary in primary education was at approximately 50 percent of GDP per capita in 2015, and the teacher's maximum salary reached 134 percent of GDP per capita (table 4.5). Given that most teachers in primary education are at lower grade levels, the average salary scale at 82 percent of GDP per capita would be a good approximation of where most primary teachers are located on the pay scale. This pay scale level is comparable to the level of OECD countries, as displayed in table 4.1. However, for secondary education, the average salary scale in Lebanon was at 134 percent of GDP per capita in 2015, and the maximum salary scale was at 169 percent of GDP per capita (table 4.6). Given that most secondary teachers are at higher grade levels, salaries for secondary teachers in Lebanon are considered high compared to OECD countries.

FIGURE 4.10

Total cost of teacher salaries per student in the public sector

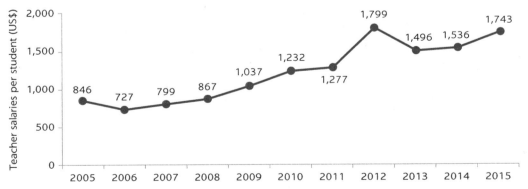

Sources: Teacher salaries expenditures based on data provided from the Ministry of Finance in 2016; enrollment numbers based on CERD statistical yearbooks, Beirut, https://www.crdp.org/statistics?la=en. *Note:* Government increased civil servants' wages in 2012. In 2013, the number of non-Lebanese children in public schools nearly doubled, bringing down teacher salaries cost per student. Note that these calculations include total enrollment but exclude second-shift students and teachers. They also exclude "supplemental teachers" financed by donors and hired to teach Syrian students (see the section on the impact of the Syrian refugee crisis at the end of this chapter). CERD = Center for Educational Research and Development.

TABLE 4.4 **Total cost of teacher salaries per student per level per country**

OECD	PRIMARY EDUCATION (US$)	LOWER SECONDARY EDUCATION (US$)	UPPER SECONDARY EDUCATION (US$)
Spain	3,067	4,052	—
Korea, Rep.	2,981	2,941	—
Portugal	2,777	3,516	4,366
Greece	2,720	3,515	—
Italy	2,692	3,100	2,963
OECD average	**2,677**	**3,350**	**3,749**
Poland	2,247	2,519	—
France	1,735	2,374	3,643
Lebanon	**1,506**		**2,745**
Turkey	1,368	1,459	1,800
Hungary	1,229	1,252	1,287
Chile	1,181	1,095	1,124
Estonia	1,015	1,350	—
Mexico	958	1,057	—
Slovak Republic	924	1,254	1,152

Source: OECD 2015; numbers for Lebanon were calculated using data provided by the Ministry of Finance.
Note: Lower secondary is equivalent to the intermediate education level in Lebanon (grades 7, 8, and 9). — = not available.

TABLE 4.5 **Teacher's salary as a share of GDP per capita (primary education)**

COUNTRY	STARTING SALARY (% GDP PER CAPITA)	AVERAGE SALARY (% GDP PER CAPITA)	MAXIMUM SALARY (% GDP PER CAPITA)
Slovak Republic	42	53	64
Estonia	50	58	66
Czech Republic	59	65	72
Hungary	46	60	74
Norway	63	68	74
Poland	63	86	108
Italy	78	97	115
Lebanon	**50**	**82**	**134**
France	72	102	131
Greece	69	103	136
Ireland	76	107	138
Austria	72	107	142
Japan	76	122	168
Chile	81	125	169

Source: OECD 2015.
Note: Sorted by average salary. GDP = gross domestic product.

TABLE 4.6 **Teacher's salary as a share of GDP per capita (secondary education)**

COUNTRY	STARTING SALARY (% GDP PER CAPITA)	AVERAGE SALARY (% GDP PER CAPITA)	MAXIMUM SALARY (% GDP PER CAPITA)
Estonia	50	58	66
Czech Republic	59	65	72
Portugal	61	112	87
Hungary	50	71	93
Netherlands	83	91	99
Finland	93	108	123
Denmark	106	116	126
Italy	85	108	132
Greece	69	103	136
Ireland	80	110	140
France	82	111	141
Austria	79	122	165
Lebanon	**94**	**134**	**169**
Japan	76	124	173

Source: OECD 2015.
Note: Sorted by maximum salary. GDP = gross domestic product.

TEACHER WORKLOAD

In 2017, Lebanon had an average student-teacher ratio of 10.7.[10] This ratio was low compared to other countries in the region (e.g., Jordan had a ratio of 15.8 and Turkey a ratio of 18.3), and to other upper-middle-income countries (figure 4.11). The general indication from the student-teacher ratio is that there is a surplus of teachers in the system.

A defining feature of the Lebanese public education system is the fact that teacher workload decreases with years of service for civil servants, and there is no enforcement of nonteaching responsibilities for more experienced teachers (table 4.7). While some OECD countries, such as Greece, also reduce the teaching workload based on years of experience, these countries require that teachers spend the remaining hours at school, assessing students, preparing lessons, correcting students' work, doing in-service training, and holding staff meetings (OECD 2015). It is essential that more experienced teachers devote time to mentorship, planning, and collaborative learning with other teachers and staff members to translate investments in teachers into actual student learning.

In addition to low levels of enforcement for nonteaching duties, it seems that in some public schools, the minimum required workload in teaching hours was not enforced, based on an analysis conducted by the World Bank using data from the Mount Lebanon governorate. On average, a civil servant spent between 10 and 15 hours on teaching tasks and a contractual teacher spent between 10 and 19 hours per week teaching. Significantly low levels of workloads accompanied by high teacher salary per student put tremendous pressure on the expenditure levels of the government. There is a need to develop policies that ensure a clearly laid out work program for teachers, with a

FIGURE 4.11

Student-teacher ratio in a sample of upper-middle-income economies

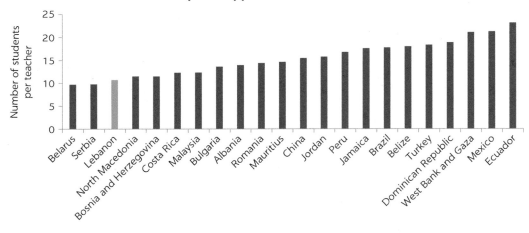

Source: Calculation using UNESCO Institute for Statistics (UIS) (database), Pupil-teacher ratio by level of education (headcount basis) (indicator), (accessed August 31, 2019), http://data.uis.unesco.org/index.aspx?queryid=180.

TABLE 4.7 **Teaching workload and seniority for basic and secondary education, 2014–15**

	BASIC EDUCATION		SECONDARY EDUCATION	
YEARS OF SERVICE	WEEKLY TEACHING WORKLOAD (H)	YEARS OF SERVICE	WEEKLY TEACHING WORKLOAD (H)	
0–20	27	0–15	20	
21–22	23	16–18	19	
23–25	22	19–21	18	
26–27	21	22–23	17	
28–29	20	24–25	16	
30–31	19	26–27	15	
32 and above	18	28 and above	14	

Source: Data provided by MEHE, Lebanon, 2015.
Note: H = hours; MEHE = Ministry of Education and Higher Education.

balance between teaching and nonteaching related tasks. Figures 4.12 and 4.13 show the distribution of weekly teaching hours for civil servants and contractual teachers, respectively. While the Mount Lebanon governorate might not be representative of all of the country, its data illustrate that there might be difficulties in enforcing teacher workload policies in all public schools, and thus there are inefficiencies in the system which need to be addressed.

Despite the difficulty of fully assessing teacher workload due to a lack of detailed data, there is some indication that the teacher workload in Lebanon is low, compared to the OECD average. Compared to high-performing systems, where a teacher's average annual working time was equal to 771 hours according to the OECD average (figure 4.14), Lebanon's working hours were significantly lower. In Lebanon, the school year consisted of 160 days at both the primary and secondary levels. This was 20 days shorter than the school year in high-performing systems, which had an average of 180 days per year. Accounting for only civil servant work hours, Lebanon's average was close to 379 working hours per year, and when contractual hours are added, the average

FIGURE 4.12

Average weekly hours taught by civil servant teachers

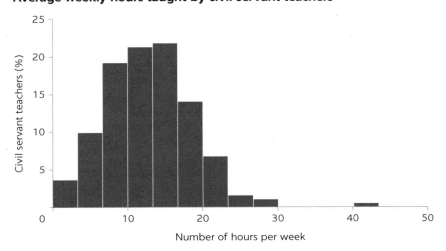

Source: Data provided by the Mount Lebanon Regional Directorate, Lebanon, 2015.

FIGURE 4.13

Average weekly hours taught by contractual teachers

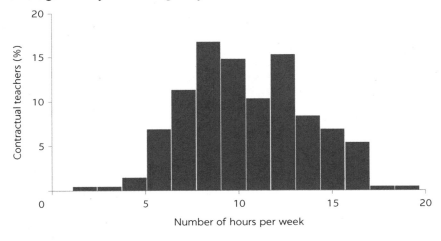

Source: Data provided by the Mount Lebanon Regional Directorate, Lebanon, 2015.

working hours per year increased to 431. This implies that the average workload of a teacher in Lebanon (civil servant and contractual) was close to 13.5 hours per week, which is far below the average international workload of 21.5 hours per week.

Limited incentives exist to attract teachers to work in hard-to-staff schools or to teach subjects in critical shortage. The MEHE is responsible for assigning public school teachers to their location of work. However, compared to high-performing OECD countries, Lebanon has limited or no official incentives for teachers to work in disadvantaged areas. A lack of incentives for teachers to work in hard-to-staff schools can result in having the least qualified teachers working in schools serving the most disadvantaged students and may exacerbate further inequity in teaching quality and learning outcomes. In Lebanon, this problem is further compounded by the fact that contractual teachers, with no proper preservice training, are more likely to be placed in hard-to-staff schools.

FIGURE 4.14

Teacher working time in hours per year (primary education), selected systems

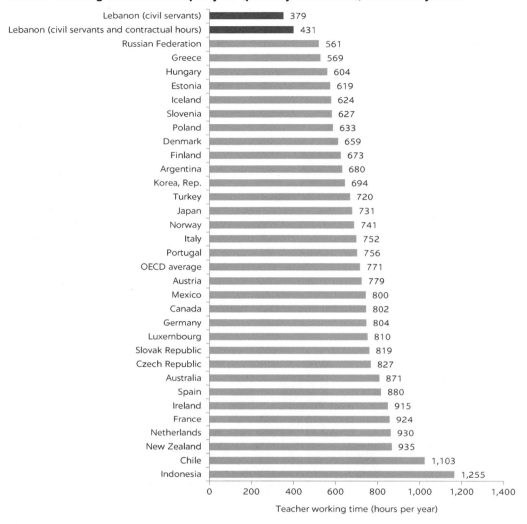

Teacher working time (hours per year)

Sources: OECD 2015; working hours for Lebanon were calculated using data provided by the MEHE and CERD.
Note: CERD = Center for Educational Research and Development; MEHE = Ministry of Education and Higher Education; OECD = Organisation for Economic Co-operation and Development.

SCHOOL CONSTRUCTION AND DISTRIBUTION

In addition to significant investments in teacher salaries, the Government of Lebanon has consistently insisted on the necessity of expanding the reach of public schools in the regions and ensuring coverage in all administrative districts in the country. This policy prompted not only the construction of new schools but also the renting of privately owned premises to house public schools. By the early 2000s, rent costs became a significant portion of the MEHE budget, with 62 percent of public schools in the academic year 2000–01 being rented schools (figure 4.15). However, during the last 15 years, the government undertook major construction efforts and increased the number of publicly owned schools by 36 percent from 2001–15. By 2015, the number of rented schools decreased to 42 percent, with rent costs consisting of 3 percent of the MEHE budget in basic and secondary education. It is important to note that the MEHE was able to decrease the total number of

FIGURE 4.15

Number of public schools by ownership over time

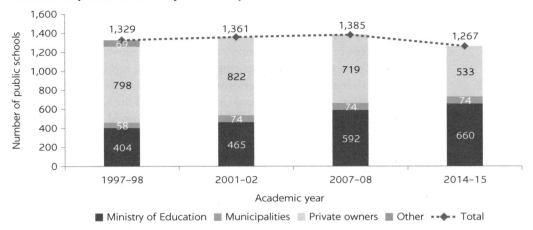

Sources: CERD statistical yearbooks, Beirut, https://www.crdp.org/statistics?la=en; and data provided by the MEHE and CDR in 2016.
Note: CDR = Council for Development and Reconstruction; CERD = Center for Educational Research and Development; MEHE = Ministry of Education and Higher Education.

FIGURE 4.16

Quality of school buildings

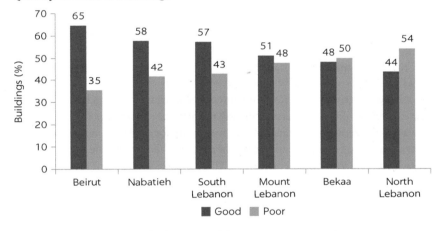

Source: Data provided by the MEHE and CERD in 2015.
Note: CERD = Center for Educational Research and Development; MEHE = Ministry of Education and Higher Education.

public schools by 7 percent from 2001–15 due to the consolidation of small schools. This is an indication, coupled with the low student-to-teacher ratio, that there are efficiency gains to be made in terms of school distribution.

The MEHE, with support from donors, has also undertaken a substantial program of rehabilitation of schools, with hundreds of schools being rehabilitated to date. Rehabilitation aimed to solve some critical issues in the quality of school buildings and infrastructure (figure 4.16), especially in the North of Lebanon and Bekaa governorates, where the majority of schools had poor quality infrastructure.

EXTERNAL EFFICIENCY AND RETURNS ON EDUCATION INVESTMENT

School inputs and learning outcomes

Regression analysis was conducted to understand how some of the internal efficiencies issues raised in this chapter are associated with learning outcomes. To this end, the available data were used to determine the impact of school variables on the learning outcomes of students, measured by student passing rates in national examinations.

School size—or the total number of students per school—was found to be the single most important factor influencing student passing rates in national examinations, with higher levels of performance for larger schools (table 4.8). On average, student passing rates improved by 10 points if the school consisted of more than 250 students. Student passing rates also improved, to a lesser extent, when the school had between 125 and 249 students, when controlling for other variables. This can be due to economies of scale realized when the schools are larger, resulting in higher efficiency.

The quality of school buildings was another important factor influencing student passing rates. Good-quality buildings usually have improved school resources, which have been shown to positively affect students' performance. Models 4 and 5 in table 4.8 show that in schools with better-quality buildings, the average passing rates were approximately 4 points more than in schools with poor-quality buildings. In model 4, for example, the average student passing rate was 55. Other factors staying constant, the student passing rate increased by 3.5 points if the school building was of good quality. The ownership of the school buildings (owned versus rented) did not seem to have any impact on student achievement. Students in rented buildings performed at the same level as students who studied in government-owned buildings. This means that the focus of the government should not necessarily be on building schools but on improving the quality of resources in the existing schools. This was true across all regions.

The analysis also showed that high salaries for civil servant teachers were associated negatively with learning outcomes. Because higher salaries are usually earned by older teachers according to the salary scale, this finding may be related to the reduction in teaching responsibility for staff with seniority. Higher salaries can also be an indication of higher teacher headcount and lower productivity leading to low student outcomes. This calls for government intervention to focus on improving the productivity of teachers, so the burden of teacher inefficiency does not fall on the students and the government's education budget. Teachers' salary grades did not seem to affect student performance. Moreover, the number of contractual teachers did not seem to have a significant effect on student learning outcomes. The reason for this was because contractual teachers were evenly distributed across schools and some of them have high-quality teaching experience as they teach in both private and public schools.

TABLE 4.8 **Impact of school inputs on student performance in public schools, 2013–14**

SCHOOL INPUT	(1) PASS	(2) PASS	(3) PASS	(4) PASS	(5) PASS	(6) PASS	(7) PASS
School size (middle 33%)	6.740***	4.776*	4.758*	4.675*	4.671*	4.265	3.691
School size (top 33%)	13.30***	11.27***	11.66***	11.62***	11.67***	10.01***	9.885***
Civil servant teacher salaries cost per student		−0.30**	−0.30**	−0.31**	−0.31**	−0.38**	−0.40*
Ownership of building (rented = 1)			0.088	0.0456	−0.061	2.209	2.386
Quality of school buildings (good = 1)				3.432*	3.55*	2.682	2.912
Type of school (basic = 1)					−8.44	−8.97	−9.07
Teachers' grades (more than 30)						0.0022	0.0014
Number of contractual teachers							−0.028
_Constant	53.27***	56.12***	55.92***	47.31***	55.28***	57.96***	58.37***
N	966	933	896	896	896	690	670

Source: Abdul-Hamid et al. 2018.
Note: *$p < 0.05$, **$p < 0.01$, ***$p < 0.001$.

Hence, school size, quality of school building, and teacher management and allocation were the main areas that stood out for further policy action. Improvement in these areas could lead to improved quality of education outcomes.

Enrollment rates

The net enrollment rate (NER) for primary education has been nearly constant over the years, at slightly below 90 percent. The NER for preprimary education has been increasing owing to significant investments in the expansion of public provision of kindergarten. However, the NER for secondary education is of serious concern and has been declining since 2009, a decline which was exacerbated by the onset of the Syrian refugee crisis (figure 4.17). Moreover, the completion rates for primary and lower secondary education have also been decreasing and have reached low levels, especially for lower secondary (59 percent) compared to countries with a similar level of development as Lebanon (figure 4.18).[11] The trend

FIGURE 4.17

Net enrollment rates, 2006–13

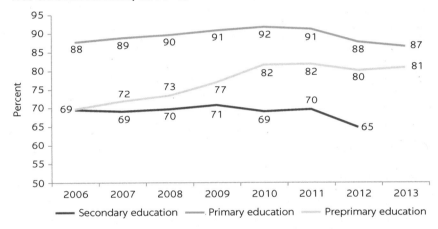

Source: Education Statistics (EdStats) 2013 (database), World Bank, Washington, DC, http://datatopics.worldbank.org/education/country/lebanon.

FIGURE 4.18

Completion rates, 2005–13

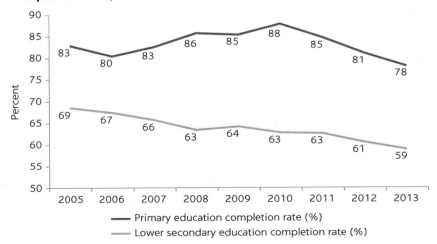

Source: Education Statistics (EdStats) 2013 (database), World Bank, Washington, DC, http://datatopics.worldbank.org/education/country/lebanon.

in enrollment rates in primary and secondary education reflects potential inequity in access to education, especially for the most vulnerable population in Lebanon.

EQUITY AND INCLUSION

The Human Opportunity Index (HOI) for Lebanon reflects inequality in access to educational opportunities in the country. The HOI is a measure that combines both access to education and how equally opportunity is distributed across selected characteristics. The HOI for Lebanon was 0.48, lower than that of Chile, Mexico, and Romania (figure 4.19). This reflects that socioeconomic characteristics, wealth, birthplace, gender, and family background had a significant impact on a child's access to education services and that personal circumstances—birthplace, wealth, race, and gender—affected the probability of a child being able to access services—education, running water, and connection to electricity.

Gender equity

Gender inequity remains in access to education services. Females stay in school longer than males. Data on individuals' school attendance recorded in the 2011–2012 CAS household survey provide a picture of participation in education by age and gender. For children, up to age 13, estimates of participation in education for both genders are high, exceeding 95 percent (figure 4.20). Nonetheless, in preprimary and primary education, enrollment rates for girls are lower than enrollment rates for boys. This enrollment gap closes at the intermediate education level; after age 13, the gap is reversed, with a much higher percentage of females remaining in school compared to males at the secondary and tertiary levels.

Wealth inequity

Children from wealthier households stay in school longer than children from poorer households. The disparity in school attainment is apparent from the 2011–2012 CAS household survey. For example, by age 17, 87 percent of children from the wealthiest population quintile were in school, while only 25 percent of children from the poorest quintile were in school (figure 4.21). Given the strong

FIGURE 4.19

Human Opportunity Index

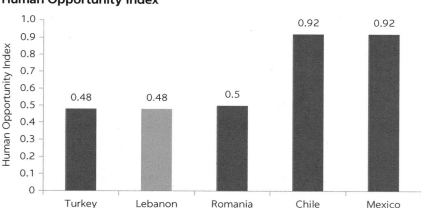

Source: Calculations based on Education Statistics (EdStats) (database), World Bank, Washington, DC, https://datatopics.worldbank.org/education/country/lebanon.

FIGURE 4.20

School participation by age and gender

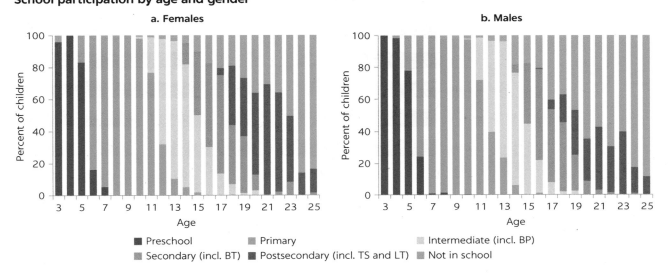

Source: CAS (database), Household-based Survey 2011–2012, Central Administration of Statistics, Beirut, http://www.cas.gov.lb/index.php /demographic-and-social-en/householdexpenditure-en.
Note: BP = *Brevet Professionnel* (3-year technical and vocational track after the primary cycle); BT = *Baccalaureat Technique* (3-year technical and vocational track after the intermediate cycle); CAS = Central Administration of Statistics; LT = *Licence Technique* (4-year technical and vocational track after the secondary cycle); TS = *Technicien Supérieur* (3-year technical and vocational track after the secondary cycle).

FIGURE 4.21

Percentage of students in school by age and wealth quintile

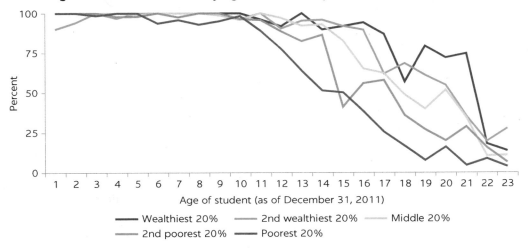

Source: Calculations using CAS (database), Household-based Survey 2011–2012, Central Administration of Statistics, Beirut, http://www.cas.gov.lb/index.php/demographic-and-social-en/householdexpenditure-en.
Note: CAS = Central Administration of Statistics.

association between educational attainment and earnings, the fact that children from poorer households tended to stay in school for fewer years than children from wealthier households perpetuates wealth inequity in the country.

The wealth quintile composition of each level of education reveals that the poorest households were underrepresented in secondary and postsecondary education (figure 4.22). The poorest 20 percent of households represented only 11 percent of secondary school students and just 4 percent of university (postsecondary) students. Conversely, the wealthiest 20 percent represented approximately a quarter of secondary students and 38 percent of postsecondary students.

FIGURE 4.22

Composition of each school level by wealth quintile

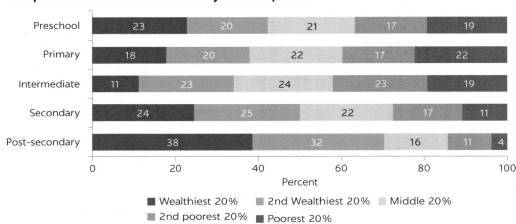

Source: Calculations using CAS (database), Household-based Survey 2011–2012, Central Administration of Statistics, Beirut, http://www.cas.gov.lb/index.php/demographic-and-social-en/householdexpenditure-en.
Note: Wealth quintiles defined by asset index. Levels include corresponding vocational and technical programs. The total for each bar is not equal to 100 percent because percentages have been rounded. CAS = Central Administration of Statistics.

This underrepresentation of poor households at the secondary and tertiary education levels creates a large inequity based on socioeconomic status. Lack of educational attainment for poor households implies lower earnings in the future and lower likelihood of upward social mobility. Additionally, especially for female youth, lack of postsecondary education is highly correlated with lack of labor market participation, and thus female youth from poor households are at high risk of exclusion from the labor market.

While socioeconomic factors themselves could be increasing the vulnerability levels of children and leading to their dropping out in lower secondary and secondary education levels, the data from the CAS 2011–2012 household survey revealed that there were significant academic challenges faced by children from the poorest households early on in their schooling years, leading to high repetition rates and increasing risks of dropouts. Children from poorer households tended to be overage starting from the primary education levels. While children from poorer households tended to be sufficiently represented in primary- and intermediate-level education, they were more likely to be part of the overage population (figure 4.23). At the primary school level, children from the poorest 20 percent population made up nearly half of all overage children. Consequently, resolving low enrollment rates in secondary education for poor children requires mitigating academic and probably socioemotional difficulties faced by those children at the lower levels of education as well.

In grade 8, the poorest students were not able to achieve minimum proficiency in mathematics and science according to the TIMSS 2011 international assessment. The difference in achievement between the wealthiest and poorest students was stark: 66 percent of the wealthiest quintile of students achieved minimum proficiency in math, while only 22 percent of the poorest quintile of students achieved this level of proficiency (figure 4.24). In other words, the wealthiest quintile was three times more likely to achieve the minimum proficiency in math than the poorest quintile. In science, the wealthiest quintile was nearly five times more likely to do so.

FIGURE 4.23

Percentage of children enrolled in each level, by age and wealth quintile distribution

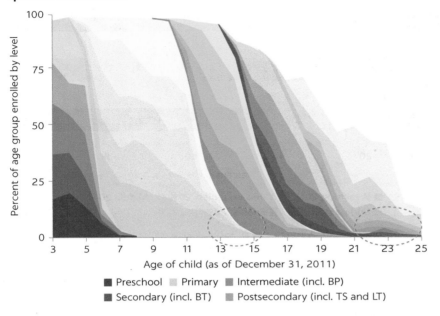

Source: Calculations using CAS (database), Household-based Survey 2011–2012, Central Administration of Statistics, Beirut, http://www.cas.gov.lb/index.php/demographic-and -social-en/householdexpenditure-en.
Note: Wealth quintiles defined by asset index. Levels include corresponding vocational and technical programs. Shades denote wealth quintiles; darker shades denote poorer children.
BP = *Brevet Professionnel* (3-year technical and vocational track after the primary cycle);
BT = *Baccalaureat Technique* (3-year technical and vocational track after the intermediate cycle); CAS = Central Administration of Statistics; LT = *Licence Technique* (4-year technical and vocational track after the secondary cycle); TS = *Technicien Supérieur* (3-year technical and vocational track after the secondary cycle).

FIGURE 4.24

Percentage of grade 8 students attaining intermediate-level achievement in TIMSS by wealth quintile

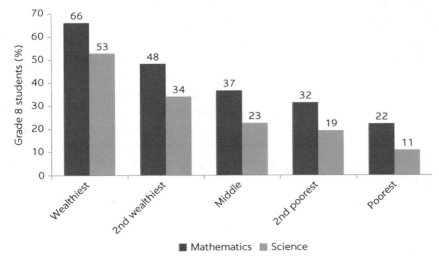

Source: Calculations using International Association for the Evaluation of Educational Achievement. TIMSS 2011–Grade 8 (database); https://www.iea.nl/data-tools/repository/timss.
Note: TIMSS = Trends in International Mathematics and Science Study.

FIGURE 4.25

Student composition of each type of school by wealth quintile

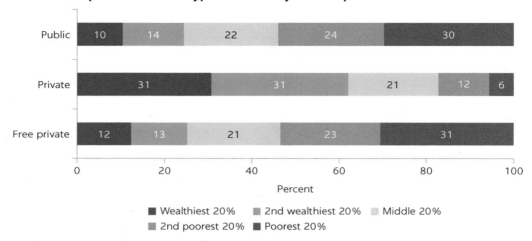

Source: CAS (database), Household-based Survey 2011–2012, Central Administration of Statistics, Beirut, http://www.cas.gov.lb/index.php/demographic-and-social-en/householdexpenditure-en.
Note: Wealth quintiles defined by asset index. The total for each bar is not equal to 100 percent because percentages have been rounded. CAS = Central Administration of Statistics.

FIGURE 4.26

Distribution of government education allowances by wealth quintile

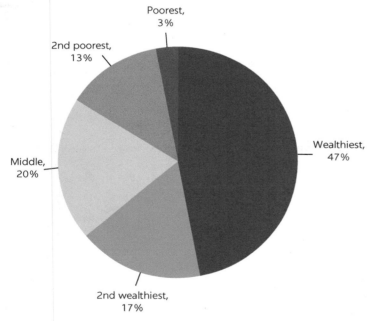

Source: Calculations using CAS (database), Household-based Survey 2011–2012, Central Administration of Statistics, Beirut, http://www.cas.gov.lb/index.php/demographic-and-social-en/householdexpenditure-en.
Note: CAS = Central Administration of Statistics.

PUBLIC-PRIVATE PARTNERSHIPS

Education subsidization programs typically aim to decrease inequity in access to quality education. In Lebanon, the government has a system for subsidizing private schools through both school allowances to civil servants and direct subsidies to "free-private" schools—schools that cannot charge tuition above 150 percent of the monthly minimum wage and in return get direct fund transfers from the government for every student enrolled. By examining the student composition of each type of school using the CAS 2011–2012 survey (figure 4.25), it is revealed that students in public and free-private schools had a similar socioeconomic background. However, even though more than one-fifth of education public expenditures are spent on school allowances for civil servants to enroll their children in paid private schools; these schools had low enrollment from the poorest households—the poorest 40 percent of children made up only 18 percent of students at private, fee-charging schools. Consequently, the school allowance subsidization program has not been effective in expanding equitable access to the poorest Lebanese.

In fact, the current subsidy system does not properly target the poorest households. On the contrary, an analysis based on the CAS 2011–2012 household survey data revealed that the poorest two quintiles (40 percent) received only 16 percent of education allowances provided by the government. Conversely, the wealthiest quintile received nearly half (47 percent) of total education allowances provided by the government (figure 4.26). In fact, for the subsidy system to be equitable and focus on learning, it should support the two poorest quintiles.

In Lebanon, students in private schools attained higher achievement than those in public schools. Using TIMSS 2011 performance benchmarks, 21 percent of students in public schools attained minimum proficiency in both mathematics and science, while more than twice as many private school students (47 percent) were able to attain this level of achievement. This difference in achievement can be decomposed into a portion attributable to the quality of education delivered by the school—and other unobserved characteristics related to school selection— and another portion attributable to differences in student background, mostly socioeconomic status. Figure 4.27 shows, for Lebanon and comparator countries with large private provision of education—Chile, Belgium, and the Netherlands— the difference in achievement between students in public and private schools, decomposed by the two portions: school quality / selection and student background / socioeconomic status.

The difference in achievement between public and private school students in Lebanon was 26 percentage points: 16 points attributable to school quality / selection and 10 points attributable to student socioeconomic status (figure 4.27). Thus, Lebanon faced high wealth inequity in terms of access to high-quality schools, in addition to high variation in quality between schools. If the poorest students in Lebanon had equal access to both public and private high-quality schools, then the difference in achievement between public and private school students would be

FIGURE 4.27

Composition of difference in achievement of minimum proficiency in math and science between private and public schools

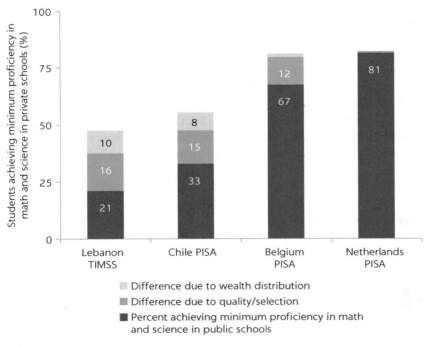

Sources: Calculation using OECD PISA 2015 Database, OECD, Paris, https://www.oecd.org/pisa/data/2015database/; and International Association for the Evaluation of Educational Achievement. TIMSS 2011–Grade 8 (database); https://www.iea.nl/data-tools/repository/timss.
Note: The difference due to quality/selection is the difference in *achievement* between students in public school and their predicted achievement if they were in private school. For the Netherlands, the net difference is shown as public school students tend to be wealthier. OECD = Organisation for Economic Co-operation and Development; PISA = Program for International Student Assessment; TIMSS = Trends in International Mathematics and Science Study.

decreased from 26 to 16 percentage points. Comparatively, Belgium, for example, had low wealth inequity as poor students and their wealthier peers had near equal access to high-quality private schools. As a result, the difference in achievement between public and private school students in Belgium was much lower (nearly 12 percentage points) and was mostly dominated by the variation in quality of schools and selection criteria. In conclusion, differences in learning achievement attributable to the quality of private schools do not exacerbate wealth inequity when the poorest students have equal access to private schools. However, when there is unequal access to private schools, these schools exacerbate the role of wealth inequity in widening the learning gap between students.

A revision of the private school subsidy model in Lebanon is needed to be able to better benefit from the large private sector provision of education while keeping inequity levels low. Countries like Belgium and the Netherlands provide good examples for how the benefits of a large private education sector could be leveraged for education provision without compromising equity in learning achievement. To decrease inequity, these countries have a financing model for the sector which is dominated by high levels of public financing of education and low levels of private expenditures in the sector (figure 4.28). Despite the large size of the private sector, the models rely on public subsidization of private schools to ensure that education expenditures remain public rather than private. In the Netherlands, public financing makes up 96 percent of private schools' costs, while in Belgium, it contributes 85 percent. In Chile, where inequity levels are lower than in Lebanon but higher than in Belgium and the Netherlands, public financing makes up only 68 percent of private schools' costs. Conversely, Lebanon has low levels of public financing for education, and despite significant portions being allocated to subsidies of private schools, private expenditures in the sector are considerably large and thus exacerbate wealth inequities in learning achievements.

Figure 4.29 compares the average amount households spend on tuition fees with their household total spending power (as measured by per capita household expenditures) based on the CAS 2011–2012 survey data. The figure shows the 10th, 50th, and 90th percentiles of household total spending power for both households with children in public schools and those in private schools. The poorest 50 percent of households sending their children to public schools have a spending power that is less than or equal to the poorest 10 percent of households sending their

FIGURE 4.28

Education financing as percentage of GDP

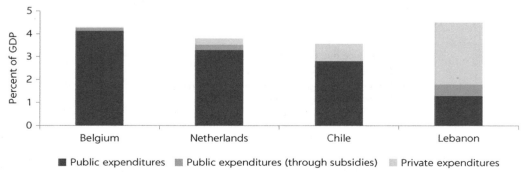

Source: OECD 2015. Figures for Lebanon were calculated using data from Ministry of Finance 2015; private expenditures estimated from tuition data from the MEHE.
Note: GDP = gross domestic product.

FIGURE 4.29

Household average education expenditures versus total spending power

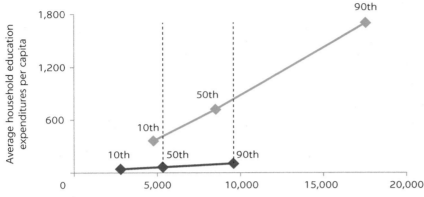

Average household expenditures on education per capita at the 10th, 50th, and 90th percentiles of household spending power

- Among households with public school children only
- Among households with private school children only

Source: Calculations using CAS (database), Household-based Survey 2011–2012, Central Administration of Statistics, Beirut, http://www.cas.gov.lb/index.php/demographic-and -social-en/householdexpenditure-en.
Note: Private schools exclude free private school category. Average education expenditures per capita (total household expenditures on education divided by number of household members) modeled using a log-transformed regression model. CAS = Central Administration of Statistics.

children to private schools. Nevertheless, the remaining 50 percent of households with children enrolled in public schools have the same spending power as at least half of the households with children enrolled in private schools. This suggests that any subsidization model for private education provision should target the poorest 50 percent of households with children enrolled in public schools.

IMPACT OF THE SYRIAN REFUGEE CRISIS ON EDUCATION SECTOR FINANCING

In addition to the government and private households financing of the education sector, the Syrian refugee crisis introduced a third parallel system of financing sponsored by donor countries and aimed at responding to the Syrian refugees' need for education services. Donor financing to the public education system for the years 2014–18 had an annual average of US$250–US$300 million, representing more than 25 percent of public education sector financing. Given that this financing was aimed to support the Government of Lebanon to enroll Syrian refugee students in public schools, and that the refugee population, as of 2018, exceeded 45 percent of the public student population, the level of donor financing was low, indicating that a significant share of the cost of education of Syrian refugees was absorbed by the Government of Lebanon and/or was partially offset by an increase in the efficiency of the system. For example, map 4.1 shows that in 2016–17, the percentage of non-Lebanese students in a public school classroom ranged on average from 15 percent in North Lebanon to nearly 40 percent

MAP 4.1

Share of non-Lebanese students in public school classrooms by region, 2016–17

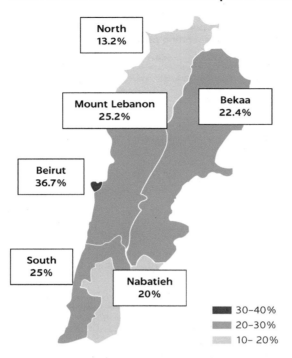

- In an avarage section of 25 students, the percentage of non-Lebanese pupils ranged from 15% in North Lebanon to 40% in Beirut in the last academic year.

- Non-Lebanese students are concentrated in early grades; 67% of those enrolled in 2016–17 were in KG1 to grade 3.

North
13.2%

Mount Lebanon
25.2%

Bekaa
22.4%

Beirut
36.7%

South
25%

Nabatieh
20%

■ 30–40%
■ 20–30%
■ 10–20%

Source: Calculations based on the data for school year 2016–17 provided by the MEHE.
Note: KG = kindergarten; MEHE = Ministry of Education and Higher Education.

in Beirut. This implies that non-Lebanese students might have filled some classrooms that were not running at full capacity before the crisis. However, in addition to filling existing classrooms, schools in the first shift have also opened new classrooms, which were nearly entirely filled by non-Lebanese students. The RACE Program Management Unit (PMU) conducted an analysis in March 2017 to measure the number of new classroom sections opened in schools in the first shift.[12] Out of a total of 991 basic education schools, the RACE PMU selected a sample of 383 schools with a high number of refugees (enrolling 55 percent of non-Lebanese students and 30 percent of Lebanese students). In the sample, 26 percent of all classrooms had five Lebanese students or less, with some classrooms having no Lebanese students at all. The MEHE reported having operated 1,500 classroom sections in first shift with less than five Lebanese students,[13] representing more than 8 percent of all classrooms.[14]

While a large portion of the donor financing was channeled through nongovernmental actors, up to half of the financing was channeled through the Ministry of Education and, in particular, through the RACE PMU. This unit was established at the beginning of the crisis to manage the response to the Syrian refugees' influx and to channel donor financing to the system. Financing through this unit did not go into the MEHE budget and was accounted for and executed separately from the MEHE budget execution, allowing for traceability of funds.

Financing through the PMU for the Syrian crisis response was largely dominated by contributions to schools for the enrollment of Syrian refugee children (at a rate of US$160 per student) and Lebanese students (at a rate of US$60 per student), in addition to the payment of teachers and staff salaries to cover

FIGURE 4.30

Financing for the education sector within the response to the Syrian crisis

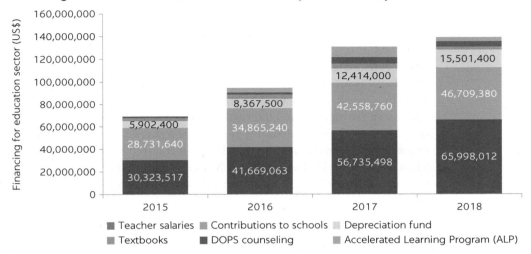

Source: Calculations based on RACE PMU data, MEHE, Beirut, www.racepmulebanon.com.
Note: DOPS = Direction d'Orientation Pédagogique et Scolaire (School Guidance and Counseling Department); MEHE = Ministry of Education and Higher Education; PMU = Program Management Unit; RACE = Reaching All Children with Education.

additional classroom sections opened in first-shift schools due to the increased enrollment and to open and operate second-shift schools which hosted exclusively non-Lebanese students. With donor financing, the MEHE recruited new teachers—supplemental teachers—to teach Syrian refugee students in first and second shifts. The MEHE also supplemented the income of existing teachers who opted to teach in the second shift. In 2016–17, there were 5,172 supplemental teachers in the system,[15] representing more than 10 percent of the teacher workforce in public schools.[16] Additionally, a total of 10,900 teachers, supervisors, and school principals (22 percent of the total schools' workforce) were working in second-shift schools during academic year 2016–17, with their salary income partially or totally dependent on donor financing.

Additional contributions from donors included the establishment of a depreciation fund to cover infrastructure needs—maintenance, rehabilitation, and so on; the provision of textbooks; the support to the School Guidance and Counseling Department (DOPS) to provide academic, health, and psychosocial counseling to schools; and the operation of an Accelerated Learning Program (ALP) for out-of-school refugee students to ease their transition into formal schooling.

Funds through the RACE PMU, which exceeded US$70 million in 2015 and US$140 million in 2018 (figure 4.30)[17] represented from 11 percent (in 2015) to up to 20 percent (in 2018) of the total budget of the MEHE. In 2018, around 12 percent of the MEHE teacher salaries were processed by the RACE PMU.

CONCLUSION

Lebanon is committed to investing in education. While public expenditures in the sector are low, it is compensated by significant investment from private households. The private education sector dominates in terms of service delivery, with nearly 71 percent of Lebanese children enrolled in private schools. The government subsidizes the private sector through both direct subsidies to a selected number of schools and through school allowances to civil servants. This subsidization is significant and represented 28 percent of public expenditures in education in 2015.

Considering both public and private expenditures in the sector, Lebanon has a comparable level of investment to other countries in the region and in the OECD. However, this level of investment is not producing high-quality education for all, as measured by poor learning outcomes in math, science, and reading in national and international assessments. The system is highly inequitable, with tremendous differences in learning outcomes and quality of education between the wealthiest and poorest children. Children from disadvantaged households have a relatively high dropout rate before secondary school, driving Lebanon's secondary enrollment rate to below the benchmark of countries with a similar level of socioeconomic development. Moreover, government expenditures and subsidization programs are not geared toward decreasing inequity and are on the contrary widening learning gaps between households as they benefit the wealthiest households much more than the poorest ones.

In the public sector, high levels of inefficiency are driving the poor performance of Lebanese public schools. Particularly, a surplus of unqualified teachers with uneven recruitment standards, salary inflation, and low workload places Lebanon high in terms of teacher salary cost per student compared to the OECD countries, especially at the secondary level. There is also large inefficiency in school distribution and geographic allocation, with a sizable number of schools having low levels of enrollments. These inefficiency indicators have been correlated with poor learning outcomes and student passing rates.

The Syrian crisis introduced additional challenges to the public education system by exacerbating fiscal stress in the system. Non-Lebanese children reached up to 45 percent of the public students in 2018. While some of the costs for enrolling these children have been covered by international donors and partners, a portion of the costs was also borne by the government.

Finally, a results-based commitment model linked to school and system improvement is key to move the system forward. The current system uses student headcount, for example, to distribute funding to schools and does not allocate spending according to different types of schools and students. The current financing model should be revisited to ensure that in the future, the allocation of funds is linked to school improvement and student performance, regardless of school size. Policy enhancement should consider four important principles of a school finance system: adequacy, equity, quality, and efficiency. The system should provide adequate resources at all levels of the education system to ensure that all students (irrespective of their socioeconomic background and other characteristics) receive a high-quality education. There needs to be a mechanism to use adjustments in education spending across governorates, districts (*cazas*), and school sizes to preserve fiscal neutrality, so that available resource allocations are not biased. Linking financial expenditures with results is key to improving education quality. Learning and education outcomes should be a strategic national interest and should guide future commitments and expenditures in the sector.

Chapter 5 seeks to analyze the efficiency and other challenges presented in this chapter from a political economy lens by reviewing the cornerstones and drivers of the education system, identifying the stakeholders and their interests, and unpacking the decision making and execution processes that govern the sector in the aim of providing a roadmap to address those challenges and unlock the potential of the Lebanese education system to produce high-quality learning for all children.

NOTES

1. CAS (database), Household-based Survey 2011–2012, Central Administration of Statistics, Beirut, http://www.cas.gov.lb/index.php/demographic-and-social-en/householdexpenditure-en.
2. World Bank Open Data (database), World Bank, Washington, DC, https://data.worldbank.org/.
3. World Bank Open Data (database), World Bank, Washington, DC, https://data.worldbank.org/.
4. CAS (database), Household-based Survey 2011–2012, Central Administration of Statistics, Beirut, http://www.cas.gov.lb/index.php/demographic-and-social-en/household expenditure-en.
5. Ministry of Finance data, 2016. Total expenditures to the education sector averaged around US$1.2 billion annually: around US$900 million on general education, US$225 million on tertiary education, and US$90 million on technical and vocational education and training (TVET).
6. Civil servants receiving education allowances for their children to enroll in tuition-charging private schools include army personnel, security forces, and public school teachers.
7. Data from UNESCO Institute for Statistics (UIS). In 2015, Lebanon ranked 6th among more than 280 countries and territories in terms of the private sector share of education enrollment, only behind Macao SAR, China, Zimbabwe, Belize, Aruba (the Netherlands), and Grenada.
8. Calculations based on 2015 tuition data of 955 private schools provided by the MEHE. Private schools are mandated to provide tuition data to the MEHE.
9. Inflation rates are estimations from the World Bank.
10. Calculation using UNESCO Institute for Statistics (UIS) (database), Pupil-teacher ratio by level of education (headcount basis) (indicator), (accessed August 31, 2019), http://data.uis.unesco.org/index.aspx?queryid=180. These figures are for first-shift schools only. The student-teacher ratio in the second-shift classes hosting refugees is much higher because of a limited supply of second-shift schools and high demand from refugee children.
11. Lower secondary is equivalent to the intermediate education level in Lebanon (grades 7, 8, and 9).
12. RACE Executive Committee Meeting. Minutes of Meeting. March 9, 2017.
13. Ministry of Education, RACE Executive Committee Meeting, Signed Minutes of Meeting, June 2017.
14. Number of classrooms in public sector from CERD 2017.
15. Ministry of Education, RACE Executive Committee Meeting, Signed Minutes of Meeting, August 2017.
16. Number of teachers in public sector from the CERD 2017.
17. Calculations based on enrollment and expenditure data from the RACE PMU, www.racepmulebanon.com.

REFERENCES

Abdul-Hamid, H., H. I. Sayed, D. Krayem, J. R. Ghaleb. 2018. "Lebanon Education Public Expenditure Review 2017." World Bank, Washington, DC. https://openknowledge.worldbank.org/handle/10986/30065.

CERD (Center for Educational Research and Development) 2015. "CERD Statistical Bulletin 2014–2015" (in Arabic). CERD, Beirut. https://www.crdp.org/files/201703140524141.pdf (accessed May 2018).

———. 2017. "CERD Statistical Bulletin 2016–2017" (in Arabic). CERD, Beirut. https://www.crdp.org/files/201712220733131.pdf (accessed May 2018).

OECD (Organisation for Economic Co-operation and Development). 2015. *Education at a Glance: OECD Indicators*. Paris: OECD Publishing.

5 Analysis of the Cornerstones of Education

MAIN MESSAGES

1. This chapter aims to study the main political determinants of education reform. It seeks to understand the role and interests of the main education stakeholders and the processes governing decision-making and policy execution in the sector. These processes include mechanisms that interest groups use to influence policy, as well as the structural features of the environment and institutions driving reform. This analysis is essential to uncovering the forces that could support or undermine different reform attempts in achieving education results. The findings in this chapter are based on a political economy analysis, conducted through a series of semistructured interviews and focus groups with the main stakeholders in the sector.

2. The education system in Lebanon presents both strong assets and major challenges for the effective and efficient promotion of student learning. It is rooted in a national philosophy, culture, and legislation that extend social services and build on active community dynamics. It is a source of national pride and receives full support from all levels of the societal and political spectrums. Moreover, the diversity in the education provision model can be an asset for the country and can provide a healthy environment for building coalitions, collaboration, and competitiveness to enhance education success. However, the system also has significant challenges related to political instability, consensual decision making, conflicts of interest, and organizational efficiency.

3. The education sector is characterized by many actors, who often have misaligned and contradictory interests impeding the achievement of education outcomes for all children. Building coalitions of actors by aligning interests in a coherent way is essential for accomplishing education objectives. Absence of a goals-oriented structure allows for interference by special interest groups. It is essential that a culture in which education delivery is a shared responsibility is promoted. For that, education objectives and responsibilities need to be continuously shared and communicated, and assessment and process evaluation reports need to be regularly produced and discussed.

4. There is a strong need to update and ensure coherence in legislative, regulatory, and normative laws and frameworks to align them toward common goals focused on student learning. The absence of objective, precise, and

transparent standards, criteria, and procedures in many aspects of education sector management, and the lack of accountability mechanisms for the application of existing standards, criteria, and procedures leave space for political interference. Processes of patronage politics and rent-seeking interfere with decision-making and divert focus from learning and results. Politicians use the education sector to provide services to their constituents, for example, through the recruitment and deployment of teachers. Furthermore, the current legal structure for decision-making involves multiple layers of approvals and procedures, which, coupled with political interference and a consociational mode of decision-making, leads to years of delay in reforms and decreases the responsiveness of the system to the needs of students, teachers, school administrators, and other stakeholders.

5. Centralization of decision-making power is a salient characteristic of the Lebanese education system. Most of the decisions made by the ministry, including the appointment and transfer of every teacher, must be approved by the minister, even though these decisions are processed by at least four or five layers of the administration. This modus operandi creates an administrative burden in the public institutions by increasing the number of transactions in the system, delaying decision making, or even resulting in no decisions being made.

6. An area of development is the need to strengthen decision-making power and capacity at the regional and school levels. This approach would need to be coupled with a reinforced system of accountability. At the school level, the Ministry of Education in recent years established a program which increases school autonomy and provides school leaders with skills and financial resources to assess the needs of their schools and make decisions on how to meet those needs. These efforts are promising, as similar programs in other countries have showed great potential in improving the school learning environment, lowering repetition and dropout rates, and improving student learning.

7. Decision making, planning, and execution processes showed high fragmentation and a lack of coordination between different entities in the system. This is observed in areas such as teacher professional development, the management and use of education data, and the assessment of student learning. The advancement of the education system in Lebanon could have been faster and more effective if a "systems approach" had been used when planning for reforms, along with structured and well-institutionalized processes. The absence of an integrated, aligned, and holistic approach in the implementation processes have made it hard to achieve a reasonable consensus, collegial cooperation, and a high sense of drive—all of which are required in a functioning education system.

8. Regarding system inputs, there is a lack of effective human resources allocation at both the MEHE and the CERD. This is due to restrictions on recruitment into the civil service and the reliance on the redeployment of teachers from schools to fill administrative gaps without the provision of training for them to acquire the skills they need to accomplish their new functions. With support from external financing from international and local actors, the MEHE and the CERD sought to fill gaps in human resources through the recruitment of consultants. However, these consultants would rarely have in their scope of work the need to build the capacity of permanent staff, and as a result, have generally worked independently, producing their required outputs and exiting the system without strengthening the institutions.

With regard to financial resources, it is essential that a public financial management function is established and that the budget formulation exercise be linked to a strategic planning function. These will help in improving the efficiency, economy, and value for money of government expenditures in the sector.

9. In education delivery, the system perpetuates a dichotomy between public and private schools. Private schools operate with a large degree of autonomy. They enroll approximately 71 percent of Lebanese students and have significant power in the sector. However, there is no quality assurance mechanism and thus there is limited accountability for results toward the government and parents. Quality assurance and accountability mechanisms are an important function intended to ensure that delivered services meet agreed-upon standards.

10. The existing education subsidy system to private schools favors particular groups and is not based on socioeconomic need. As a result, it perpetuates inequity in access and quality of education. The government needs to revisit this subsidy system with an equity lens and a focus on results. This will ensure that the most vulnerable children have access to high-quality learning opportunities.

11. In the public education system, the government should focus on building its technical capacity for analyzing and forecasting needs in school construction and teacher allocation. A technical approach to these two essential mandates would decrease political interference, contribute in increasing internal and external efficiency, and drive improvements in student learning.

12. Information management is a key aspect of planning and decision making. To be effective, decisions need to be based on technically sound information collected at all levels of the education service delivery chain. The flow of information should include feedback loops to assess and evaluate the impact of policy decisions and to adjust policies to better meet the needs of students, teachers, and other actors. Despite significant investments in data systems in Lebanon, there has not been any formulation of a clear policy and framework for information management, leading to fragmentation and divergence in vision and responsibilities for collecting and analyzing data across different units at the MEHE and the CERD. There is a need for a clear policy which sets roles and responsibilities, eliminates duplication, and sets standard mechanisms for data collection, validation, storage, manipulation, reporting, and utilization. This policy would create a stronger enabling environment for a reform in data systems, ensuring sustainability, cost-saving and efficiency, data credibility, and evidence-based decision making.

13. Well-functioning governance is essential for good results. It is crucial for the success of the future education agenda to ensure a system shift from running an operation and focusing on inputs to monitoring and achieving results. There need to be updated rules and processes that affect the way in which powers are exercised at the national level, particularly around financing, quality assurance, accountability, and effectiveness.

INTRODUCTION

The education system in Lebanon faces numerous challenges to achieving education results, including improving student learning, decreasing inequity, and increasing the efficiency of the system. Lebanon has passed through multiple attempts for reform to address those lingering challenges, but many plans have failed to be transformed into real action and tangible achievements. This chapter aims to study the main political determinants of education reform. It seeks to understand the role and interests of the main education stakeholders and the processes governing decision-making and policy execution in the sector. These processes include mechanisms that interest groups use to influence policy, as well as the structural features of the environment and institutions driving reform. This analysis is essential for uncovering the forces that could support or undermine different reform attempts in achieving education results.

The findings in this chapter are based on a political economy analysis, conducted through a series of semistructured interviews and focus groups with the main stakeholders in the sector, as well as a detailed literature and document review. At least 65 stakeholders were interviewed through this process, including former ministers of education, current and former governmental officers in education institutions, private and public school stakeholders, and representatives from local and international organizations active in the sector.

EDUCATION STAKEHOLDERS: ROLES, RESPONSIBILITIES, AND INTERESTS

Education systems need both alignment and coherence

Aligning the interests of all education stakeholders and actors ensures that the whole system works for performance. It reduces the effect of contradictory interests that distract from achieving education objectives. To be truly aligned, parts of the education system must be coherent with one another. Alignment means that student success and learning is the goal of the various components of the system; and coherence means the components reinforce each other in achieving educational goals. By integrating both into the system and directing stakeholder interests accordingly, Lebanon will be able to overcome technical and political barriers and establish a system which is conducive to student success and is sustainable in the long term. By considering these real-world barriers and mobilizing everyone who has a stake in education, Lebanon can support innovative educators on the front lines and direct education systems toward all-inclusive and sustainable learning. Box 5.1 provides an example of alignment of objectives based on learning standards.

As illustrated in figure 5.1, many actors and groups of stakeholders contribute to the education process, each with their own individual interests and incentives. Many of the inputs to the learning process are choices made by the actors or choices made in reaction to the actual or anticipated choices of other actors. Bureaucrats, politicians, and nonstate players make decisions that influence education access, quality, equity, and learning. For instance, teachers react to changes in school leadership, school principals react to community demands, and parents react to changes in government policy. To this end, the system should generate incentives for stakeholders to align their interests in a coherent manner. However, in many cases, misalignments between stakeholders and different vested interests divert systems away from learning. In those cases, political challenges compound technical ones; undermining the entire education development process. Political influence processes such as patronage or rent-seeking behavior interfere to divert focus and resources from promoting

Example of alignment of objectives

Learning standards clearly lay out the competencies that students are expected to master in each grade. Teachers are expected to translate these standards into detailed lesson plans so that students can learn and acquire the competencies laid out in the curriculum effectively. All these steps should ideally have an in-built audit and monitoring trail.

An efficient and timely process implies that there will not be any undue delays and bureaucratic procedures that increase public and private costs, leading to missing intended targets. It further implies that the system will have in-built processes for life-cycle costing, retrofits, extension of system capability, and the like.

FIGURE 5.1

Education stakeholders in an education system

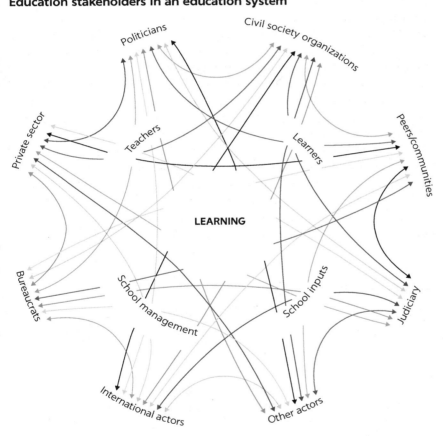

Source: World Bank 2018.

and improving student learning to serving individual interests of stakeholders; for example, by dispensing services to specific target groups based on political affiliation, religious confession, and geographical area, among other criteria. This can happen at various stages, from setting policy goals to designing, implementing, evaluating, and sustaining reforms. Another example is in the implementation of decentralization policies, which in theory aim to increase local capacity and responsiveness but can be transformed into political maneuvering to delegate accountability for results to local actors without conferring the authority or resources to achieve them.

Value of building coalitions

To align the interests of different stakeholders, it is essential that a culture in which education delivery is a shared responsibility is promoted to achieve high-level education outcomes for all. For that, education objectives and responsibilities need to be continuously shared and communicated, and assessment and process evaluation reports need to be regularly produced and discussed.

Many actors and organizations, both public and private, contribute to shaping the Lebanese education sector. Among the public actors, the legislative (the Parliament) and executive power (the Council of Ministers) play an essential role in setting up the framework of action for the sector. Execution of education policy is led by (1) the minister of education; (2) the Directorate General of Education (DGE) within the Ministry of Education and Higher Education (MEHE), responsible for the management of schools; (3) the Center for Educational Research and Development (CERD), responsible, among other things, for educational research, curriculum revision, and teachers' in-service training; and (4) the Lebanese University, responsible for preparing teachers and providing teaching diplomas. The main external monitoring and regulatory body is the Education Inspectorate, a division within the Central Inspection Body, responsible for monitoring education services in the public sector, including at the school level. Finally, other governmental actors include the Council for Development and Reconstruction (CDR), which executes large construction works, and governmental institutions mandated to support administrative reforms, such as the Office of the Minister of State for Administrative Reform (OMSAR), and fiduciary management, such as the Ministry of Finance, which supports the government's budgeting process (figure 5.2).

FIGURE 5.2

Governmental actors in education sector reform

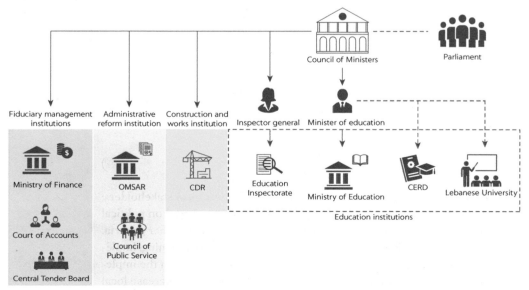

Note: CDR = Council for Development and Reconstruction; CERD = Center for Educational Research and Development; OMSAR = Office of the Minister of State for Administrative Reform.

As for the nongovernmental actors and organizations, the most notable ones that contribute to shaping the education sector and service delivery are the following: (1) private schools; (2) teachers' unions and associations; (3) local authorities, represented mainly by elected municipal councils; (4) parents and students; (5) CSOs and NGOs; and (6) international actors and organizations.

Governmental agencies

The legislative power: The Parliament
The Lebanese Constitution has provided the elected national Parliament with the powers to set the legislative framework governing education and to allocate financial resources for the delivery of education services. The Parliament also determines teachers' employment conditions in both the public and private sectors. Within the Parliament, a specialized Committee for Education and Culture, composed of 12 members of Parliament (Lebanese Parliament 2017), studies education-related bills to be submitted to the General Assembly of the Parliament for discussion and voting. The committee also holds regular discussions with the Minister of Education, the Director General of Education, and other education public officials, to understand the needs of the sector and to seek clarifications and inquiries when studying draft laws. The legislative power covers a broad spectrum of issues, from approving national curricula and education plans, to passing bills that are more from an executive nature such as the appointment of teachers. This broad power the legislative holds can in fact be the cause of significant delays witnessed in reforming many aspects of the sector—one such aspect is the organizational structure and administrative processes of the Ministry of Education, as explored in box 5.2.

Moreover, according to stakeholders interviewed for this study, including members of Parliament and former ministers, legislative work in Lebanon has been scattered both in terms of themes and momentum, and has rarely been conceived through a comprehensive lens. This approach has led to many gaps in education-related legislation, even in establishing fundamental rights, such as the right to compulsory and free education, as explained in box 5.3.

BOX 5.2

Legislation on the organizational structure of the Ministry of Education

The Legislative Decree 111, adopted in 1959, and amended by Decree 58 of 1982, restricts the power of establishing directorates and services within ministries and institutions to the Parliament, rather than the executive power represented by the Council of Ministers or by individual ministries. As a result, most of the current organizational structure and administrative processes of the Ministry of Education date back from the 1950s, with little to no update since then.

According to organizational specialists interviewed at the Council of Public Service and OMSAR, the fact that only the legislative power can introduce reforms in administrative processing and organizational structures is a major impediment to improving service delivery and operations at the Ministry of Education and other public institutions, given the significant time the legislative branch would need to pass such laws and the different priorities the Parliament must address.

The executive power: The Council of Ministers

According to Article 65 of the Lebanese Constitution, the executive power at the national level is vested collectively in the Council of Ministers, which sets the general policy of the government, drafts bills and organizational decrees, and makes decisions necessary for implementing them. The Council of Ministers holds the mandate for approving appointments of senior public officials. This process is generally conducted in a consociational manner, by taking into consideration representation of different religious confessions across public positions, and thus introducing more complexity to the assignment process compared to processes where only competency-based criteria are used. As a result, significant delays accompany appointment processes and many essential positions sometimes remain vacant or are assigned on an interim basis.

Given its mandate, the Council of Ministers has a critical role in large-scale education reform—one such example is the adoption of the "New General Education Curriculum" in 1997. The factors leading to this major accomplishment are detailed in box 5.4.

Education policy execution bodies

The Minister of Education and Higher Education. In Lebanon, the Taef Agreement, promulgated as constitutional law in 1990, has provided extensive powers to the ministers in charge of their respective ministry. The current legal framework places the minister at the head of the entire education system and makes this role the most pivotal one for the advancement of educational reform.

With the absence of a national education strategy other than the 1994 Plan for Education Reform, ministers over the last 20 years have come to introduce different initiatives based on their individual vision, focus, and style. Given the short terms of most ministers, as outlined in box 5.5, it was increasingly difficult that any initiative introduced by a minister would be successfully institutionalized and that normative instruments setting standards and due processes would be adopted and sustained in the system.

BOX 5.3

Legislation on compulsory and free education

The right to education has never been clearly stated in the Constitution. Compulsory education was affirmed for primary education in 1959, then in 1998, and was extended in 2011 to cover all basic education stages, generally by a single article of law without any guidance on how it should be implemented. The same could be said about free education, which has never been explicitly defined by law.

BOX 5.4

Factors leading to the adoption of the 1997 curriculum

According to interviewees, several factors have made this possible, including the following: (1) political will at all levels of the state to reform the national general education curriculum after more than two decades of strife due to the 1975–90 civil war; (2) the fact that the previous curriculum was nearly 30 years old, dating back to 1968, and thus was largely obsolete; (3) the allocation of financial resources by the government to the CERD to undertake this endeavor; (4) a strong leadership and mobilization capacity exercised by the president of the CERD; and (5) the consultative approach used for drafting the new curriculum by mobilizing around 450 teachers and specialists from various education backgrounds and religious communities, thus ensuring large national ownership of the process and its results.

Analysis of the Cornerstones of Education | 133

BOX 5.5

Short terms of ministers of education

An examination of the list of ministers who have exercised their functions since the start of the general education reform process in 1992 shows that 13 different individuals have been appointed as ministers of education, with an average term of less than 2 years (22 months) for each one, varying between 3 months and 35 months. Moreover, many ministers served long periods of their terms on a caretaking basis due to the resignation of the government and the delays in forming a new government. The short terms of ministers of education negatively affected the sector by creating constant disruptions to the leadership and vision in the sector. In a context where no national education strategy existed other than the 1994 Plan for Education Reform, the sector was frequently driven by individual and mostly fragmented initiatives introduced by each minister.

Ministers hold management powers over all ministry personnel; they also hold the power for assigning positions, roles, and functions, to staff from the ministry, with the exception of the director general position,[1] which is appointed by the Council of Ministers. This power over administrative staff allowed subsequent ministers to reshuffle staff across different positions or assign different roles and responsibilities to staff, based on political affinity. Additionally, many ministers frequently recruited external advisors, who were appointed on a consultancy basis at the ministry, sometimes creating parallel structures by taking over tasks from public officials.

Moreover, the minister holds the mandate of deploying and distributing teachers across schools. Given the size of the teacher workforce, this is a power that is commonly under political pressures and demands for rendering services to constituents by facilitating employment and employment conditions through preferred assignment to schools, subjects, and the setting of teaching hours. While the legislation allows the minister to delegate the mandate for teacher deployment to the Director General of Education, some interviewees argued that the legislation should be adjusted to transfer this mandate to the Director General of Education, similar to what Lebanese legislation has allowed for armed and internal security forces.[2] This approach, according to interviewees, in addition to the setting of clear norms for teacher recruitment and deployment, would decrease the level of political interference in the teacher deployment process.

The Directorate General of Education. The highest public official responsible for the management of general education is the Director General of Education (DG). The DG is the head of the DGE, which groups several specialized directorates, all linked to support the management of schools and the provision of services to schools. Among those directorates, there are centralized ones responsible, among other things, for primary education (including kindergarten and intermediate education), secondary education, private education, national examinations, guidance and counseling services, cultural affairs, and projects and programs. Also among the directorates are Regional Education Offices (REOs), one for each governorate, responsible for the management of primary schools[3] and the provision of services at the regional level.

It is important to note that financial matters and budgeting lie outside of the DGE, but under the minister of education, through the Directorate for Common

Instability in the Director General of Education position, 1994–2007

During the period from 1994–2007, five directors general have held this position; two of them came from within the Ministry of Education on an interim basis and for very short periods, while the others came from outside the ministry.

Administrative Services, which provides finance-related services to the DGE, as well as to the Directorate General of Higher Education and the Directorate General of TVET.

The DG is assumed to be the head of the institutional memory of the ministry, given that they are supposed to enjoy employment stability as opposed to the constant change of ministers. However, as detailed in box 5.6, an examination of the list of individuals who occupied this position from 1994–2007 shows that the director general position was marked by instability. According to most of the interviewees, this instability, compounded with the powers concentrated in the position of the minister, has weakened the role of the DG in leading education reforms and relegated the position to a mere day-to-day administrative role.

For reform to succeed and be institutionalized and sustained in the long term, the role of the DG is critical as it combines the institutional memory and lessons learned from previous reforms with the stable leadership that would not only design but also oversee execution of reform initiatives. To this end, systematic and institutional strengthening of the DG's position is needed to allow them to lead long-term education reform in the face of inevitably changing governments and ministers. This will allow the DG to assist the new minister in providing lessons learned from previous reforms, ensure the continuity and sustainability of educational projects, and build long-standing coalitions with other education stakeholders for successful implementation.

The RACE PMU. Within the MEHE, the Program Management Unit (PMU) was established in 2014 by the minister of education to manage the education sector's response to the Syrian refugee crisis under RACE. The establishment of the RACE PMU was supported by external donors and international actors, which were seeking a rapid response to the crisis and provided financing for the recruitment of consultants at the PMU. Having a separate unit focused on the response to the refugee crisis, outside of the regular administrative structures, aimed to avoid overburdening the system, given the large size of the Syrian refugee children population, and to increase responsiveness to the crisis, as well as to facilitate the flow and tracking of financial contributions. The RACE PMU's annual budget is significant and corresponds to approximately 20 percent the size of the MEHE's general education budget.[4] Some of the RACE PMU's activities include, among others, planning the location and number of second-shift schools, transferring funds to schools to cover enrollment fees for Lebanese and Syrian children, paying salaries for second-shift teachers, rehabilitating schools, collecting enrollment and attendance data, and monitoring education service delivery in second-shift schools.

The Center for Educational Research and Development. The CERD is an essential driver of education reform and service delivery in Lebanon. The CERD is an administratively and financially autonomous institution under the custodianship authority of the minister of education. Through its different academic units, it is the main body responsible for review and design of the national curriculum and was behind the successful overhaul of the national curriculum in 1997. The CERD develops and owns the copyright of Lebanese national textbooks and other educational content it produces. In addition to textbooks, the CERD sets specifications for educational material and equipment based on the curriculum. Other mandates of CERD include the provision of in-service training for teachers and staff, as well as education research and publication of education statistics.

The president of CERD and four elected members among the center's specialists constitute a "Board of Specialists," which provides guidance to the Council of Ministers on education matters. While the CERD has been in the lead on the content of the curriculum and teacher training, it has no direct reporting or management lines with schools and relies on the coordination with the DGE to disseminate content to schools and education staff. That coordination, highlighted in box 5.7, is crucial for any successful reform to translate into successful results at the school level.

Given the challenges in the education sector to yield high student learning outcomes and the crucial role assigned to the CERD in driving the quality of education in Lebanon, a number of interviewees identified areas of improvement where the CERD could capitalize on to improve education quality:

1. Reinforcing the strategic positioning of the CERD to focus on a clear and specific long-term vision for reforming and improving the education system. This vision will help the CERD in amplifying the effectiveness and the efficiency of its work by prioritizing activities that can help the system in achieving long-term outcomes.
2. Strengthening alignment, integration, and harmonization between activities conducted by the CERD and related activities implemented by other public education actors (DGE, Education Inspectorate, Lebanese University). For example, there is a need for better alignment on teacher professional development activities and on the establishment and use of data systems.
3. Establishing relevant processes and procedures for measuring and evaluating reforms in the system, as it is essential that any long-term vision for the CERD and the education system be monitored in terms of progress and adjusted in terms of execution and objective to yield better results.
4. Conducting periodic assessments and introducing new curricula reform. The 1997 curriculum reform in fact stipulated that assessment and revision of curricula would take place every 4 years. However, this did not materialize for many reasons, including the lack of financial resources and capacity, organizational, and structural constraints.
5. Expanding and strengthening teacher support programs. Despite the large number of training offerings provided by the CERD through 36 teacher training centers spread across all regions, there still exist structural constraints to provide adequate learning opportunities to all teachers and cover skills and competencies that teachers need. There is also little evidence collected on the impact of teacher support programs and their ability to translate into improvements in teacher classroom practices and student learning outcomes.
6. Reforming the CERD staff recruitment and assignment practices, including improvement in working conditions and compensation systems. Shortcomings in recruitment practices have led to capacity gaps at

BOX 5.7

Coordination between the CERD and the DGE

The law foresees coordination between the CERD and the DGE through a Consultative Body chaired by the minister and composed of senior public officials at the MEHE and CERD. Interviewees in this study admitted that the Consultative Body rarely meets to discuss education matters related to its mandate.

the CERD. As a matter of comparison, when the CERD was founded in 1971, the conditions for employment of specialists were better than those of professors at the Lebanese University, in a way that attracted highly qualified Ph.D. holders through a selective process. With time, conditions of employment (for example, salaries and types of contracts) have not remained competitive, hindering the CERD's ability to fill staff capacity needs.

The Lebanese University—the Faculty of Education. The Lebanese University is the only public higher education institution in Lebanon. It is financially and administratively independent but falls under the custodianship authority of the minister of the MEHE. The Faculty of Education within the Lebanese University plays an essential role in general education by providing preservice training to teachers, school principals, and counselors. While private universities in Lebanon could also provide teacher preparation programs, formal accreditation of those programs is contingent on meeting standards set by the Lebanese University. Box 5.8 explores, in more detail, instances of coordination between the Lebanese University, CERD, and MEHE on the preservice preparation of education staff.

The monitoring and regulatory bodies

The Education Inspectorate. The Education Inspectorate is one of five divisions of the Lebanese Central Inspection authority, reporting directly to the Council of Ministers.[5] This body is responsible for monitoring the functioning of public schools, including the decisions made by the various administrative levels of the ministry. Educational inspectors conduct

---

BOX 5.8

Coordination between the Lebanese University, MEHE, and CERD

While in the past, the Center for Educational Research and Development (CERD) used to provide preservice training for secondary school graduates and others interested in joining the teaching profession, the recent legislative framework has consigned this task to the Lebanese University. The coordination between the Lebanese University, CERD, and Ministry of Education and Higher Education (MEHE) on the preservice preparation of education staff is thus crucial for improvement in the education system. Recent years have seen several initiatives of increased coordinated work toward that end. In November 2017, a joint effort by the CERD, MEHE, and Lebanese University resulted in the development and adoption of a professional competency framework for teachers, teacher trainers, and counselors. Building on this achievement, the Lebanese University would undertake a reform of its teacher preparation programs to align them with the new common and approved teacher standards. Moreover, while the Lebanese University does not currently grant a professional degree for education administrators, joint efforts with the MEHE and the CERD have set up a preparation program for individuals selected to be appointed as school principals. This program delivered by the Lebanese University allows nominated individuals for the position of school principal to acquire fundamental skills in school management to better succeed in their newly assigned roles. Following this experience and also given the lack of relevant counseling programs at the Lebanese University, an ongoing discussion between the MEHE and the Lebanese University is focused on the establishment of a professional degree program to prepare teachers selected to take on a counseling role at the Ministry of Education.

regular school visits to examine financial and administrative records, conduct classroom observations, ensure compliance with applicable laws and decrees, and write inspection reports, which are transmitted to Central Inspection and the Ministry of Education. The Education Inspectorate contributes in driving public schools' management at all levels to improve education quality and efficiency, by monitoring the work of all public administration employees and imposing disciplinary sanctions on staff not complying with rules and regulations. However, the inspectorate has no power to enforce decisions and/or actions made by the minister of education, who, as stated earlier, holds broad executive power in the sector. This issue is highlighted in box 5.9 and has been pointed out by many interviewees as an obstacle to the Educational Inspectorate's effectiveness in driving significant impact in the system. Another challenge to the effectiveness of the Education Inspectorate, according to interviewees, is the understaffing of the department, with less than 40 inspectors still active, after a freeze on hiring and attrition due to retirement.

It is important to note that education inspectors are specialized in specific grade levels (kindergarten, primary, secondary) and/or in specific subjects (science, math, Arabic language, and so on). When they visit schools, they are actively engaged in observing classrooms and discussing instructional methods with teachers and school principals. This mandate, according to some interviewees, creates a duplication in duties and responsibilities with Direction d'Orientation Pédagogique et Scolaire (DOPS), which is under the DGE. Contrary to the Educational Inspectorate, DOPS is an integral part of the MEHE, and has thus greater access to administrative tools to enforce the MEHE's directives on education quality and service delivery.

DOPS within the DGE. DOPS is a department within the DGE and, given its role in monitoring school-level practices, could be considered as an internal regulatory body which provides internal feedback to the system for improvement of service delivery. However, unlike education inspectors, DOPS counselors do not have a compliance enforcement role; they do not impose any sanctions or disciplinary actions for noncompliant teachers, they instead focus on the provision of follow-up, feedback, guidance, and coaching for teachers. DOPS has approximately 600 counselors, recruited from public schools (see box 5.10 on recruitment of counselors), who provide counseling services to schools through regular visits and follow-ups in four main areas: (1) pedagogical counselors, specialized in specific grade levels and/or school subject, conduct classroom observations and provide coaching and guidance to teachers for improving the teaching and learning environment; (2) psychosocial counselors provide advice and guidance to schools on addressing the psychosocial and socioemotional needs of children; (3) health counselors conduct awareness sessions and support schools with regard to health issues such as school cleanliness and student hygiene; and

---

BOX 5.9

Limitations of the Education Inspectorate

All interviewees holding or having held administrative positions within the ministry affirmed that the Education Inspectorate is essential for ensuring compliance with rules and regulations because it can impose disciplinary sanctions on public employees found to be noncompliant. However, the inspection power exercised by the Education Inspectorate focuses on legislation passed by Parliament and decrees passed by the Council of Ministers but does not encompass decisions made by the minister.

BOX 5.10

Recruitment of DOPS counselors

In the last 4 years, DOPS has witnessed a significant increase in the number of counselors recruited, reaching more than 600 counselors, which is double the number originally envisioned for the department. Counselors were mainly recruited from secondary schools, given the perception that secondary school teachers were the most qualified personnel within the ministry. Some interviewees in this study argued that the targeting for recruitment of secondary school teachers as counselors has adversely affected schools by emptying them of their most qualified cadre and pushing schools to resort to fast recruitment of less qualified contractual teachers with lenient criteria for selection, given the urgency to fill teacher shortages. Another concern expressed by interviewees was the lack of preparation of counselors to perform their mandates, given that high qualification in teaching skills does not necessarily translate into high qualification in coaching and counseling skills.

(4) special education counselors lead the ministry's effort in providing inclusive education to children with special needs.

There was a consensus among the interviewees on the necessity of strengthening the legislative and regulatory framework for the role of DOPS because, while the establishment of DOPS was created in a budgetary law during the 1980s, to date, there is no regulatory and implementation framework adopted to organize their functions at the ministry.

Fiduciary monitoring and regulatory bodies. In financial and budgetary matters, the Ministry of Finance and the Court of Accounts (COA) play a crucial role in the annual budgeting process and in conducting prior reviews and audits of expenditures. In procurement, the Central Tender Board (CTB) regulates procurement procedures across all government institutions. Finally, the State Council is responsible for ensuring that the administrative decisions and actions of the government are compliant with the laws adopted by the Parliament.

Other governmental agencies

OMSAR: Organizational and administrative reforms. OMSAR was established in the early 1990s with the mandate to lead administrative reform of the public sector. According to interviewees in this study, there are many areas where the structure of the Ministry of Education could have been strengthened to improve efficiency and accountability in employment and administrative decisions. During the last 20 years, several attempts have been made within the framework of OMSAR's work and with the participation of organization specialists of the Council of Public Service, but these attempts have not been successful due to the instability of government and lack of political will. For example, in relation to professional and administrative positions in the DGE, an adjustment in the organization is needed to guarantee the continuation and implementation of projects in the face of changing governments. This implies a balancing of roles and responsibilities across multiple senior public officials rather than a concentration of power with a limited number of staff. However, the implementation of such reform has been extremely complex due to the fragile equilibrium in staff positions, where balance of power is largely based on the representation of various sectarian groups in key positions at the ministry. This distribution based on sectarian affiliation constricts the flexibility of recruitment and assignment of staff. As a result, it is not uncommon to have at the ministry one public official holding two or three different positions.

The Council of Public Service: Teacher recruitment reforms. The Council of Public Service deals with all matters related to employment in the various administrative structures of the government. Along with OMSAR, it plays an important role in the reform of the organizational structure of the ministry, the establishment of new professional or administrative positions, and the recruitment of public servants including teachers. According to interviewees in the study, there is a need for reform in teacher recruitment, and the Council of Public Service could play a more active role to facilitate the recruitment of civil servants for teacher positions in public schools by working collaboratively with the MEHE, the CERD, and the Lebanese University to achieve the following: (1) increased capacity to forecast teacher needs in the system, (2) improved deployment of teachers to schools based on a technical analysis of school needs, (3) strengthened capacity to enforce teacher recruitment and deployment policy and to monitor compliance, (4) improved entrance requirements for the teaching profession, and (5) a strengthened and coordinated system for preservice teacher preparation delivered consistently to all candidates for the teaching profession.

The Council for Development and Reconstruction. The CDR is considered the planning arm of the government for infrastructure investment and is under the custodianship authority of the president of the Council of Ministers. It is responsible, among other things, for building and rehabilitating public schools (financed from the government budget or by grants and loans). The MEHE identifies schools to be built or rehabilitated, and the CDR executes works through contractors and then delivers the schools to the ministry. The CDR exercises its discretionary power to engage in negotiations with the ministry on the terms of agreement for undertaking the works. Interviewees in this study pointed out several instances where initiation of works had been stalled or delayed due to differences in priorities and terms proposed between the ministry and CDR, despite the availability of financing to complete school construction and the need for construction, particularly to replace rented schools. These examples highlight the importance of aligning interests in a timely and efficient manner among different education sector stakeholders.

Nongovernmental agencies

Private education institutions

With more than 70 percent of Lebanese students enrolled in private schools, Lebanon is a frontrunner among countries where enrollment in private schools outnumbers enrollment in public schools. Subsidized private schools also play an important role, with around 13 percent of children enrolled in those schools, mainly at the primary school level. Paid private schools usually attract children from middle and upper socioeconomic households who seek to increase their children's chances to access higher education institutions and better career opportunities. It is worth mentioning, however, that there are significant differences between private schools in terms of tuition and quality of education.

BOX 5.11

The power of private schools

The right to establish schools, particularly by religious communities, has been guaranteed by the Lebanese Constitution since 1926 as an extension of the privileges these communities were granted when Lebanon was under the Ottoman Empire's rule. This right was extended to individual citizens. The great majority of general education private schools remain under the authority of religious communities. Most of these establishments are organized in the "Federation of Private Education Establishments," which considers itself a partner of the Ministry of Education in the provision of educational opportunities to citizens, but which constitutes, at the same time, a powerful political lobby representing these establishments.

As explored in chapter 2, a large segment of private schools is religiously affiliated, and some are linked to foreign institutions and organizations such as the French Ministry of Education; accordingly, many private schools belong to networks of private schools, such as the Catholic Schools, the Makassed Schools, the Mabarrat Schools, and others. Box 5.11 describes the organization of private schools. Despite the large degree of autonomy provided to private schools to operate in the country, the Government of Lebanon is mandated to ensure that all education institutions are compliant with agreed-upon standards and rules. Particularly, the Government of Lebanon regulates the curriculum, national examinations, and accreditation of programs and degrees. The government also regulates through laws and decrees teachers' employment conditions, including the determination of salaries in both the public and private sectors. Other laws that the government enforces concern the financial transparency of education institutions and the engagement of parents in school decision making.

The lobbying of private education institutions has mainly focused on the following five issues during the past years: (1) the need to preserve the status of subsidized schools and the timely transfer of funds from the government to those schools; (2) the assertion of autonomy of these institutions and their resistance to forms of direct supervision or monitoring by the ministry, on the grounds that the ministry lacks the expertise necessary to perform such monitoring; (3) the opposition to laws and regulations perceived as an interference in private schools' management or decision making, such as the opposition to presenting financial balance sheets to school parents' committees; (4) the participation in consultation on laws and decrees concerning teachers' employment conditions, particularly their wages, in light of the repercussions of any salary increase for the overall school budget and the ensuing increase in school tuition; and (5) the desire of these institutions to participate in discussions around education policy and reform, including teacher policy, curriculum, and national examinations.

Given that private schools deliver education services to more than two-thirds of children in Lebanon, they represent a powerful force in driving education sector reform or can be a strong opposing force to policies they perceive as infringing on their autonomy and freedom of operation. For any reform to succeed, it is thus essential that in-depth consultations be held with private schools' associations, in addition to other imposing actors such as teacher unions and parents' associations, which could present a substantial counterweight and balance in policy reform discussions.

Teachers' unions and associations

Teachers are the most influential stakeholders in the education process. They are the main actors implementing reforms in classrooms and driving student learning. From their classroom experience, they also provide inputs and feedback to policy makers. As an example, teachers contributed to the development of the 1997 general education curriculum as the CERD mobilized around 450 teachers to participate in this national endeavor. They thus have played a crucial role in the curriculum revision process.

In addition to their essential educational role, teachers, when organized in associations or unions, are a political force and have collective bargaining power. They have vested interests in improving their employment conditions. Teachers have two specific areas they lobby for: (1) higher salaries and benefits (such as promotions into higher salary grades and education allowances); and (2) conditions of employment (such as permanent appointments, and decrease in workload). Teachers' lobbying has large effects on public and private spending on education, as well as on the efficiency and equity of the system.

The teachers' associations and unions landscape in Lebanon is diverse, with at least eight different associations representing teachers of different education sectors (public, private); education levels (primary, secondary); and employment status (permanent staff, contractual). Teachers' associations can play a significant role in education reform in Lebanon, when they are not driven by partisan politics and when their interests are aligned with interests of other actors in the system. Nevertheless, teachers' associations have, in many cases, been disruptive to the education process, specifically through their ability for large mobilizations in protests and strikes. Recent years have seen a wave of disruptive strikes, which culminated in 2014 in the cancellation of the national examinations due to teachers' withholding from correcting the exams, prompting the Ministry of Education to issue certificates of completion for all grade 9 and grade 12 students. Box 5.12 cites more examples of roles played by teachers' associations in recent years.

Regional and local authorities

Regional and local authorities play an important role in expanding access to education to their constituencies and in improving the learning environment in schools.

The regional governor, appointed by the Council of Ministers, is mandated by law to assist the MEHE in ensuring the availability of well-equipped schools in the region.[6] In practice, this mandate has been translated into a consultative role, as they are consulted before the establishment or closing of a public school.

BOX 5.12

Examples of roles played by teachers' associations

Teachers, associations have played both positive and more controversial roles in the system. For instance, the Association of Secondary School Teachers has exerted strong leadership, along with other associations, by lobbying for the expansion of access to secondary education and for ensuring that the quality of education in the early years is equitably improved to decrease dropping out by the most disadvantaged students. They also supported the Ministry of Education's proposal for restricting all steps of the teacher recruitment process to the Council of Public Service, including the advertising of positions, shortlisting of candidates, interviews, and recommendations for appointment to avoid all forms of favoritism in the teacher selection process. Conversely, the associations of contractual teachers have consistently lobbied for the unconditional protection of contractual teachers and for contractual teachers to be hired as permanent teachers, representing a significant pressure point for the government, given that they represent more than half of the teacher workforce.

Municipal councils, which are elected for 6-year mandates, have regularly assisted the Ministry of Education in providing education services. In terms of expanding access to public schools, municipalities have been instrumental in providing land to the national government to undertake school construction activities. In some cases, municipalities have built schools and offered them to the ministry. Municipal councils have also contributed significantly in improving the school learning environment. In many municipalities, local authorities have invested in the physical environment of schools through the provision of school furniture and equipment (especially ICT), the maintenance of school premises, and the provision of fuel for heating. Moreover, municipal councils have also contributed to the learning experience of children through the offering of remedial classes for students with learning difficulties and the provision and salary payment of temporary teachers (offered teachers) for subjects such as foreign languages, computer science, music education, theater, and sports.

While the Municipalities Law,[7] as explored in box 5.13, provides a broad mandate to municipal councils—including the expansion of access to public schools, the financial contribution to public schools' operations, and the regulation and monitoring of education service delivery in both public and private schools—their role has not been consistent across all municipalities in the country because of several challenges. First, there has been little fiscal space in municipalities' budgets to invest in education, particularly for smaller municipalities. Legislative proposals to make compulsory the financial contribution of municipal councils to public schools have been opposed by the members of Parliament who argued that schools located in municipalities with limited financial resources would be at a disadvantage. Second, there has been little political pressure from constituencies to engage municipalities in education service delivery. The household survey presented in chapter 3 reveals that among critical actors for education reform, municipalities came at the last position, with only 18 percent of parents attributing an important role in the education sector to municipal councils. As a result, most municipalities have focused their limited resources to address other priorities in their localities. Third, even when municipalities are committed to playing a role in improving education services for their constituencies, they are typically faced with challenges in their lack of capacity to do so effectively, thus

---

BOX 5.13

Municipal councils' role in education

Lebanese law (particularly Municipalities' Law) provides municipal councils with several mandates related to education, including:

1. Contributing to the expenses of public schools, including tuition fees (Article 49);
2. Monitoring education activities and operations in public and private schools, and reporting back to the relevant education authorities (Article 49);
3. Establishing or contributing to the establishment of public schools, museums, libraries, playgrounds, and other social, cultural, and artistic institutions (Article 50); and
4. Approving the establishment, transfer, or closing of public schools (Article 51).

Moreover, the law provides municipal councils the mandate to regulate transportation within the municipality, including transportation to schools (Articles 49 and 50).

resorting to focus on investments in infrastructure rather than the learning process at schools. Moreover, there are no implementation frameworks or processes for municipalities to exert their mandate of regulating and monitoring public and private schools, and there is no information flow mechanism to provide education sector data and feedback from/to municipalities, making execution of this mandate implausible.

Decentralization efforts in the education sector to equip municipal councils with a larger role in supporting, regulating, and monitoring education service delivery should thus take into consideration local capacity and equity concerns to ensure that all municipalities have adequate resources to invest in learning. Implementation frameworks and processes should be defined to support municipalities in executing their mandate, including the strengthening of information systems and feedback loop mechanisms.

Parent associations

Unlike teachers, parents do not have a collective bargaining power since they are generally not organized; and although their participation in education decision-making could in principle improve school accountability and learning outcomes, findings from both the political economy interviews and the public perception study indicate a low rate of participation from parents, partly because of the lack of accountability of the school management toward parents and the lack of authority for parents to effectively influence decisions on education-related matters. Nevertheless, parents can influence the education process through two means: (1) freedom of choice in the selection of schools; and (2) parent associations' role in private and public schools.

The Lebanese education sector provides parents with great freedom of choice in the selection of schools for their children. There is a large range of private education provision, including religious and nonreligious institutions, schools affiliated with foreign institutions, and subsidized (or free) private schools. Parents can also choose from any of the public education offerings without restriction by neighborhood of residence, as long as they can secure transportation to the school.[8] In fact, the household survey presented in chapter 3 reveals that around one-quarter of households with children in schools admitted that their schools were far from their home. The large degree of freedom of choice provides more opportunities for parents to independently appraise the offering of public and private schools and select the school that would in their opinion provide the best education to their children, tuition and transportation costs being the main prohibitive factors. That being said, and in support of freedom of choice, the government has a system to provide subsidies to a segment of parents and schools to partially cover the cost of private education. However, these subsidies are based on employment status and are not targeted to low-income families. The implication of the government policy on school subsidies is the decrease in the socioeconomic diversity of the student population in public schools. In other words, public schools in Lebanon serve primarily low-income households. As revealed by the perception survey presented in chapter 3, public school parents tended to have lower education achievements and less experience with the education sector. Moreover, public school parents were significantly less likely to be engaged with their children's school. As a result, the current subsidization system indirectly reduces the role and influence of parents in education sector improvement and creates impediments to public school improvement. Box 5.14 explores the relation between the current subsidy system and parents' role in public school improvement.

BOX 5.14

The private school subsidy system and parents' incentives for public school improvement

The political economy interviewees revealed tensions between parents' freedom of choice in schools and parents' incentives for supporting improvement in public schools, particularly in the light of government subsidies for some parents to enroll their children in private schools.

It is evident that the education system in Lebanon provides a large degree of freedom of choice for parents in selecting schools between different public and private education options. Even among public schools, parents have freedom of choice. For example, when a public school enrolling approximately 1,000 students recently had a change in leadership, it saw its enrollment cut by 80–90 percent after parents perceived the change in leadership as causing a serious deterioration of the quality of education at the school. Most students transferred to other public schools because there are no neighborhood residence restrictions for enrolling in public schools in Lebanon, while other students transferred to subsidized (also known as "free") private schools.

Subsidized private schools, largely operated by religious associations, receive a financial subsidy from the central government per student enrolled. Originally, they were envisioned to provide education services at the primary school level in neighborhoods, towns, and villages where there were no public schools. Nowadays subsidized private schools coexist with public schools in the same locations and compete for students, given that they charge low or no tuition fees. Subsidized private schools currently enroll 14 percent of Lebanese students at all grade levels, and 22 percent of primary school children in Lebanon, which is close to the 28 percent of primary school children enrolled in public schools.[a]

In addition to subsidies to schools, the Government of Lebanon provides subsidies to a segment of parents (mainly all public sector employees) to cover school tuition. These subsidies are not based on income level, they are rather based on employment status. Government employees and some private sector employees receive, through different mechanisms, school allowances to enroll their children in private schools. In particular, civil servants in the education sector—including senior officials, administrators, school principals, and teachers—receive school allowances and likely enroll their children in private schools. Some interviewees pointed out that these school allowances might decrease public civil servants' incentives to support public schools.

a. CERD 2018. Figures exclude second-shift public schools, which host only refugee children.

Lebanese law also provides influence to parents through their role in parents' committees in private schools or parents' councils in public schools. The biggest focus of those parents' associations is the budgeting exercise, as parents negotiate with schools their annual budget and spending priorities, which, in private schools, lead to the determination of tuition fees. Private school parents' committees can be consulted by the MEHE (for example, on tuition fee–related matters) and can raise complaints to the MEHE to initiate an audit and review of schools' tuition fees. In public schools, parents contribute to a parents' council fund at each school, which is separate from the school fund. While the latter (US$100 per student) is used for covering recurring operational costs—such as electricity, water, and telephone bills—the parents' council fund (US$60 per student) can be used to support the learning process by purchasing learning materials, organizing extracurricular activities, and, in some cases, hiring additional teachers for elective subjects such as arts, music, theater, computer science, and sports. The parents' council works with the school management to ensure proper allocation of those funds. The parents' council can also support the school by organizing fundraising efforts.

Despite the involvement of parents in the budgeting process, accountability of schools toward parents with regard to expenditures is low. In fact, the current law provides parents' associations in private schools the power to negotiate the annual budget but does not require the school management to disclose the school balance sheet, making it difficult for parents to effectively engage in the budgeting process and to hold the school accountable for its financial management. This issue had been raised by parents, but the federation of private schools has continuously lobbied against any legislation forcing schools to disclose their balance sheets to parents.

On education-related matters such as instruction methods, curricular content, and assessments, parents' committees have a mandate in conveying parents' opinions and concerns to the school management. However, parents have little power to influence the education process.

Student organizations

Before the civil war, Lebanon had active student organizations which contributed to the shaping of the education sector. Some of these organizations included those of secondary school students, students from teacher training institutes, and students from the Lebanese University. Their advocacy helped in the expansion of public schools across the country, the expansion of public tertiary education, and the strengthening of students' rights, among other social and political causes. However, their role has been greatly diminished since the civil war. Because students are the main beneficiaries of the education sector, it is important that their role in the education reform process be reinforced.

Civil society organizations

Civil society organizations (CSOs) have traditionally not played a primary role in the education sector. Their contributions were the strongest in areas that the Ministry of Education did not have the capacity to fully cover, such as providing education services to children with special needs; partnering with schools to engage children in cultural, artistic, and sports activities; and delivering awareness sessions in schools about specific topics not typically covered by the Lebanese curriculum, such as environment education or sexual health education. CSOs' role became more prominent with the recent refugee crisis, as children's needs for education services in the country multiplied and funding for CSOs drastically increased. The CSOs started to provide nonformal education (NFE) opportunities, in addition to retention and homework support, among other activities targeting Syrian refugee children and vulnerable Lebanese.

Activities by CSOs have traditionally been fragmented, with little coordination among themselves and with other stakeholders such as the Ministry of Education. The Syrian refugee crisis and the rise in prominence of CSOs' role in the sector prompted the MEHE to seek to establish a framework for CSO coordination and operation in the sector. One such mechanism is the NFE framework, explored in more detail in box 5.15, which clearly defines the types of NFEs to be delivered by CSOs, in addition to requirements and qualifications that CSOs should have to deliver those programs. This mechanism supports the MEHE in regulating the work of CSOs, while also providing guidance and resources (for example, an NFE curriculum and learning materials) and capacity building (training CSO employees).

Moreover, also in the scope of the response to the refugee crisis, the MEHE has instituted a system to accept expressions of interest from CSOs to facilitate

BOX 5.15

NFE framework as an example of MEHE-CERD-CSO partnership

The Syrian crisis resulted in an influx of hundreds of thousands of refugee children into Lebanon. With support from the international community, the Ministry of Education and Higher Education (MEHE) sought to provide formal education to those children in public schools. Nevertheless, more than half of refugee children (UNICEF 2018), as of 2018, were still out of formal education. For refugee children who lost several years of schooling because of displacement, it was difficult to enroll in school without bridging a skill gap necessary to enroll at an age-appropriate level. Civil society organizations (CSOs) and nongovernmental organizations (NGOs) have started providing nonformal education (NFE) services to fill refugee children's skill gap and support their transition into formal schooling. As of 2018, approximately 15 percent of refugee children were exclusively enrolled in NFE programs (UNICEF 2018).

The MEHE also recognized the importance and complementarity of the work of CSOs and NGOs in NFE. With support from the international community, the MEHE devised an NFE framework, which included the definition of each type of NFE program to be delivered, in addition to requirements and qualifications that CSOs should have to deliver those programs. The MEHE sought expressions of interest from all CSOs and NGOs interested in delivering any of those programs. CSOs were evaluated based on their qualifications and were selected to deliver specific programs they qualified for. The list of CSOs was then shared with international donors and organizations which are interested in financing the operation of the eligible CSOs. The MEHE also worked with the CERD to develop curricula for the NFE programs, in addition to training for NFE teachers and facilitators. Training was then delivered to eligible CSOs, and resource materials were distributed.

To increase coordination, a network of CSOs and NGOs was created, and representatives from this network were elected to participate in an NGO committee set up by the MEHE. The aim of this committee was to strengthen coordination between different CSO actors and the ministry and to share experiences and lessons learned. It is also a channel through which CSOs can share ideas and feedback with the MEHE.

donor financing to CSOs to implement activities, such as the provision of NFE, the rehabilitation of schools, the provision of transportation to students, and the delivery of services to children with special needs. The last area is an increasing area of collaboration between the MEHE, CERD, and CSOs, given the expertise that CSOs have in providing support to children with special needs and the MEHE's goal of transforming public schools into inclusive schools. Nevertheless, the MEHE's partnership with CSOs is still at a nascent stage, and there remain many areas of development for strengthening this relationship.

One of the main concerns raised by some interviewees was the unpredictability of financing for CSOs, making them at times unreliable partners. Interviewees pointed out that many CSOs have seen their financing increase only recently following the Syrian refugee crisis and the strong interest of donors in providing support to refugees; however, looking beyond the crisis, recent trends show a significant decrease in financing available to CSOs, leading to the discontinuation of some activities. Sustainability was thus the main factor raised by education stakeholders to create effective and complementary partnerships with CSOs in education service delivery. Another area of concern was related to the MEHE's ability to monitor activities, implementation by CSOs and to evaluate and assess their impact, notably in cases where the MEHE has set clear operation frameworks such as the NFE framework. Partnership with CSOs on monitoring and evaluation is crucial to leverage innovations by CSOs and draw lessons learned that could benefit the entire system.

International cooperation agencies

International cooperation agencies have played a significant role in shaping reform in the sector. As discussed in chapter 2, Lebanon has a long-standing history of engagement in international commitments in education, including, more recently, the Millennium Development Goals (MDGs) and the Sustainable Development Goals (SDGs). Technical assistance provided by international cooperation agencies was crucial in the development of sector strategies and setting some reform priorities, such as the expansion of early childhood education, the strengthening of data and information systems, and the integration of technology in education. Lebanon also maintains historical bilateral partnerships with several countries/partners on education matters, including France, the European Union, the United Kingdom, the United States, and others.

International cooperation agencies had strong leverage with the MEHE in the processes of setting education strategies (such as the RACE initiative), probably owing to the technical assistance they provided to develop those strategies and their intent for financing those plans. Nevertheless, donors and international partners have had different levels of effectiveness in their efforts to support the implementation and execution of those strategies. An example of success in execution is the provision of formal education and NFE to Syrian refugee children under the RACE initiative, reaching 357,587 Syrian refugee children (UNICEF 2018). This achievement was made possible by several factors including political will from the Government of Lebanon, strong alignment between all international donors and the MEHE under RACE, the large size of financing allocated to RACE, and the assignment of a focal point within the MEHE to lead the execution and delivery of this initiative. Conversely, an example of a strategy which has not yet materialized in implementation is the National Educational Technology Strategic Plan (NETSP), developed by the MEHE in 2012, with support from USAID. This strategy was a 5-year plan to support the integration of technology in teaching and learning. However, 7 years after inception, the strategy has not yet been operationalized. Despite its alignment with government priorities and the involvement of government actors in the conception and drafting of the plan, there was no leader/champion within the education system assigned to take it forward into implementation. This example highlights the need for international actors to put greater focus on strengthening implementation capacity when supporting the development of key reforms. While donors, especially USAID, continued to support the implementation of some activities within the NETSP, the vision in the strategy was far from being realized.

Interviewees identified political stability as a key element undermining the effectiveness of international actors in driving reform in the system. Many bilateral and multilateral projects were delayed or discontinued following a change of the concerned minister. For example, the Second Education Development Project (referred to as "EDP 2"), a US$40 million project financed by the World Bank, was approved in 2010, but only made effective by the Government of Lebanon 2 years later in 2012 due to political instability. Then, following changes in ministers and the onset of the Syrian crisis, the project spent 3 years not disbursing more than 5 percent of project funds. It was only after 2015 that project implementation gained momentum and reached 98 percent in disbursements by 2018. Part of the success of the project in its last 3 years of implementation emanates from political will and the appointment of the DG as head of the project, thus streamlining all project activities into the institutional processes.

Another aspect of collaboration between the MEHE and international actors is the ability to institutionalize lessons learned and reforms resulting from these partnerships. Given that most bilateral and multilateral projects have been implemented through parallel institutional arrangements, such as the setup of specialized PMUs, it has been difficult to streamline these projects' activities into the regular operational structure of the MEHE and the CERD. As a result, there have been very few instances where bilateral and multilateral projects have been successfully institutionalized and carried forward by the institutions.

DECISION MAKING, PLANNING, AND POLICY EXECUTION

In Lebanon, decision-making, planning, and policy execution processes are complex due to the consociational form of governance, typically requiring lengthy consultations with several stakeholders to reach a consensus before making decisions. Effective and timely education policy decision making, planning, and execution are instrumental factors for the progress of any education system to ensure flexibility and responsiveness to the ever-changing needs and requirements of the sector.

Decision making

Centralization of decision making

Decision-making power in the sector is highly centralized and skewed toward the highest levels of administration. Most of the decisions made by the ministry, including the appointment and transfer of every teacher, must be approved by the minister, even though these decisions are processed by at least four or five layers of the administration. This modus operandi creates an administrative burden in public institutions by increasing the number of transactions in the system, delaying decision making, or even resulting in no decisions being made. To highlight the size of the administrative burden, the political economy interviews found that—at the level of the DG, for example—more than 30,000 transactions are processed per year, which corresponds to an average of 120 transactions per working day.[9] Most of these transactions go through the minister as well for final approval. The high number of administrative transactions leaves little space for education sector decision makers to carry out higher-order planning and management tasks.

The political economy interviews charted two areas of improvement for improving the efficiency of the system in terms of decision making at the central administration level. The first area dealt with the automation and digitization of administrative operations and transactions. Interviewees pointed out that recent efforts in this area have contributed in expediting the processing of transactions and facilitating the tracking of transactions across administrative layers, though much more effort is needed in this area. The second area dealt with power delegation. According to the organizational specialists interviewed within this study, transfer of power to the lower levels of administration is not possible without the adoption of new legislative and regulatory texts by the Council of Ministers and the Parliament. Nevertheless, senior officials at the Ministry of Education, including the minister and the DG, can consider delegating systematically some of their powers to the lower layers of the administration, thus alleviating administrative burden, speeding up decision making, and increasing responsiveness in the system. Similarly, heads of departments could delegate some of their functions to members of their team to alleviate some of the administrative workload.

Beyond the central administration, strengthening the capacity of the REOs is necessary for providing stronger follow-up to schools, increasing accountability at the regional and local levels, and building stronger ties between schools and communities. Decentralization of powers from the central administration to regional offices is a common advocacy point for many governmental and nongovernmental stakeholders. However, international evidence from developing countries tells a cautionary tale about decentralization (Kingdon et al. 2014). The literature concludes that the supposed benefits of decentralization do not accrue in practice because of the realities of politics of influence at the community level. A particular concern is elite capture, where local elites close all space for wider community representation and participation in school affairs. There are several global examples where decentralization had negative or no impact on the education sector, such as in Mexico and Indonesia. An international review by Mulkeen reveals some of the politics that could be at play—for instance, in Lesotho, community pressure resulted in schools employing local persons in preference to better-qualified outsiders; in Gambia and Uganda, school principals had difficulty applying disciplinary actions against teachers living in the same community; and in Uganda, teachers working in their district of origin were more likely to be absent (Mulkeen 2010).

While international evidence of the effectiveness of decentralization in education is mixed, there is stronger evidence for the effectiveness of strengthening school-based management (SBM). The literature found that strengthening decision-making, planning, and budget execution at the school level had a positive association with improvements in school learning environment, repetition and dropout rates, and student learning (Santibañez 2006). To succeed, programs aimed at transferring decision-making power and financial resources to schools should be coupled with a strengthened system for school accountability. In Lebanon, the Ministry of Education has introduced a major reform in recent years to improve school-based management and school leadership capacity through a series of professional development activities with school principals followed by the provision of school grants. The School Improvement Plan (SIP) program sought to increase school autonomy and provide school leaders with skills and financial resources to assess the needs of their schools and make decisions on how best to meet those needs, working in collaboration with school stakeholders such as teachers, students, and parents. Box 5.16 explores in more detail the Lebanon SIP program.

The role of politics in decision-making

Politicians in Lebanon exercise substantial power in making education policy decisions. As described earlier in this chapter, most decision-making and execution functions are centralized in the position of the minister of education. Given that ministers are appointed based on political considerations, politics dominate decision making in the sector. A key observation from the political economy interviews was that, in numerous cases and given the centralization of power in the position of the minister, ministers have adopted an approach of recruiting special advisors on whom they rely on for guidance on policy making, giving limited space for relying on a team or structure within the public administration.

BOX 5.16

The SIP program, an example for improving decision making at the school level

The School Improvement Plan (SIP) program's main objective is to improve and strengthen decision-making at the school level by equipping school principals with skills and financial resources to design a school improvement plan and implement it using a grant transferred from the Ministry of Education to the school.

Internationally, school grants have been widely used by central governments to decentralize and devolve autonomy to stakeholders at the school level (Lugaz and De Grauwe 2016; IIEP 2017). The premise is that school actors—namely, school principals, teachers, students, and parents—know better what goes on in their schools and are better able (than policy makers) to identify and address their needs. It is also assumed that local stakeholders are intrinsically motivated to improve education and, therefore, can manage and monitor the use of resources more effectively (Heneveld and Craig 1996). The successful implementation of school grant programs largely depends on (1) the self-management capacity of local stakeholders, in particular, their ability to conduct a candid self-assessment, and develop and implement a school improvement plan; and (2) and the provision of timely resources, both financial and nonfinancial (time, administrative personnel, and so on), to implement the school grants programs.

In Lebanon, the program consisted of first building the leadership capacity of school principals. School principals followed an initial Leadership Development Program (LDP) delivered by the Faculty of Education at the Lebanese University as a requirement for all principals. Upon successful completion of LDP, school principals were then trained in the SIP methodology, which included a principal self-assessment, a school needs assessment, followed by the design of a school improvement plan and its implementation. The training was coupled with ongoing coaching at the school, where the school principal worked in collaboration with the school administration staff, teachers, students, and parents to conduct all the steps in the SIP methodology. The school improvement plans were reviewed centrally by the MEHE; however, the process included capacity building for the Regional Education Offices with the hope that in future iterations, the school improvement plan would be reviewed by the Regional Education Offices. Following the review of the SIP, the MEHE transferred grants of US$7,000 to the schools, which implemented the grants and reported on expenditures to the MEHE. While there was no formal evaluation of the SIP program, interviews with school principals revealed the positive impact that this program had on building the leadership skills of school leaders and increasing school-level autonomy and decision making.

A review of the educational background and professional experience of advisors recruited at the Ministry of Education in the past two decades revealed that many of them did not come with experience or technical knowledge of the education sector and that their appointment was primarily driven by political affiliation. This approach not only strengthened the influence of politics in education sector decision making, but also in many cases marginalized and weakened the public administration by creating parallel structures for decision making.

Political interference is not limited to the minister's political party, but due to the consociational form of governance in Lebanon, political interference comes from all sides of the political and religious spectrum. Therefore, many reform decisions require lengthy processes of consultation with politicians and religious leaders to garner a consensus. When politicians unite and work in alignment with national interests, considerable progress can be achieved. For instance, the 1997 curriculum reform was only successful owing to significant political

BOX 5.17

The case of the Lebanese history curriculum

Adoption of the history curriculum is an example where political interference and the need for a consensus led to the stalling of reform. The current history curriculum dates back to the 1960s and covers the history of Lebanon up to the independence of the country, leaving all contemporary history aside. Within the scope of the 1997 curriculum reform, the history curriculum was reviewed, especially given its importance in achieving one of the main objectives of the 1994 Plan for Education Reform, which is to contribute to the creation of a national identity and to enhance the sense of belonging and integration in the country. A Technical Committee established by the CERD conducted complex, long, and detailed consultations and negotiations with representatives from major political parties and religious communities to reach a consensus on the curriculum content. While there was a possibility of a breakthrough, delays in the formal approval process reignited differences of opinion, and the new textbooks were canceled altogether. Subsequent ministers have tried to renew efforts to reach a consensus and finalize and approve the curriculum, but with no success to date.

will and a national consensus reached through the Taef Agreement. However, reaching a consensus is not an easy task, as it is difficult to align the interests of all parties toward a common vision for the sector. For example, the 1997 curriculum reform remains unfinished, given that the history curriculum was not agreed upon and approved; moreover, the curriculum had not been revised since 1997, even though the initial vision was to conduct reviews and revisions every 4 years. Box 5.17 explores in detail the case of the history curriculum.

Patronage politics and rent-seeking

Political interference in the sector can also take the form of patronage politics and rent-seeking. Patronage politics supports and rewards specific groups not for their merit but for their affiliation (e.g., political, religious, kinship, etc.); and rent-seeking is an attempt by individuals or groups to gain economic benefit by influencing policies or their implementation.

Patronage politics drives public education systems to spend more on salaries and large-scale procurement, as opposed to spending on classroom-based inputs (e.g., instructional material, performance-based incentives to teachers, etc.) (Corrales 2005). Patronage suggests that it is more convenient for policy makers to expand educational coverage—for example, by building more schools or hiring more teachers—than to fix existing inefficiencies within the system, because the former involves spending on political actors whereas the latter may involve reducing resources allocated to underperforming political actors (Kingdon et al. 2014). The Ministry of Education is the second-largest employer in the public service, behind only the armed and internal security forces, making it propitious for patronage politics in recruitment practices. The political economy interviews revealed several examples of patronage politics, such as (1) the appointment of school principals without following due process, (2) the appointment of contract teachers, (3) the redeployment of teachers from one school to another or to administrative positions at the MEHE and the CERD, (4) the selection of localities for school construction, and (5) the selection of schools to benefit from the provision of equipment and furniture. This form of decision making has a negative impact on the allocation of resources in the system, decreasing efficiency and widening inequity.

Rent-seeking is another type of political pressure exerted on the education system. A prominent example of rent-seeking is in the design of the education subsidization programs in Lebanon, which benefit a particular group based on status while excluding other groups that might have the most need. As a result, rent-seeking leads to a more powerful group securing a larger share of the "educational pie" than poorer households (Gradstein 2003). For instance: (1) Only a limited number of schools can have access to direct subsidies from the government. These schools are mainly religiously affiliated and receive subsidies because of their status rather than performance. There is no clear and transparent mechanism for other private schools to acquire the same status and receive subsidization from the government. (2) Civil servants receive school allowances from the government to enroll their children in private schools. School allowances are provided based on employment status rather than income and poverty status. The government does not provide school allowances to low-income families.

Legislative, regulatory, and normative texts and frameworks

Legislative and normative texts provide the structure and organization of the decision-making process by granting powers, setting boundaries, regulating systems, clarifying authorization and accountability channels, and determining financial structures.

In Lebanon, the legislative and regulatory foundations of general education are characterized by a large number of fragmented texts amounting to thousands of pages, some of which date back to the early years of independence, and most of them based on the legislative decrees of 1959 and their subsequent amendments. A common practice in Lebanon is that new laws, decrees, orders, decisions, bylaws, and other regulatory texts generally contain a provision to abrogate whatever provisions in older texts contradict the new text. This practically means that provisions of previous texts continue to be in force as long as they do not contradict the new text. Texts sometimes deal with multiple subjects at the same time. Other times, a same topic is scattered over various texts, with overlapping or even contradictory information. Interviewees in the study emphasized that, when making a decision or taking an action, there needs to be a high level of expertise and effort from public administrators to be able to navigate effectively from one text to another and understand subtle differences between texts. Consequently, decision makers often find difficulties in effectively and efficiently implementing some of their mandates due to a lack of clarity and precision in legal texts.

In fact, the absence of objective, precise, and transparent standards, criteria, and procedures in many aspects of education sector management and the lack of accountability mechanisms for the application of existing standards, criteria, and procedures leave space for political interference and patronage politics. Furthermore, the current legal structure for decision making involves multiple layers of approvals and procedures, which, coupled with political interference and consociational mode of decision-making, leads to years of delay in reforms and decreases the responsiveness of the system. Box 5.18 explores one example of delays incurred in an approval process.

BOX 5.18

The approvals processes could be lengthy

As an example, the establishment of a directorate would require approval from Parliament after going through a governmental and parliamentary process, taking up to 3 years. Then, the determination of the directorate's administrative components and the adoption by the Council of Ministers of the description of their duties and responsibilities and conditions of recruitment and employment would take approximately another 3 years, as it necessitates approval from various supervisory and regulatory bodies. Finally, the selection and provision of employees could often take more than 2 years. Thus, the entire process of establishment of a directorate could take up to 8 years and require very close follow-up from the leadership of the education sector. Unfortunately, the momentum for such a reform is hard to sustain, especially with the frequent changes in governments. For example, in 2008, the MEHE led an initiative which developed a new organizational structure for the ministry, including detailed descriptions of the units, functions, and roles and responsibilities. The change in government and the minister of education shortly after the completion of the restructuring exercise brought this effort to a standstill.

To streamline decision making in the sector, there is a need to review the legislative and regulatory framework—including laws, decrees, orders, decisions, bylaws, and other regulatory texts—for better consolidation and cohesion and to maintain alignment in provisions. Interviewees in this study advocated for the modernization, unification, and simplification of the legislative and regulatory texts governing the management of educational affairs. Some of the most salient issues—which, according to interviewees, needed to be prioritized to produce consolidated legislative and regulatory frameworks—included (1) the quality assurance mechanism for both public and private schools; (2) the management of information and data about the sector; (3) preservice and in-service teacher professional development; and (4) the management and allocation of teachers to schools.

Planning and information management

Strategic planning

The organizational framework of public institutions in Lebanon, including the MEHE and CERD, dates to the 1950s and lacks the critical planning functions of a modern administration. For example, the MEHE does not have units or positions within the institution that are mandated to undertake strategic planning, budget planning and formulation, performance management, monitoring and evaluation, internal audits, and other essential tasks.

In recent years, the MEHE and the CERD have leveraged international actors and partners to seek technical assistance to produce strategic plans, such as the ESDP in 2010 and the RACE strategic plans in 2014 and 2016. These strategic plans were used to solicit donor financing for implementation.

Information management and feedback loops

Information management is a key aspect of planning and decision making. To be effective, decisions need to be based on technically sound information collected at all levels of the education service delivery chain. The flow of information should include feedback loops to assess and evaluate the impact of policy decisions and to readjust policies to better meet the needs of students, teachers, and other actors in the system. A strong information management and feedback loop system supports the establishment of data-driven decision-making processes, which could help in countering political influence in the education sector's decision-making process.

An Education Management Information System (EMIS) governs the collection, storage, analysis, utilization, and dissemination of data for policy making. An effective and well-functioning EMIS has four key dimensions: (1) the enabling environment and foundation, such as laws, policies, frameworks, culture, and infrastructure, human, and budgetary resources, which make data collection, management, utilization, and access possible; (2) the technical soundness of the system, which ensures that key processes, structures, and integration capabilities provide the right technical support; (3) the quality of the data, which establishes the mechanisms required to collect, store, produce, and utilize information in an accurate, secure, and timely manner; and (4) effective utilization of data in decision making by all users (policy makers, teachers, students, and parents) across the education system.

The issues concerning data systems have been in discussion in Lebanon for more than two decades with very slow progress due to a weak enabling environment. In fact, many attempts have been made to implement effective data systems to manage information about students, teachers, staff, school buildings and facilities, and administrative transactions. However, to date, education sector data remain largely fragmented, incomplete, and unavailable on time for decision making. In recent years, some progress has been achieved; but success has been uneven, with multiple data systems being developed and used at the same time by different units across institutions. For example, the MEHE has developed and deployed a School Information Management System (SIMS), described in detail in box 5.19, which collects data directly from schools; in parallel, the CERD, which is the body that publishes national educational statistics on a yearly basis, rolled out an improved online data system (CASE) in 2016 that collects similar data from schools. Additional information management systems were also deployed for monitoring specific activities such as school attendance in second-shift schools or student examination scores. This situation creates inefficiencies and duplication of effort, as well as inaccuracies and discrepancies in the data collected due to divergence in systems and mechanisms used across different units.

Despite significant investments in data systems in terms of time, financial, and human resources, there has not been any formulation of a clear policy and framework for information management, leading to fragmentation and divergence in vision and responsibilities for collecting and analyzing data across different units at the MEHE and the CERD. There is a need for a clear policy which sets roles and responsibilities, eliminates duplication, and sets standard mechanisms for data collection, validation, storage, manipulation, reporting, and utilization. This policy would create a stronger enabling environment for information management reform, ensuring sustainability, cost saving and efficiency, data credibility, and evidence-based decision making.

Monitoring and evaluation

An integral aspect of effective planning and execution is the role of monitoring and evaluation. However, this function does not exist in the organizational

BOX 5.19

A review of the SIMS

In 2010, the MEHE embarked on a project in collaboration with the United Nations Development Programme (UNDP), the European Union, and the World Bank to implement an operational Education Management Information System (EMIS)[a] to support evidence-based policy making by providing education stakeholders access to timely and reliable data for effective analysis of policy options, increased internal efficiency, and improved targeting of resources designed to enhance student outcomes. The project witnessed significant delays and substantial financial cost (up to US$10 million[b] as of 2018 in hardware and software investments), prompting the MEHE to reduce the project's objective to the operationalization of a School Information Management System (SIMS).

A review of SIMS, conducted by the World Bank in 2018, on the four key dimensions of an EMIS: (1) enabling environment, (2) system soundness, (3) quality of data, and (4) use for decision making, revealed the following:

Enabling environment. As for all information management systems, there was no clear policy framework driving the management and use of SIMS in Lebanon. Policy gaps exist in many areas, including (1) definition of roles and responsibilities and ownership of data, and how the data are to be collected, analyzed, and utilized; (2) budget needs to maintain the system for sustained functionality; (3) utilization or confidentiality requirements for education data, to reduce risks of infringements on data rights and student information; (4) indicators needed to monitor education performance, planning, and management; (5) guidelines on reporting and disseminating data indicators to education stakeholders; and (6) mandates for training staff on the effective use of the system.

System soundness. Through SIMS, the MEHE has been able to automate the data collection process at the school, regional, and central levels. In particular, modules for school and student demographic data have been fully developed and functioning, with total compliance from public schools in inputting the required data. These modules ease the process of student enrollment, prevent ghost entry, and facilitate the transfer of students from one school to another.

Moreover, student assessment results are available, which enable schools, regions, and the ministry to determine pass rates in schools. Nevertheless, the creation of unique identifiers for students and teachers is still pending; and the activation of other modules, such as teacher and asset modules, has not been launched. Moreover, there are no data analysis functions embedded effectively in SIMS.

Quality of data. SIMS has contributed to improvements in education sector data accuracy by moving the system from paper-based to digitized data collection decreasing errors due to manual data entry. Nevertheless, there are limited methods to verify the accuracy of the data collected. The only verification mechanism is conducted by the Regional Education Offices, where they verify enrollment data submitted by schools against the personal certificates of each student. Moreover, data security and access are issues. The entire system is managed and operated by the information technology (IT) team, which has the authority to make changes to the collected data at any point. The MEHE staff do not have direct access to the data and need to request any data from the IT department. Thus, the full potential of technology has not been leveraged to enhance data access and security measures. If only schools and the concerned ministry staff had editing rights, and the IT team had only viewing rights, some of the security issues could have been addressed as there would have been no interference from external departments or agencies.

Use for decision making. Currently, the MEHE is not using the SIMS data for evidence-based policy making. SIMS also remains underutilized as a tool for monitoring and evaluation. There are some instances where the SIMS data have been used for planning purposes, notably for the logistical preparations of the national examinations; but most planning and management of education affairs are based on data collected outside of SIMS by the different units and departments concerned. At the school level, SIMS has been mainly seen as a compliance tool, with no relevance to the school's operation and management. The lack of data analysis tools in SIMS makes schools feel less empowered to benefit from SIMS data in their school

continued

Box 5.19, *continued*

management practices. Nonetheless, there is some evidence of schools leveraging SIMS to improve school-level decision making, by using data to determine teacher schedules, take student attendance, and monitor school performance. These individual initiatives highlight the great potential of strengthening information management systems and establishing feedback loops to improve education service delivery at all levels to achieve higher student learning.

a. UNDP 2010. The EMIS components were to include the following: (1) EMIS data warehouse and Decision Support System; (2) SIMS; (3) Geographical Information System; (4) Document Management System, including archiving system, workflow, and document management; (5) Human Resource Management; (6) Question Bank System / Examination Management System; (7) Official Exams Grade Collection System; and (8) website and digital management system.
b. Estimation from the IT project manager at the MEHE.

BOX 5.20

Example of feedback loops and evidence-based planning and decision making

Calibrating, adjusting, and correcting during implementation are features of a well-functioning system. Overseeing schools and providing them with feedback and support in relation to achieving goals is a fundamental component of such a system. For example, a school routinely assesses student progress based on learning standards. The results of these assessments are fed directly into classroom practices, where teachers use them to adjust lesson plans and schedule additional time for areas in which students are facing difficulties. Student assessments are also an important input for a comprehensive system aimed at monitoring, evaluating, and supporting teachers.

structure of the MEHE or the CERD, and there is no cadre entrusted to carry out this task. Monitoring and evaluation are only carried out within the scope of donor-financed projects and are generally fragmented. No impact evaluation[10] or strategic assessments have been conducted for major reforms in the sector in contemporary times (for example, curriculum reform, teacher professional development, school-based management), and implementation process evaluations are also scarce and do not follow a consistent methodology. Additionally, the reporting and dissemination function is inconsistent and absent from many areas, making it more difficult to evaluate and assess performance.

Monitoring and evaluation allow for the establishment of feedback loops in the system and a culture of evidence geared toward the improvement of student learning. When evidence is provided, rational decisions can have political and national concurrence. The system should incentivize stakeholders to align their interests in a coherent manner based on evidence. This is crucial, given that the politicization of education has proven to slow education reforms, even when clear vision and direction were available. The example of several Latin American countries bears testament to this (Bruns and Schneider 2016). Box 5.20 provides an example of feedback loops and their use in planning and decision making.

Budget planning and formulation

Even in the presence of strategic plans, the budget formulation exercise has been consistently disconnected from the strategic planning process and has been largely performed as an accounting exercise with its own drivers and parameters. In fact, there is no dedicated team for budget planning at each directorate general. The exercise is led by the Accounting Department within the Joint Services Directorate at the MEHE, reporting directly to the minister. The lack of a technical team (for example, economists), which could conduct budgeting and costing exercises to support the MEHE's strategic plans is also one of the reasons such initiatives have not materialized, even when they were funded by donors, such as the Medium-Term Expenditure Framework funded by the European Union in 2014.

At the preparatory phase, the DG, in coordination with the minister, issues directives to the Accounting Department setting budget priorities for the upcoming fiscal year. The Accounting Department compiles the expenditure sheets from the DGE, in addition to other data requested by the department. The compilation is a transactional task that is not driven by a strategic underpinning. Based on the DG and the minister's directives, parameters defined in the previous year budget, and the national accounting law, the Accounting Department submits a draft budget to the minister for approval.

The head of the Accounting Department embodies the institutional memory when it comes to the budget cycle, driving the budget formulation process and as a by-product controlling it, raising concerns on matters of transfer of know-how, agenda setting, and transparency. It is often observed that directorates fail to provide all the data required to formulate the budget, which forces the Accounting Department to prepare its own estimates. This irregularity is exposed when the budget cycle goes into the implementation stage. Spending units (for example, directorates) incur expenses according to their own work plans, which may or may not be included in the MEHE's budget. Thus, postexecution arrangements such as conciliatory contracts are imposed on the administration to address the fait accompli expenses.

The formulation of the overall MEHE budget does not fully integrate current and capital spending. The two items are often addressed separately, and in most cases, are accounted for on an ad hoc basis. For example, building a school (that is, a capital project) ensues future recurring costs (for example, wages, maintenance, utilities). However, future recurring and future operational (and maintenance) costs are generally neglected and not incorporated in the original planning. Moreover, when capital projects are agreed upon and executed through external parties (for example, the Council of Ministers and the CDR), the MEHE is asked to assume, unexpectedly, the cost of maintaining and operating the new facilities constructed.

The CERD prepares its own budget. This should, in principle, reflect the sector strategy, and it is submitted to the minister for approval. Once endorsed, it is entered as a line item in the MEHE's budget under "contribution to the CERD" and is directly transferred to the CERD upon ratification of the budget by the Parliament. The MEHE administration is then expected to address the implications that ensue. If, for instance, the CERD's strategy called for the introduction of course material which relies on new equipment to be procured, then the MEHE would have to allocate the corresponding expenses in its budget to procure the new equipment.

External financing through grants and loans is also generally not integrated into the MEHE's budget. In recent years, due to the Syrian refugee crisis and the strong interest of donors in financing education for refugees, external financing amounted to up to 20 percent of the MEHE's budget in 2018.[11]

Once drafted by the Accounting Department and approved by the minister, the MEHE budget is negotiated with the Ministry of Finance. There are no specialized sector working groups leading those negotiations or any structured mechanism governing the process, and thus the process is mostly driven by cost-saving considerations from the Ministry of Finance, rather than strategic considerations. In case of disagreements, the issues are raised to the respective ministers or to the Council of Ministers.

Budgets are then submitted to the Council of Ministers to be presented to the Parliament for ratification, a process that has been extremely difficult in the past years. In 2005–17, no budget was approved during those 12 years, compelling ministries to follow the same budget as the previous year and thus obstructing the budget planning and formulation process altogether.

At the school level, public schools also get financial resources through tuition from parents. These enrollment fees, which correspond to US$160 per student per year, have been subsidized in recent years by the Government of Lebanon and by international donors following the Syrian refugee crisis. On an annual basis, schools prepare their budgets, which are largely composed of recurrent operational expenses—such as electricity, water, and telephone bills—but can also include budget elements focused on improving the school environment and learning, including the procurement of equipment and furniture, organization of events and field trips for students, and, in some cases, the recruitment of additional teachers for elective subjects such as art, music, theater, computer science, and sports. Upon preparing the budget, the school submits it to the Regional Education Office, which has the responsibility of verifying school-level expenditures and reporting back to the central MEHE administration. The size of the school budget varies from one school to another, depending on the total number of students enrolled, but a medium-sized school of approximately 200 students can expect an annual budget of US$32,000. Moreover, as discussed earlier in this chapter, some schools can receive grants. These additional financial resources are also budgeted by the school and reported to the Regional Education Office.

Policy execution

This subsection deals with policy execution from two angles—first, discussing general administrative processes such as budget execution and allocation of human resources, and then exploring execution of key mandates in the education sector, including among others, the deployment and professional development of teachers, the development of curricula, and the construction of public schools.

Budget execution and audit

The organizational framework of public institutions in Lebanon lacks basic public finance management roles. Budget execution is initiated by the DG, who directs the Accounting Department to execute payments. There is no unit or staff mandated to carry out financial management functions, such as defining financial requirements of activities, forecasting use of financial resources, monitoring and evaluating the use of resources, and exploring corrective options if needed.

There is no internal audit function at the MEHE or anywhere else in the Lebanese administration. The external audit function is conducted by the COA and the Central Inspection body, which report to the Council of Ministers. The COA and Central Inspection prepare annual reports submitted to the Parliament identifying administrative irregularities and including general recommendations. In recent years, irregularities identified in the external audit reports were administrative in nature, often with exceptional circumstances being cited to justify those irregularities. More strategic recommendations were often overlooked. The COA and Central Inspection have the power to impose fines or recommend prosecution when violations have been determined. However, recent years have shown that this mandate was only exercised for low-level administrative irregularities. There were also no major actions taken by Parliament as a result of the external audit reports.

Resource allocation

The translation of the learning strategy and curriculum competencies into an actionable resource allocation plan is not systematized and lacks mechanisms for equity and proper targeting based on need. Consequently, despite having some strong foundations in terms of availability of inputs and resources such as textbooks, learning materials, and equipment, the education system needs significant reform in how resources are allocated to schools to effectively transform those inputs into gains in learning and education outcomes. In addition to gaps in equitable resource allocation, there are large inefficiencies in the allocations which create delays in the deployment of those resources and their use for learning. An example of such inefficiency is in the textbook allocation mechanism, as portrayed by box 5.21, which quantifies gaps in textbook quantity and availability, quality of print, and durability, and uncovers inefficiencies in the supply chain.

Human resource allocation

For the execution of any policy reform, human resources must be allocated effectively and efficiently. There is a chronic lack of effective human resource allocation at both the MEHE and the CERD. Recruitment into the civil service can only be executed for positions and scope of work set by the Council of Public Service. However, the list of job families as outlined by the Council of Public Service is outdated and does not include critical positions, such as different education specialists, economists, and IT officers. There is also a misalignment between the job description requested by the Council of Public Service and the skills and scope of work required by the MEHE and the CERD.

Because recruiting education administrators and specialists into the public service is extremely challenging, the MEHE and the CERD resort to a redeployment of teachers from schools to the central and regional administration to fill administrative gaps. However, most teachers do not have the essential training for effectively managing administrative tasks. For example, to fill gaps in accounting positions at the Accounting Department, teachers are mobilized and provided with basic training from the Institute of Finance (linked to the Ministry of Finance), but this training does not constitute a proper and embedded program to develop necessary public finance management skills.

With support from external financing through bilateral and multilateral projects with international actors, the MEHE and the CERD sought to fill gaps in human resources through the recruitment of consultants. For example, in the

Textbook allocations

A World Bank study of the Lebanon public sector textbook distribution system for the 2017–18 school year was conducted with the aim to assess, strengthen, and improve the efficiency of the Lebanese textbook supply chain, including the monitoring of the quantity and quality of textbooks deployed to schools. The study collected data on the number of textbooks available in public schools and measured the quality of these textbooks against suggested Lebanese textbook technical specifications. Key stakeholder interviews were conducted with the MEHE, CERD, textbook publishers, printers, distributors, bookseller association members, and school principals. These interviews enabled the analysis of the existing textbook procurement process and the textbook supply chain currently in use in Lebanon, as well as the system used to manage and monitor the supply chain. Lebanese technical specifications were also evaluated and compared with technical specifications used by comparator countries. Interviews were undertaken with publishers, and textbooks' life expectancy and costs were compared between Lebanon and comparator countries. The results of this investigation supported why textbook durability is important and highlighted the benefits that could be achieved by increasing textbook life and by improving the efficiency of the textbook supply chain.

A sample of 40 schools was selected in coordination with the MEHE from across all governorates to study the supply of textbooks in public schools in Lebanon. Of the sample, 35 were first-shift schools and 5 (12.5 percent of all 40 schools) were second-shift schools. The study included all general education grades from kindergarten to grade 12. There were two rounds of textbook inventory data collection to check textbook availability over a 3-month period. The first took place from November 1 to November 11, 2017, and the second was completed from February 5 to February 22, 2018. All 40 schools selected were visited for both rounds of data collection, with a school principal questionnaire conducted during the first round.

Textbook supply chain. In the Lebanese public education system, the procurement of textbooks is done by individual schools. Every year, in March/ April, the CERD collects enrollment data and projects the number of students expected to enroll in the coming year in public schools. The CERD contracts with a publisher and sends orders for textbooks (every 2–3 years, new tenders for publishers are produced by the CERD). The publisher sends unit orders to printers. Printers print textbooks and supply them back to the publisher, which then supplies them to distributors (or distributors collect from the publisher); then distributors deliver to bookshops (or bookshops collect from distributors). Schools are then assigned to bookstores based on a distribution agreed upon with the association of bookstores. Schools often place multiple orders for textbooks, given the fluctuating enrollment numbers (especially with the enrollment of Syrian refugees who might enroll 1 month or more after the start of the school year). Bookshops deliver to schools multiple times (or schools collect from bookshops themselves) depending on orders and availability. Schools pay bookshops multiple times for multiple orders; then they claim reimbursements for textbook purchases back from the MEHE through regional offices, which collect school claim forms. Regional offices submit school claim forms to the central MEHE administration; the latter verifies school claims (requesting amendments or more information) and reimburses the cost of textbooks to schools. This process in the past 3 years has taken more than 1 year from schools placing orders for textbooks to receiving the full reimbursement from the MEHE, creating disincentives for schools, especially ones with low budgets to purchase textbooks early in the school year, given the time needed for reimbursement. Furthermore, the number of layers in the chain from the CERD to publishers, printers, distributors, bookstores, and schools creates inefficiencies in the system, including an inflation of the cost of textbooks due to the need for all the middle actors (publishers, printers, distributors, bookstores) to make an economic profit.

Textbook availability and quantity. The study showed that there are significant delays in getting all textbooks to all students. In November 2017, more than 1 month after the start of classes, the study counted only 17,292 textbooks for 27,814

continued

Box 5.21, *continued*

students (62 percent) for all grades from kindergarten to grade 12. In February 2018, nearly 5 months after classes started, that number climbed to 23,141 textbooks for 28,125 students (82 percent) for all grades from kindergarten to grade 12. The target ratio of 1:1 textbooks-to-students was not achieved more than halfway into the school year. These delays raise significant concerns on the ability of schools to perform well without the proper access to essential resources such as textbooks.

Textbook durability and quality of print. Testing textbooks' durability and quality of print at the level of the schools revealed that nearly half of textbooks (46 percent) tested in the sample schools failed to meet the Lebanese national textbook technical specification requirements. Comparatively, in testing samples of textbooks in private schools, more than three quarters of textbooks (77 percent) tested passed higher standards than the Lebanese national technical specifications and had a life expectancy of 4–5 years. The Lebanese textbooks' technical specifications include more detailed specifications than in comparator countries. However, key specifications, which could improve textbook durability and quality, such as binding style, need to be updated. The binding style adopted by the Lebanese specifications lead to a high possibility of textbooks not lasting more than 1 school year, which has also been the policy of the Lebanese government: to provide every student with a new textbook per subject each year.

Textbook cost and cost-efficiency. The unit cost per textbook in Lebanon is the lowest when compared to two neighboring countries—Jordan and Turkey. However, it is not the most cost-effective. The durability of the Lebanese national textbook does not exceed 1 school year, given the binding style adopted in printing and the national policy to provide every student with a new textbook per subject each year. Strengthening the binding style requirements for textbooks could increase their lifetime to up to 4 years. While this would imply an increase of 40 percent in unit cost, given that this additional cost would be spread over multiple years, the overall cost of textbooks over 4 years would be much smaller and would be only 35 percent of the total cost of renewing all textbooks every year.

To ensure an effective and sufficient annual supply of textbooks to public schools in Lebanon, the following recommendations resulted from this study:

1. **To develop a new documented national textbook policy,** which will contain all the policies and procedures for textbook supply, including, but not limited to, technical specifications, supply chain, rental plan, management systems, monitoring and control, and textbook usage in schools;

2. **To update textbook technical specifications** to improve durability and printing and binding quality;

3. **To optimize the textbook supply chain processes** (textbooks ordering, delivery and reimbursement processes, penalties for textbook suppliers for late deliveries and noncompliance with technical specifications);

4. **To develop, deploy, and implement a Textbook Management Information System** as a textbook supply measure and to enhance communication, monitoring, evaluation, administration, and control of the textbook supply chain; and

5. **To develop guidelines for textbook management** (storage, preservation, and usage) at a school level to increase textbook life and to train all teachers and students in textbook conservation.

absence of IT functions in the public service structure, the entire IT department at the MEHE was recruited through consulting contracts executed by the UNDP. Bilateral and multilateral projects have also been implemented through the setup of PMUs filled exclusively by external consultants, with very few exceptions. These consultants would rarely have in their scope of work the need to build capacity of the MEHE and the CERD staff, and as a result, have generally worked independently, producing their required outputs and exiting the system without strengthening the institutions' human resources.

Teacher recruitment, management, and deployment

Teachers are recruited into the profession from various educational backgrounds with no consistent requirement that teachers should follow a preservice teacher preparation program. This is a relatively recent development, as in the mid-1980s, the law stipulated the need for a pedagogical diploma or certificate, issued by the CERD's teacher training institutes or by the Faculty of Education at the Lebanese University, before the appointment of teachers into the profession. Currently, only a university degree is requested for recruitment, with no specific attention to the specialization of the degree. As a result, many teachers are recruited into schools, with basic to no knowledge or skills in pedagogy, and while some of them are proficient in specific school subjects (for example, math, economics, and the Arabic language), many teachers get assigned to teach a subject which is different from the one they are proficient in. Moreover, the political economy interviews with school-level stakeholders and with officials from the Lebanese University and the CERD indicated the necessity of teacher preservice programs to instill in teachers a sense of belonging to the teaching profession and a commitment to education as a public good.

Due to structural reasons—such as restrictions in recruitment of additional teachers as civil servants, and technical reasons, including the MEHE's inability to accurately forecast teacher recruitment and deployment needs—recent years have witnessed a tremendous surge in the recruitment of contractual teachers. However, in addition to the inconsistency in teacher preparation requirements, the education sector lacks a coherent policy on the recruitment of contractual teachers, leaving space for political interference in those processes and creating inefficiencies in the sector, as discussed in chapter 4. Political interference is also pronounced in the deployment of public teachers, with pressures to transfer teachers from one school to another during the school year or transfer from a school where they are needed to where there is a surplus of teachers.

Teacher professional development

Teacher professional development is carried out by several entities within the education system, with currently no clear mechanism established to support coordination between those entities. In-service teacher training for public school teachers is delivered by the CERD through its regional teacher training centers. All teachers are requested by the MEHE to participate in at least one training session per year; however, the CERD data show low levels of compliance with this requirement. Moreover, teachers select the training sessions they would like to attend, most commonly for convenience reasons or personal interests, rather than professional development needs. For example, a public school principal in the study's focus group mentioned an instance where two teachers registered for a training session on the use of interactive whiteboards in the classroom, even though the school had no such technology. According to the school principal, they were interested in strengthening their education technology skills to get higher standing at the private schools they were concurrently teaching in. Beyond training delivered in the CERD regional centers, the CERD trainers do not have the jurisdiction to provide in-school follow-up support. The latter is the mandate of pedagogical counselors from the School Guidance and Counseling Department (DOPS) within the DGE at the MEHE. DOPS counselors conduct school visits, perform classroom observations, and provide feedback and support to teachers and school principals. In addition to the DOPS counselors, educational inspectors, who report to the General Inspectorate under the

Council of Ministers, also conduct school visits and can perform classroom observations and provide feedback to teachers. This follow-up in schools, whether from DOPS or the Educational Inspectorate, is not conducted in a consistent and standardized manner. First, the choice of schools and teachers to be visited is nearly entirely under the coach or inspector's prerogative, with no clear policy outlining how in-school support to teachers should be managed and evaluated. Second, personnel are asked to cover their own transportation, creating disincentives for coaches and inspectors to visit remote schools. Finally, there is no standardized approach to teacher performance assessment and coaching, with different assessment and observation tools being used and with no coaching programs being defined.

The three bodies providing in-service professional development belong to different and independent institutions, operate following separate procedures, and have distinct pay scales. Consequently, there is currently no feedback loop between training and in-school coaching, with the two functions being dissociated and performed independently. Some recent efforts in coordination between the three bodies have started to bear fruit. In November 2017, the Ministry of Education adopted—following more than 5 years of work between the CERD, DOPS, the Educational Inspectorate, and the Faculty of Education at the Lebanese University—professional standards and competency frameworks for teachers, teacher trainers, pedagogical counselors, and psychosocial counselors. This first step is a building block for streamlining efforts in how teacher performance is assessed and how teacher support programs are delivered.

Reform in curriculum, instruction, and assessment

The last major national curriculum reform was undertaken in 1997. Since that date, very few changes have been made to the curriculum, mainly limited to the reduction in the content of some subjects through canceling some chapters. The interviews conducted in the study revealed three principal barriers to the successful execution of curriculum reform.

The first shortcoming was that the 1997 curriculum reform was not accompanied by a clear implementation plan on how the curriculum would translate into the classroom and would produce a real transformation of teaching and learning processes. For instance, the reform did not include provision of a suitable learning environment and resources, with most public schools lacking the essential teaching and learning resources, as well as information and communication technology (ICT), equipment to properly implement the curriculum. These included, among others, science laboratory equipment, music, theater, and art equipment, and learning materials for second foreign languages. In addition to the physical learning environment, training of teachers on the implementation of the curriculum was insufficient, as it focused more on the content of the new curriculum and did not sufficiently deal with improved instruction and pedagogical practices. Thus, there was little change in instructional practices in the classroom, and teachers relied more heavily on memorization to cover the content of the curriculum.

Second, while the new curriculum advocated for new approaches in learning assessments, there was no clear strategy and framework for measuring and assessing learning at the national level and no direction to schools on how teachers could apply the proposed assessment programs to better monitor learning outcomes and provide support to students.

Finally, the new curriculum was supposed to be reviewed systematically every 4 years. However, there was no established mechanism for conducting proper assessments of the curriculum and for undertaking significant revisions. There were also no financial and human resources allocated and no technical capacity built for such a task.

While the CERD is mandated to study the curriculum and advise on needed revisions, the experience from the 1997 curriculum reform highlighted the necessity for strong engagement from the MEHE and school-level actors to better plan the translation of the curriculum at the school level if any curriculum reform is to yield concrete improvements in teaching and learning in the classroom.

Construction of public schools

Since independence, the government has had a policy of expanding the number of public schools across the country. However, this expansion was not conducted in a systemized way using a thorough analysis of demographic and educational data; instead, it was largely influenced by the political interests of politicians seeking to provide benefits to their constituencies by constructing schools in their localities and creating employment for teachers and school administrators. As a result, a sizable number of public schools were built but ended up not enrolling enough students. As a result, in the last four decades, the number of public schools has decreased by 13 percent from an all-time high in the early 1980s.[12] Part of this decrease was due to construction of schools in localities where there was no sufficient need for public schools and part was due to the strong competition from private schools in attracting students from all socioeconomic backgrounds.

This finding was confirmed by the Ministry of Education in 1983, which stated that the expansion of public schools "was not complemented with well thought through plans for suitable potential locations for the schools, a comprehensive policy for construction of the schools and their equipment, and a coherent policy for teacher training, ensuring suitable quality and sufficient quantity"(Directorate of Primary Education, Ministry of Education 1983, 55).

While experts agree that there is a need to build and expand public schools in remote areas of Lebanon—particularly in Akkar, Baalbeck-Hermel, and other areas—the lack of a technically sound needs assessment and political interference have impeded efforts in achieving an effective, efficient, and equitable distribution of public schools across the country. As a result, there were many lost opportunities for progressing on public school construction, including a relatively recent grant from the French Development Agency (Agence Française de Développement, AFD) for the construction of 20 schools. The grant was retracted by AFD after political interference led to an onerous and long process for the selection of school sites.

The political economy analysis revealed that a school construction needs assessment is a strategic and technical necessity. The assessment should be conducted in a transparent and clear manner based on data about population projections. It should also be done in an integrated manner by looking at all sorts of education provision, including public and private providers, and all levels of education, including technical and vocational education. This assessment would provide a solid ground for decisions on locations of new schools and would decrease political interference to a certain extent.

Public-private partnership in education service provision

Education service provision in Lebanon is dominated by the private sector, with the government being mandated for regulating and monitoring the operation of private schools. Two main policy aspects govern the relationship between the public and the private education sectors—the quality assurance and regulatory role of the government and the financing and subsidy structure of the sector.

The Division of Private Education, under the DGE, is the main entity responsible for regulating private education in Lebanon. This unit reviews applications for establishing new private schools, oversees existing schools, and keeps track of private school students and teachers' data (Division of Private Education, MEHE 1971). Lebanon has been successful at ensuring compliance with registration and licensing requirements, controlling tuition increases, and enforcing the application of the Lebanese curriculum and the national examinations.[13] Aside from a focus on general compliance, there has been little capacity built in government institutions to play a structured and consistent role in quality assurance of both public and private schools, and monitoring of education quality in private schools has been nearly absent, despite large government expenditures on private education subsidies. Interviews within this political economy study emphasized the difficulty for the government to establish any regulatory and monitoring system for private schools, without full support from private education providers, as they would consider such an act as an intrusion on the freedom of the education provision right maintained in the Constitution. To succeed, such an endeavor would have to be based on a true partnership with private schools by engaging them in the decision-making process and in education policy planning and execution. Moreover, it would need to be built on clear, structured, and coherent criteria, standards, and procedures, applied in an equitable and fair manner to all schools, and focused on education quality and learning.

With regard to education financing, the Government of Lebanon provides several types of education subsidies to some private schools directly or to some households with children enrolled in private schools. However, the subsidy system in Lebanon is based on employment status rather than on other equity criteria such as income level. In fact, it is mostly public sector employees who are the largest beneficiaries of education subsidies to enroll their children in private schools. Reforms in education financing, though required for equity purposes, are difficult to accomplish due to strong resistance from private school providers and from unions of public sector employees. Box 5.22 provides a more detailed overview of Lebanon's PPP model for education service provision.

Education of Syrian refugees

The provision of education services to Syrian refugees is governed by the Government of Lebanon's RACE strategy. The governance structure is led by the RACE Executive Committee, which is chaired by the minister and includes officials from the MEHE and the CERD, in addition to all major donors to RACE, given their strong interest in this topic. The direct costs of formal education for refugees in the public sector have been financed by donor countries using a unit cost model, which includes enrollment fees covering operational expenses of schools (electricity, water bills, and so on), teacher salaries, and in the case of second-shift students, a fixed depreciation cost covering expenses incurred due to the increased use of school infrastructure and equipment. However, the success of the MEHE in enrolling large numbers of children in public schools and the unpredictability of external financing led to recurrent financing gaps for

Lebanon's PPP model for education

In Lebanon, households invest a significant percentage of their disposable income on education expenditures, with an average of 6.55 percent of household expenditures being allocated to education, a percentage which reaches an average of 10 percent of expenditures for households with the highest spending power.[a] Nevertheless, and despite high levels of expenditures from households, the Government of Lebanon also invests significantly in private education through various subsidy systems:

- **Direct subsidy to private schools.** A sizable proportion of private schools are directly subsidized by the Government of Lebanon. In 2017, those schools represented 24 percent of all private schools.[b] Most subsidized private schools are religiously affiliated. Every academic year, subsidized schools are required to submit to the MEHE data related to their teachers and students, in addition to other compliance information and legal documents regarding their status. A committee established for guiding and overseeing free private schools at the MEHE's Division for Private Education reviews the documents to ensure that all information is accurate and complete. The decision for funding is raised by the head of the division and the DGE to the minister of education for approval. The MEHE provides subsidies to schools by paying a unit cost fee of approximately 100–125 percent of the minimum wage per student (in 2018, this was equivalent to US$450–US$560 per student per year) (Division of Private Education, MEHE 1971). The World Bank's public expenditure review showed that direct subsidies to private schools represented an average of 7 percent of government education spending over the period from 2013–15 (see chapter 4).
- **School allowances to public civil servants.** All public civil servants in Lebanon, including military personnel, security forces, teachers, and others receive from the government a school allowance per child. The World Bank's

public expenditure review showed that school allowances represented an average of 21 percent of government education spending over the period from 2013–15 (see chapter 4). A report published by the Ministry of Finance in 2007 stated that in 2006, about 19 percent of government education expenditures were provided to children of civil servants through school allowances and almost 90 percent of civil servants had their children enrolled in private schools (Ministry of Finance 2007).

- **School allowances for private sector employees through the National Social Security Fund (NSSF).** The NSSF law provides a legal framework for private sector employees with children enrolled in schools or universities to benefit from an education allowance per child from the fund. This allowance is mostly financed through monthly contributions from private sector employers. The amount of the education allowance is determined through a decree by the Council of Ministers, upon the proposition of the minister of labor.[c] As of July 2018, there has been no decree enforcing such an allowance, and thus the number of private sector employees receiving a full education allowance has been limited. Nevertheless, some private sector employers have already started providing such an allowance as a means to attract top talent, among other reasons.

In parallel with the subsidy system, the Government of Lebanon is mandated by law to regulate the provision of education in private schools as well as ensuring compliance with laws and procedures and monitoring the quality of education. The Division of Private Education, under the DGE at the MEHE, is responsible for this role.

In terms of compliance, the government has set certain requirements for school infrastructure and equipment, in addition to some rules regarding school administration and operation. With regard to curricula, the Ministry of Education ensures that (1) schools teach the Lebanese curriculum to prepare

continued

Box 5.22, *continued*

students for official exams, but they can also teach other curricula simultaneously; (2) schools teach the history of Lebanon, geography, civics, and other related subjects using textbooks approved by the minister of education; and (3) no subject is taught using textbooks that have been disapproved by the minister.[d]

The Division of Private Education has a number of controllers who are dispatched to private schools to oversee and evaluate their work according to relevant laws and regulations. Due to the limited capacity of this controlling body,[e] most school visits are conducted at only subsidized private schools and focus mainly on administrative compliance. Inspectors from Central Inspection are also mandated to conduct inspection in

private schools receiving direct subsidies from the government.

The current model of PPPs in Lebanon is thus based on substantial subsidies to the private sector driven mainly by employment benefits to public sector employees and some private sector employees, with a regulatory role of the government limited to a control for administrative compliance. The model does not leverage the strong standing of private schools in Lebanon to expand equitable access to schooling for the most vulnerable children; it does not focus on the government's role in ensuring learning and good quality education for all; and it does not benefit from school-level partnerships to improve public sector education provision.

a. CAS (database), Household-based Survey 2011–2012, Central Administration of Statistics, Beirut, http://www.cas.gov.lb/index.php /demographic-and-social-en/householdexpenditure-en.
b. In academic year 2016–17, there were 370 subsidized private schools among a total of 1,547 private schools (CERD 2017).
c. NSSF Law; https://www.cnss.gov.lb/index.php/management/lois; https://www.labor.gov.lb/Temp/Files/f18fd301-c38a-45c8-b0e2 -2da6134641ad.pdf; https://www.cnss.gov.lb/index.php/book-famille; https://www.cnss.gov.lb/index.php/publicrelations/dalilmadmoun.
d. Decree for Establishment of New Private Schools, http://www.legallaw.ul.edu.lb/LawView.aspx?opt=view&LawID=168800.
e. The Division of Private Education currently has only two controllers, down from 25 due to retirement of civil servants. When needed, teachers from the public education system can be assigned to carry out the controller's functions.

the MEHE. These situations have been solved through lengthy negotiations with donors to increase financing but have generally impeded the MEHE's ability for long-term planning by perpetuating a recurrent state of funding emergency.

The Government of Lebanon's policy toward the education of refugee children was generally a policy of inclusion in the public education system, with significant enrollment of refugee children into first-shift classrooms in public schools and the creation of second shifts catering solely to Syrian students. Even though private schools in Lebanon enroll more than 70 percent of Lebanese students (see chapter 2), the government's policy, which donors complied with, did not include an engagement with the private sector for provision of education to refugee children. Nevertheless, given the freedom of choice in education provision in Lebanon, some Syrian families elected to enroll their children in private schools, which, as of March 2018, hosted approximately 17 percent of Syrian students.[14]

In terms of curriculum and instruction, Lebanon's policy was for the exclusive use of the Lebanese curriculum for the education of Syrian refugees. The MEHE has, however, encouraged teachers in second shifts where only Syrian children were enrolled to increase the use of the Arabic language in the teaching of math and science, due to the language barriers for Syrian refugees who are not used to learning those subjects in a foreign language (French or English). Lebanon also relied on the recruitment of exclusively Lebanese teachers for the provision of Syrian refugee education. The number of new teachers recruited for this task alone in the first year exceeded 5,172 teachers,[15] representing more than 10 percent of the teacher workforce in public schools.[16] Moreover, a total of 10,900 teachers, supervisors, and school principals (22 percent of the total school workforce) were working in second-shift schools during academic year 2016–17, with their salary income partially or totally dependent on donor financing. Even in first-shift schools, the MEHE reported having operated 1,500 classroom sections with less than five Lebanese students in academic year 2016–17,[17] representing more than 8 percent of all classrooms in first-shift public schools.[18] Nearly one-third of first-shift public schools had more non-Lebanese children than Lebanese children.[19] The large number of teachers, who are dependent upon external financing and the enrollment of Syrian refugee children in public schools, represents a tremendous sustainability challenge for Lebanon. Given the difficult political economy around the recruitment and management of teachers in the country, the government is likely to face difficulties in managing these teachers, once Syrian children are no longer in Lebanon and external financing is diminished.

CONCLUSION

The political economy of the education sector in Lebanon presents both strong assets and major challenges for the effective and efficient promotion of student learning.

The system has solid assets to advance and improve, as it is rooted in a national philosophy, culture, and legislation that extend social services and build on active community dynamics. More specifically, the education system has distinguishing and promising features that set a strong foundation for a competitive education system:

1. The education sector is a source of national pride and receives full support from all levels of the societal and political spectrums.
2. Citizens value education and are willing to spend large amounts of their resources to ensure good education for their children.
3. The diversity in the education provision model can be an asset for the country and can provide a healthy environment for building coalitions, collaboration, and competitiveness to enhance education success. A large degree of participation from the private sector and freedom of choice for parents can, in theory, create competition for better results.
4. There is diversity in education offerings, including foreign languages, curricula, and international accreditations.
5. The government is committed to bringing quality innovations to teaching and learning to all schools with the support of all communities and political leadership. There are also increasing drive and willingness by local schools and local leadership to innovate and collaborate on education issues, including the creation of networks for sharing resources and improving education quality.
6. In the public education system, there is an increased level of autonomy at the school level, with authority for managing budgets, including the financing and procurement of resources such as textbooks. This autonomy is accompanied by oversight from two actors—public administration at the regional and central levels, and the community through parents' and schools' committees.
7. Teachers have freedom of association, which fosters diversity and inclusiveness in the teaching profession.

8. There is a pool of qualified graduates from higher education, who can be mobilized to reinforce capacity at the management level of the system and in the teaching body.

9. The CERD, higher education institutions, and nongovernmental institutions have an interest in advancing research on education.

On the other hand, the system faces structural challenges, which need to be considered when planning and executing reforms. The most salient obstacles are related to political instability, consensual decision making, conflicts of interest, and organizational efficiency:

1. Decision-making, in the public sector, is highly centralized and politicized. Processes of patronage politics and rent-seeking interfere with decision-making and divert focus from learning and results. Politicians use the education sector to provide services to their constituents, for example, through the recruitment and deployment of teachers.

2. The system perpetuates a dichotomy between public and private schools. Private schools operate with a large degree of autonomy. They enroll approximately 71 percent of Lebanese students and have significant power in the sector. However, there is no quality assurance mechanism, and thus there is limited accountability for results toward the government and parents.

3. The existing education subsidy system favors particular groups and is not based on socioeconomic need. As a result, it perpetuates inequity in access and quality of education.

4. Decision making, planning, and execution processes showed high fragmentation and lack of coordination between different entities in the system. This is observed in areas such as teacher professional development, the management and use of education data, and the assessment of student learning.

The advancement of the education system in Lebanon could have been faster and more effective if a "systems approach" had been used when planning for reforms. The absence of an integrated, aligned, and holistic approach from implementation processes has made it hard to achieve a reasonable consensus, collegial cooperation, and a high sense of drive—all of which are required in a functioning education system. For example, it is important to ensure that the allocation of resources is not leaning toward one area more than another; that short-term professional appointments are not the norm; and that reform topics are not short-sighted. These problems are perfectly simple to correct, given a reasonable structure that allows for a contingency plan of action.

Better integration and long-term process arrangements in intervention plans can accelerate improvements in education results. In several countries (for example, Chile, Poland, and Vietnam), aligning various activities coherently toward a long-term agenda has paid off well. Logical and objective processes that are applied in an efficient and timely manner and that are linked to performance in terms of achieving the desired outcomes have been quite successful. These processes need to be implemented throughout the entire lifespan of an activity or a project, including setup, borrowing, allocations, procurement, deployments, and operation configuration and execution. It is also important to follow these structured processes at all levels of the system, as each of these embodies inherent constraints or limitations.

As the system in Lebanon has grown more complex over time and the number of actors and interactions has increased, uncertainty has multiplied. All these indicate that revised public policy for education is needed to move the system forward. To direct the system to cope with the new challenges and achieve higher education outcomes, there is an urgent need for a new education plan based on evidence and on coordination and dialogue among all education stakeholders in the country.

NOTES

1. In addition to the director general, exceptions on appointment by the minister include all blue-collar jobs such as drivers, construction workers, electricians, and others.
2. In the armed forces, powers regarding armed personnel are assigned to the respective highest chiefs, namely the general commander-in-chief of the army, the director general of the Internal Security Forces, and the director general of General Security.
3. REOs cover mostly primary education (including kindergarten and intermediate education). Secondary schools report directly to the centralized secondary education directorate.
4. Ministry of Finance. Average of 3-year period (2013–15).
5. Lebanon Central Inspection, http://www.cib.gov.lb/website.htm.
6. Legislative Decree 116, dated 12/6/1959.
7. Legislative Decree 118, dated 30/6/1977.
8. Some non-Lebanese parents might face difficulties or restrictions not experienced by Lebanese parents. For example, public schools with a proportion of non-Lebanese students exceeding 50 percent might not be able to enroll additional non-Lebanese children.
9. Assuming 250 working days per year.
10. The CERD conducted its first randomized controlled trial (RCT) in 2019 for a teacher support program. The MEHE also launched in 2019, its first RCT of its improved coaching system to be completed by 2020. These initiatives were supported through the World Bank's Support to RACE 2 Program.
11. Calculations based on enrollment and expenditures data from the RACE PMU, www.racepmulebanon.com. External financing is executed through separate joint accounts between the MEHE, UNICEF, and United Nations High Commission for Refugees.
12. Data computed from Kobeissi 2012.
13. Or equivalent examinations such as the French Baccalaureate or the International Baccalaureate.
14. There were 46,429 Syrian children enrolled in private schools in Lebanon, as of March 2018 (Ministry of Education data and CERD Statistical Bulletin 2018, https://www.crdp.org/files/201803190157241.pdf).
15. Ministry of Education, RACE Executive Committee Meeting, Signed Minutes of Meeting, August 2017.
16. Number of teachers in public sector from CERD 2017.
17. Ministry of Education, RACE Executive Committee Meeting, Signed Minutes of Meeting, June 2017.
18. Number of classrooms in public sector from CERD 2017.
19. Ministry of Education, RACE Executive Committee Meeting, Signed Minutes of Meeting, June 2017.

REFERENCES

Bruns, B., and B. R. Schneider. 2016. "Managing the Politics of Quality Reforms in Education: Policy Lessons from Global Experience." Background Paper, *The Learning Generation: Investing in Education for a Changing World,* International Commission on Financing Global Education Opportunity, New York.

CERD (Center for Educational Research and Development). 2017. "CERD Statistical Bulletin 2016–2017" (in Arabic). CERD, Beirut. https://www.crdp.org/files/201712220733131.pdf (accessed May 2018).

——. 2018. "CERD Statistical Bulletin 2017–2018" (in Arabic). CERD, Beirut. http://crdp.org /files/201908271242061.pdf (accessed May 2019).

Corrales, J. 2005. "The State Is Not Enough: The Politics of Expanding and Improving Schools in Developing Countries." Working Paper, Project on Universal Primary and Secondary Education, Amherst.

Division of Private Education, MEHE (Ministry of Education and Higher Education). 1971. "The Committee for Overseeing and Guiding Free Private Schools." MEHE, Lebanon. http://www.legallaw.ul.edu.lb/LawView.aspx?opt=view&LawID=166901.

Gradstein, M. 2003. "The Political Economy of Public Spending on Education, Inequality, and Growth." World Bank Policy Research Working Paper 3162, World Bank, Washington, DC.

Heneveld, W., and H. Craig. 1996. "Schools Count: World Bank Project Designs and the Quality of African Primary Education." Africa Region Findings and Good Practice Infobriefs 59. World Bank, Washington, DC. https://openknowledge.worldbank.org/handle/10986/9974.

IIEP (International Institute for Educational Planning). 2017. "Improving School Financing: The Use and Usefulness of School Grants." An Intensive Research Program, UNESCO, Paris. http://www.iiep.unesco.org/en/our-expertise/school -grants?language=en.

Kingdon, G. G., A. Little, M. Aslam, S. Rawal, T. Moe, H. Patrinos, T. Beteille, R. Banerji, B. Parton, and S. K. Sharma. 2014. *A Rigorous Review of the Political Economy of Education Systems in Developing Countries*. Education Rigorous Literature Review. London: Department for International Development.

Kobeissi, H. 2012. "History of Private Schools in Lebanon." International Research Seminar, "Policies and Politics and Teaching Religion", Byblos, November.

Lebanese Parliament. 2017. "Parliamentary Committees (2017–2018)" (in Arabic). Lebanese Parliament, Beirut. https://www.lp.gov.lb/Resources/Files/667d2c37-4e8b-430f-9493 -f392e6518b66.pdf.

Lugaz, C., and A. De Grauwe. 2016. *Improving School Financing: The Use and Usefulness of School Grants: Lessons from East Asia and the Pacific*. New York: UNICEF.

Ministry of Education. 1983. "Public Education Reality and Prospective (Arabic)." Republic of Lebanon, Beirut.

Ministry of Finance. 2007. "Public Services and Support Outreach and Gaps." Republic of Lebanon, Beirut. http://www.finance.gov.lb/en-us/Finance/Rep -Pub/SP-MOF /Selected%20Presentations%20by%20MOF/English/Public%20Services%20and%20 Support.pdf.

Mulkeen, A. 2010. *Teachers in Anglophone Africa: Issues in Teacher Supply, Training, and Management*. Washington, DC: World Bank.

Santibañez, L. 2006. "School-Based Management Effects on Educational Outcomes: A Literature Review and Assessment of the Evidence Base." CIDE Working Paper 188, Centro de Investigación y Docencia Económicas, México City.

UNDP (United Nations Development Programme). 2010. "Technical Support to the Ministry of Education and Higher Education for the Implementation of the Education Sector Development Plan." Project Document, UNDP, Beirut.

UNICEF (United Nations Children's Fund). 2018. "We Made a Promise: Ensuring Learning Pathways and Protection for Syrian Children and Youth." Brussels Conference, April 2018, https://reliefweb.int/sites/reliefweb.int/files/resources/Brussels%20conference%20 education%20report.compressed.pdf.

World Bank. 2018. *World Development Report 2018: Learning to Realize Education's Promise*. Washington, DC: World Bank.

6 The Path to the Future of Education

INTRODUCTION

The education system forms one of the key social and economic pillars of Lebanon—a system characterized by a multitude of stakeholders with various functions and interests under a politically unique and sensitive environment. This makes the structure, design, and delivery of education in Lebanon a complex endeavor. Despite these complexities, there is a consensus among stakeholders on education's critical role in buttressing long-term economic development and social cohesion. Enhancing the education system in Lebanon is crucial to addressing some of the most pressing developmental challenges of the country, such as strengthening human capital, reducing poverty, fostering social mobility, and boosting economic productivity and competitiveness with an increased supply of high-skilled workers. Therefore, reforming the education system is a national priority, an economic necessity, and a social responsibility, which requires continuous adjustments and a long-term vision. In the spirit of the Sustainable Development Goal (SDGs) on improving education quality, the Ministry of Education and Higher Education (MEHE) and the Center for Educational Research and Development (CERD) are revisiting Lebanon's education strategy and are looking to work with all stakeholders in crafting an updated strategic direction to move the education system forward. To this end, the R4R program, established in 2016 under a renewed vision, has gathered efforts to provide a holistic understanding of the system and hence help the Lebanese education institutions in the design of enhancements that are technically sound, politically feasible, and administratively implementable.

REVISITING THE LAST EDUCATION STRATEGIC PLAN

The latest sector-wide national plan was adopted by Lebanon in 1994. It called for strengthening the education system with a focus on building a national identity through relevant curricula and a stronger alignment between education and the labor market. While significant progress on the plan's six objectives was accomplished, these achievements are still below intended targets, even after 25 years of effort.

The 1994 Plan for Education Reform faced major challenges, which were not overcome due to the lack of a clearly engineered operational agenda identifying and addressing core systemic issues in the sector. Table 6.1 summarizes the achievements and challenges for all six objectives of the 1994 Plan for Education Reform.

While the system expanded in early education, and continues to do so with relative success, enrollment rates in secondary schools are subpar when comparing Lebanon with countries at a similar level of development. Even though secondary education is noncompulsory, low enrollment rates in secondary education, as well as tertiary education, affect the poorest Lebanese and reflect education inequity at all levels. Furthermore, technical and vocational tracks, which can provide viable alternatives to academic tracks and contribute to reducing dropouts from the education system, are largely untapped. A new Technical and Vocational Education Strategy, launched in 2018, would seek to revitalize this sector.

Creating links between what is learned in school and what is needed in the labor market is a priority. The education system is still not producing the cadre that meets the needs of the private sector and the economy, as evidenced by the poor learning outcomes compared to international benchmarks. Changing labor market needs require graduates with high proficiency in 21st-century skills and with an increased ability for lifelong learning. The education system should have a clear vision based on a robust educational philosophy and focused on student learning and student-centered outcomes. Without this clear vision and specific plans for achieving this vision, aligning education with the labor market will continue to be a challenge. The education sector should be responsive to the economic and social development needs of the country, with a focus on emerging sectors such as science and technology, high-value-added sectors, and regional and international economic cooperation.

DEVELOPMENT TARGETS FOR THE EDUCATION SYSTEM

The analysis in this volume highlights many challenges that need to be addressed to move the system to a higher level of development and toward better educational outcomes. Planning for the future of the education system, some of the lingering targets that the country needs to tackle include the following:

1. Improving educational outcomes and achieving international averages. Based on international assessments, at Lebanon's current economic and social development levels, students are currently lagging in math, science, and reading proficiency by an average of 1.5 years of instruction.
2. Increasing enrollment rates in secondary and higher education for the poorest 40 percent of the population, as these rates are low when comparing Lebanon with other countries at the same income level.
3. Decreasing inequities and learning gaps between and within schools, across education sectors and geographical areas.
4. Aligning and harmonizing critical education delivery operations, including processes around school management; teachers' recruitment, deployment,

TABLE 6.1 **The 1994 plan for education reform: Summary of achievements and challenges**

OBJECTIVE	ACHIEVEMENTS	MAJOR CHALLENGES
1. Strengthen common national identity	• Successful reform and adoption of a new curriculum in 1997, including the agreement on the civics education curriculum	• Heavy political and sectarian interference in education service delivery in both public and private schools • Legal and regulatory framework not supportive for focus on common national identity • No agreement was reached on the history curriculum
2. Build academic knowledge and required competencies	• Curriculum reform in 1997 • Participation in international assessments (for example, TIMSS, PISA) and launch of several national assessment initiatives (such as EGRA)	• Student learning outcomes are low compared to countries at similar level of development and compared to the level of expenditures by government and parents • No systematic analysis and use of international and national assessments conducted to inform policy making
3. Improve pre-tertiary education	• Expansion of early childhood education to 3 years of schooling and significant increase in enrollment rates at the preprimary levels • Adoption of professional standards for teachers, teacher trainers, pedagogical counselors, and psychosocial counselors • Improvement in school leadership skills and provision of school grants to improve school-based management	• Enrollment in secondary education is low compared to countries at similar level of development • Strong inequity in access and quality of education; large learning gap between low-income and high-income students; • Education subsidy system not serving the most vulnerable families • High inefficiency in the system, especially in the allocation and distribution of teachers and resources
4. Achieve an enrollment balance between academic and vocational tracks and strengthen the connection with higher education	• Expansion in technical and vocational education and training (TVET)	• Little progress on improving quality of TVET • Poor links between TVET and labor market • Certification in TVET is based on theoretical knowledge rather than applied skills required by the job market
5. Align education with the labor market	• Curriculum reform of 1997 sought to increase relevance of education to the labor market	• Little focus on building 21st-century and ICT skills • No continuous update of curriculum to focus on competencies and skills needed for the labor market • Education system not producing graduates with the required skills for the private sector, as reported by private sector employers
6. Achieve advancement in the sciences and technology	• Development of a strategy for the integration of technology in teaching and learning • Expansion and provision of science laboratory in public schools	• Little progress in implementation of the education technology strategy • Low satisfaction rates of public school parents in math and science teaching • Curriculum, instruction, and assessment methods in science place a greater focus on memorization rather than scientific inquiry and application of scientific method • Student learning outcomes in math and science, as measured by international standardized assessments, are much lower compared to countries at the same level of development

Note: EGRA = Early Grade Reading Assessment; ICT = information and communication technology; PISA = Program for International Student Assessment; TIMSS = Trends in International Mathematics and Science Study; TVET = technical and vocational education and training.

and work conditions; teachers' professional development and support; and data and information flow.

5. Building a comprehensive and modern curriculum, which focuses on the development of competencies and skills that are essential for Lebanon's social and economic development.

FRAMING THE THEORY OF CHANGE USING SYSTEMS THINKING

To achieve those targets, the R4R research program followed systematic methods of inquiry to study the entire education system in an effort to initiate dialogue and inform policy about how to move the system forward. Previously, country-level analyses of the factors that support education outcomes have focused on measures of school inputs such as school buildings and their quality, pupil-teacher ratios, teacher characteristics, and availability of textbooks and learning materials. The capacity of the education system to translate these inputs into education outcomes has not been researched thoroughly. Assessing the quality of an education system is an immense task. At the global level, Newman, King, and Abdul-Hamid (2016) used comparable outcome data across countries—learning outcomes, completed years of schooling, people's view of their education system, and the World Bank's policy databases (Newman, King, and Abdul-Hamid 2016). This analysis concluded that countries with well-tied system policies have, on average, better education outcomes, when controlling for their level of education expenditures and per-capita GDP. In the same vein, the R4R research analyzed system-level parameters and available data on education processes and inputs to study how they interact with each other to produce education outcomes in Lebanon.

SUMMING UP THE SYSTEM AND FRAMING THE DRIVERS AND INTERCONNECTIONS

To understand the complex interactions and the ecology of the Lebanese education system, this first volume of the R4R research program has looked at the political economy surrounding the education sector and has identified the strengths and challenges of the Lebanon education system. Using a systems-thinking and diagnostic approach, a thorough political economy analysis was conducted into the stakeholders, drivers, processes, and factors that shape education policies and institutions, and guide operations to produce and utilize education outcomes. The diagnostic also identified context, enablers, and constraints for policy change and implementation. The analysis encompassed how education policies are developed; how education consumables—such as curricula, textbooks, and learning materials—are produced, distributed, and used by learners; how education services are provided/delivered and monitored; and how the results are measured in terms of fulfilling the learners' and society's needs and aspirations. It included the identification of the most influential actors in the education arena, as well as their vested interests.

The scope and scale of the system analysis provided an opportunity to draw a summative framing of the overarching elements of the education system in Lebanon around six macro and intermediate dimensions that constitute the foundations of an education system and form an enabling environment for education service delivery: (1) standards and norms; (2) resources and expertise; (3) delivery of instruction, school and teaching services, and school management relationships; (4) governance and leadership; (5) information, evidence, and feedback; and (6) accountability and quality assurance. At the center of the education system, links and connectors across the system represent the enabling functionalities for stronger alignment, connection, and integration.

Figure 6.1 illustrates the key findings from the system diagnostic methodology, including strengths and weaknesses across the system and between the various elements and levers that constitute the Lebanese education system.

The diagnostic along the six dimensions of the education system led to the following:

1. **Standards, vision, and norms:** Overall, there are solid foundations for a renewed functionable and operational strategy in terms of policy framework, culture of choice, expectations and demand for high-quality education, and direction for the curriculum. However, the current education system is guided by an old vision, and there is a need for a modernized and strategic focus to move the system forward and achieve growth in human capital. This new strategic focus should methodically tackle the issue of equity at all levels of the system, including in the allocation of education resources.

FIGURE 6.1

The Lebanon education system's foundations: Diagnostic results

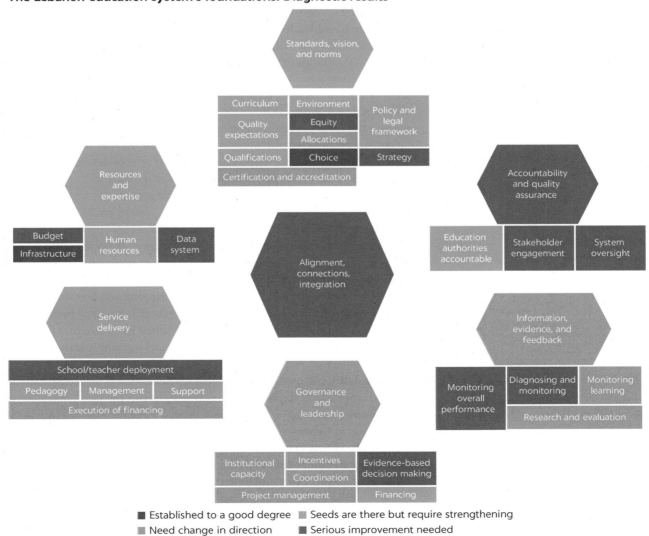

2. **Resources and expertise:** Generally, investment in inputs is adequate in Lebanon, but requires strengthening in terms of efficiency and efficacy. The current infrastructure is covering the sector needs and has been improving well over time. Budgeting is an issue in all sectors in Lebanon, including education. Human resources have promising capacity but are underutilized and inefficiently managed through the system. Data systems have been consuming significant resources but have not yet been properly established.

3. **Service delivery, including instruction and management at the school level:** While this area has solid foundations in its promotion of good pedagogy, support services, and strong management at the central and local levels, there is significant space for strengthening the system for better efficiency and higher learning outcomes. Major issues in relation to teacher deployment and ensuring compliance with teaching and working loads persist, and human resources reform is needed to ensure top qualifications, full utilization, and efficient distribution and deployment of teachers and school staff. Another delivery issue is with the execution of school financing, as the delay in disbursement to schools affects the whole teaching and learning process; one example is the delay in the procurement of textbooks by schools for all their students.

4. **Governance and leadership:** While there are financing policies and clear budget commitments to the education sector, there is a need to strengthen the institutional capacity, the management of reforms and projects, and the coordination between major players in the education system, especially in critical areas related to teachers, data, and curriculum. One major weakness of the system is its ability for evidence-based decision making in relation to investment in the sector, especially in matters related to teacher recruitment and incentives, school construction and rehabilitation, and the improvement of teaching and learning methods. Another major area of development is the need for institutional capacity building based on a theory of change tackling national challenges and the need for sustainable growth.

5. **Information, evidence, and feedback:** The system could benefit from explicit strategies targeting diagnostics and monitoring of performance at all levels. Strategies need to be accompanied by clear and specific mechanisms for monitoring and evaluation to enable the system to measure and quantify the areas and processes that are associated with the achievement or non-achievement of goals. Also, support for the teaching and learning process could benefit from evaluation and rigorous research to promote better teaching and end results. Norms need to be established to ensure that feedback loops are institutionalized to improve teaching and learning practices and the management of schools.

6. **Accountability and quality assurance:** This dimension is the weakest in the system, especially in terms of external oversight and the lack of systematic and sustained stakeholder engagement in support of education. The education system in Lebanon is well crafted to allow freedom of choice and the offering of a variety of options to parents and schools, but it does not do well in ensuring accountability and returns on investment in terms of learning.

7. **Alignment, connections, and integration:** Alignment, connections, and integration are the backbone of any system; and in Lebanon, they are also the most vulnerable areas in the education system. The following analysis and figures illustrate key examples in the Lebanese system where integration of

efforts and reaching alignment between stakeholders are crucial for achievement of better education outcomes:

a. The allocation of resources needs to take into consideration the harmonized connections between the learning strategy, curriculum competencies, the deployment of resources, and the delivery of teaching and learning activities. Currently, there needs to be a serious change in direction of how resources are allocated to schools, moving beyond the use of number of students as a metric for resources allocation and focusing rather on translating the learning strategy and learning goals into a resources' allocation plan (figure 6.2). Hence, allocations need a change in direction to be based on a learning strategy to ensure achievement and student mastery of curriculum competencies and 21st-century skills. At the same time, from a learning perspective, different strategies need to be implemented to make sure that allocations are equitable and that schools serving vulnerable groups are getting the right resources on time.

b. Moving from resources allocation to service delivery, the example of teacher professional development is illustrated in figure 6.3. There are good assets in this area in terms of a strong focus on honing teachers' skills, with a recently adopted teacher competency framework and the use of different modes of delivery including training, coaching, and hybrid models using technology. Moreover, while most of these services are well-institutionalized, there are serious gaps in the system,

FIGURE 6.2

Alignment, connections, and integration in resource allocation

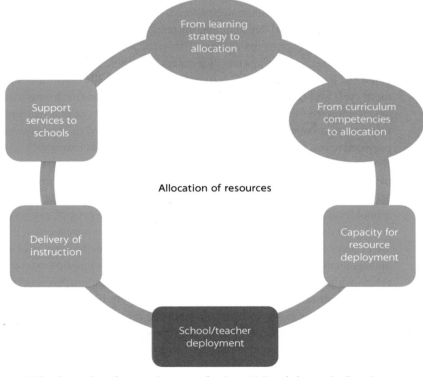

■ Seeds are there but require strengthening ■ Need change in direction
■ Serious improvement needed

FIGURE 6.3

Alignment, connections, and integration in teacher professional development

■ Seeds are there but require strengthening   ■ Need change in direction
■ Serious improvement needed

which require improvement. The system could be strengthened in terms of integration and coordination between the functions of different actors providing professional development for teachers to focus on a teacher as an engine of change in the system. These collaborative efforts need to tackle the development journey of teachers over their career. This can be enhanced if the teacher profile is integrated systematically in the development cycle and the different training, coaching, and mentoring activities are coordinated to focus on teachers' individual gaps and national learning metrics. Additionally, there needs to be a change in direction in incentives provided to teachers along their professional development journey.

c. In the area of governance, leadership, and management of the system, the overarching administrative parameters of the Lebanese education system are strong in providing a good level of autonomy in management at the school level. There is also good alignment between the central, regional, and local education authorities. However, due to system bureaucracy, the lower level of management is affected by delays. At the highest level of management, there are good foundations in capacity for building external relationships and seeking external financing for development projects, but there are substantial gaps in harmony and collaboration between stakeholders, creating significant impediments to reform. Furthermore, the management of development projects is in serious need for a change of direction to focus on results, strengthening of institutional capacity, and sustainability. An overall change in direction in the governance of the sector is needed to ensure integration and collaboration in the management of critical activities such as curriculum revision, teacher professional development, responses to crises such as the Syrian refugee crisis, and most importantly, the focus on learning and on equity (figure 6.4).

d. Another key area which needs strengthening is the culture of evidence and the alignment in strengthening information flows and feedback loops. There needs to be better alignment and integration of efforts in data-driven actions, especially in Lebanon's financially constrained and fragile context. Stronger interactions and connections between planning and improvement of education outcomes are also needed. A change in direction is needed to ensure that information flows are aligned to focus on learning and higher efficiency through evidence-based processes, cost-efficiency measures, and targeting mechanisms to provide better support to children who are most in need (figure 6.5).

e. The alignment and integration in quality assurance is in serious need of improvement (figure 6.6). To work effectively, a quality assurance system depends on clear rules to guide relationships, expectations, and responsibilities of all stakeholders and ensure effective delivery of quality education in public and private schools. Clear and specific laws within a compliance framework are needed to define interactions between internal and external oversight processes, inspection mechanisms, incentives, and penalties. This framework is currently underdeveloped in the Lebanese education system. While there are good seeds in terms of common expectations for quality between all stakeholders and a defined internal oversight system, there is a disconnect from the external oversight system. Moreover, the existing inspection and incentive mechanisms need a serious change in direction to focus on results including quality and equity

FIGURE 6.4

Alignment, connections, and integration in governance, leadership, and management

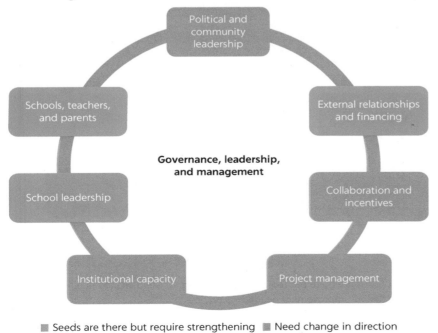

Seeds are there but require strengthening ■ Need change in direction

FIGURE 6.5

Alignment, connections, and integration in information, evidence, and feedback

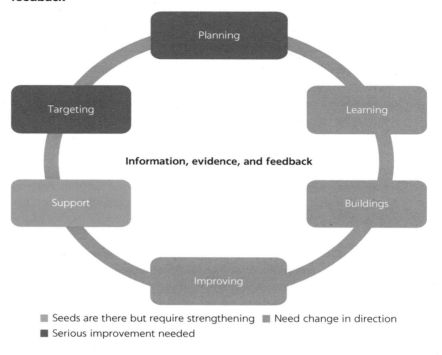

FIGURE 6.6

Alignment, connections, and integration in quality assurance

FIGURE 6.7

Alignment, connections, and integration in system renewal in education

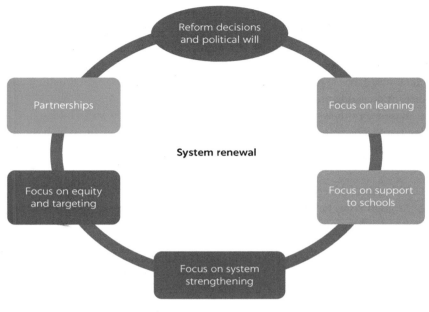

■ Seeds are there but require strengthening ■ Need change in direction
■ Serious improvement needed

rather than administrative compliance. A well-communicated agenda for shared responsibility is required to energize interactions on quality assurance and system oversight between citizens and those with decision-making power, those with convening power, and those who are delivering education services.

f. A critical area that affects the system is the lack of coordination on a well-defined framework for renewal of the education sector based on a pragmatic theory of change. This area needs serious improvement to put the system on a new path to reach its potential (figure 6.7). The connections and linkages for system renewal require serious improvement in their focus on equity and targeting, as well as on system strengthening. Moreover, the focus on learning and on support for schools should be reinforced. The system can rely on the good seeds it has built in terms of partnerships with local and international stakeholders, but it should also streamline reform decisions and garner political will across the system.

FORWARD-LOOKING REFORM ANGLES

The current practice for identifying goals is strong, but the culture to ensure the achievement of targets is not well developed. An important step to achieving higher learning outcomes in Lebanon is to strengthen the three weakest dimensions of the system—system governance and leadership; the culture of evidence, information flow, and feedback loops; and the accountability and quality assurance mechanisms. These three dimensions support the system in guaranteeing that delivered services meet certain standards while maintaining the fiscal and financial sustainability of the system. The analysis also uncovered the need for updating system-wide alignment, connections, and integration to ensure coherence and alignment toward common goals among key stakeholders, elements, drivers, principles, and laws. These are crucial to establishing and institutionalizing practical and well-directed processes.

Based on the system diagnostic, and framing the theory of change into a "systems" lens, this research uncovers the following reform angles which should constitute a foundation for dialogue to shape the path to the future of the education sector, and which are further discussed in the rest of this chapter:

1. Energizing the ecological layers and political will to strengthen education
2. Strengthening governance, institutionalization, and internal organization
3. Reducing gaps and inequity within and between schools
4. Evaluating and scaling up innovations servicing schools
5. Strengthening the regulatory framework guiding school performance
6. Strengthening data systems to track budgets, personnel, and infrastructure
7. Improving institutional capacity

ENERGIZING THE ECOLOGICAL LAYERS AND POLITICAL WILL TO STRENGTHEN EDUCATION

The mandates of the education system in Lebanon are based on the support and actions of multiple actors from the government, political parties, society, and local communities. Hence the norms that guide an education strategy must derive from an in-depth understanding of the political economy and the interaction between all those actors. The internal contests of organizations involve not just the micropolitics of individuals and departments but also the social groups, interests, and resources of the surrounding context. As a result, for education reform to succeed in reaching the beneficiaries (i.e., children), there must be consideration for the ecology of the system centered around the child. This ecology is identified by five layers that have an active role in shaping the development of a child during his/her school life and guiding the interaction of the education system with the outside world. These layers align clearly with the Bronfenbrenner ecological layers (Bronfenbrenner 2009): (a) microlayer, which refers to the institutions (schools and communities) that directly shape the child's behavior; (b) mesolayer, which refers to the interactions between parents and schools; (c) exolayer, which is the setting in which the student does not actively participate but is affected indirectly by it, such as the Ministry of Education; (d) macrolayer, which describes the cultural contexts surrounding the individual (student), such as socioeconomic status and ethnicity; and (e) chronolayer, which refers to events (such as wars, conflicts, and refugee crises) and transitions over the life span of the individual (figure 6.8).

These layers interact with each other to influence outcomes at the child's level. To this end, the following key recommendations focus on energizing

FIGURE 6.8

Bronfenbrenner layers

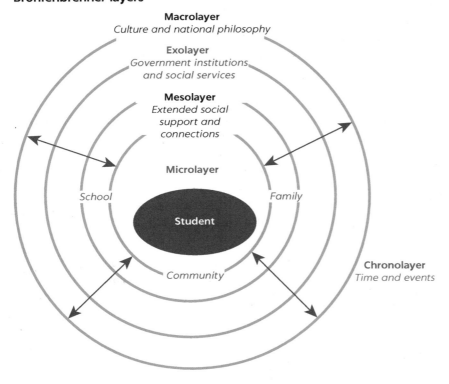

Source: Adapted from Bronfenbrenner 2009.

political will and mobilizing support for the education system across all the ecological layers:

1. Activating the role of parents in schools to expand their participation beyond membership in parent committees and to play more active and decisive roles in the processes of school improvement and effectiveness.
2. Fostering dialogue and consultations with CSOs and with local communities, as they can be powerful advocates for education interventions to strengthen education quality and they are essential in providing material and emotional support to parents and schools.
3. Engaging with teachers' unions in a systematic way on issues to improve teacher effectiveness in schools, especially that unions in Lebanon have bargaining power and are active in their advocacy work. Teachers' unions could be asked to present ideas for improving the system and support government efforts.
4. Engaging and building coalitions with associations of private schools, as they can play a bigger role in improving education.
5. Systemizing the role of municipalities and local governments in providing equitable access to high-quality education.
6. Partnering with universities, think tanks, and research associations, which have the capacity and expertise in research to build evidence that can inform education policy and to provide services such as capacity building for planning and research and preservice teacher preparation.

7. Engaging employers and the private sector to strengthen links between education and future labor market needs and to ensure that students acquire necessary and relevant skills that facilitate their transition from school to tertiary education and work.
8. Systemizing the engagement of the Ministry of Education with the Parliamentary Committee on Education and parliamentarians.

STRENGTHENING GOVERNANCE, INSTITUTIONALIZATION, AND INTERNAL ORGANIZATION

There are several governance and institutional areas that need to be strengthened for the education system in Lebanon to operate more effectively and efficiently. The education system analysis revealed issues around how different education entities interact with one another:

1. At the government and interministerial level, financing and execution of funds are lengthy and complicated processes that cause delays in the implementation of reforms and activities. The lack of application of structured and systematic budgeting processes could lead to overspending or spending before commitment of funds.
2. At the education sector level, there are fragmentation and a lack of unified and coherent education data and information feedback loops. This shortcoming might cause delays and discrepancies in information flow between different actors, including from the upper level of management of the sector to the school level and back.
3. At the Ministry of Education level, there are multiple actors working in parallel on similar areas of work (for example, teacher professional development, education data management), leading to significant challenges in the management and operation of the system. The lack of systematic coordination in key functions is not healthy for the system and could lead to inefficiencies, disorientation, and duplication of effort, such as duplicate collection of administrative data from schools, or different guidance received by teachers from distinct units working on teacher professional development. Harmonization and alignment are needed between the key directorates, departments, and units within the ministry to ensure effectiveness of service delivery.

These challenges in the institutional management and organization reflect negatively on the education system, and their effects can jeopardize the success of future strategies for moving the system forward. The current institutional imbalance and misalignment can significantly inhibit upper management's ability to control the system and to effectively manage and deploy resources. A review of roles and responsibilities is crucial to foster harmony in the management of the system and the execution of services. To this end, the government should update and ensure alignment and coherence among key elements, principles, laws, and regulatory frameworks. Clear standards and norms that are followed by practical steps for execution are essential to support the next phase of education reforms.

There is a need to reinforce and align the system's internal dynamics to be focused on student learning. Creating a goals-oriented structure helps in shielding the system from interferences, individual judgments, and special interests.

Failure to internalize and operationalize an appropriate goals-oriented structure and vision has long-lasting consequences, especially in an environment with a complex internal political structure such as Lebanon. Moreover, the lack of alignment toward common goals creates higher vulnerability to external events and shocks, such as the recent Syrian refugee crisis, which has significantly affected the education sector in recent years.

Alignment between the different implementing actors should be made first at the strategic level to agree on a unified vision for the sector, centered around improved student learning, and the roles and responsibilities of each implementing actor in achieving this vision. This coordination and consultation with the different stakeholders need to happen as early as possible in the process of strategy setting. To reach strategic alignment, the government needs to establish and reinforce collaborative leadership and administration mechanisms, while also managing and resolving interdependencies and conflicts of interest. Strategic alignment is an equilibrium state which should be continuously strived for; but, given the dynamic nature of the conditions in Lebanon, it is often a moving target. Clearly, a strategy that worked in a particular situation might not always be appropriate with changing conditions. The vision and strategy-setting approach should thus be iterative and dynamic to allow increased responsiveness to those changing conditions affecting different stakeholders. Short- and long-term strategies need to be revisited proactively and need to embed fiscal and technical space for a flexible response in case of changing conditions. Recent examples of changing conditions include both external shocks such as the Syrian refugee crisis and internal political and economic changes such as the civil servants' salary increase. As a result, both alignment and resilience need to be strengthened for the system to better respond to the challenges in the sector.

Moreover, integrating and planning for design, production, and execution processes at the vision and strategy setting stage will enable this strategic alignment to translate into a coordinated and aligned approach in implementation. There is a need to establish and institutionalize logical and objective processes for the execution of common goals. These processes should be linked to performance in terms of achieving the desired outcomes. They should be applied in an efficient and timely manner throughout the life span of an activity, including setup, financing, allocations, procurement, deployments, operation configuration, and execution.

Finally, the system should create feedback loops and foster a culture of evidence. It is crucial for the success of any reform to ensure a shift from running an operation and focusing on inputs to monitoring and achieving results. Good governance will seek to enact (a) open and accessible communication with the public; (b) active participation by citizens (and not only politicians) as much as possible in policy formation; (c) clear accountability apportioned among all relevant entities; and (d) transparency in the assessment and evaluation of effectiveness in achieving results.

REDUCING GAPS AND INEQUITY WITHIN AND BETWEEN SCHOOLS

There are large gaps in terms of inputs and results between schools in the country. These differences between schools exacerbate inequalities that might lead to negative future consequences due to poor learning outcomes and societal imbalances. Monitoring and measuring gaps between schools and looking for means to systematically reduce them should be a priority for the government. Many countries monitor gaps between schools (especially those with different institutional frameworks), while others use within-school or within-class tracking methods. Many European countries, for example, use between-school tracking, while American schools more frequently use within-school ability grouping. In Lebanon, given the different types of schools and the different institutional frameworks, tracking and reducing differences between schools are necessary for addressing inequity. For example, this monitoring could measure regional differences and better track the performance of schools catering to students with special needs. In all cases, monitoring gaps should be part of a national strategy and should be well communicated to ensure effectiveness in creating a proper climate for learning in all schools.

In addition to monitoring gaps, the government should work on reducing them. A critical point for reducing gaps between students is the investment in early years, as it has been proven globally to yield better outcomes for children from all socioeconomic backgrounds, with stronger benefits for poorer children. Moreover, strengthening school-level capacity, through the following activities, is essential to reducing gaps:

1. Strengthening school-level capacity in planning and budgeting to be able to plan for results.
2. Raising the share of funding from central and local governments provided directly to schools using a needs-based resource allocation mechanism.
3. Engaging local authorities, including municipalities, in supporting school improvement plans and sharing the responsibility for school performance.
4. Speeding up responses to schools' needs through faster execution and feedback loops from schools.
5. Bringing schools together and encouraging donations and support, including funds pooling among schools.
6. Sponsoring platforms and events where private and public schools can participate and engage together to share knowledge.

While it is critical to bridge gaps within the public education system, there are also significant differences within the private education system, which require the government's attention. However, the MEHE is not the sole authority responsible for reducing gaps, and there is a need for innovations and better networking and collaboration between schools, associations, and the government. Box 6.1 presents one example of an initiative that aims to decrease gaps among schools in one region in South Lebanon (Saida) and can provide lessons for the development of other school networks in the country.

EVALUATING AND SCALING UP INNOVATIONS SERVICING SCHOOLS

Many aspects of the current model of education provision are showing positive results in schools, as reflected by the positive public perception of parents, teachers, and school administrators. In this area, there are several activities that stand out as innovations that would need to be scaled up. To do so, it is important that first these activities are rigorously and scientifically assessed and evaluated for their impact and effectiveness, and that they are planned in a systematic,

BOX 6.1

Example of the school network in Saida and its neighboring towns

The School Network of Saida and neighboring towns was established in 2004 with logistical and financial support from the Hariri Foundation for Sustainable Human Development. Under the leadership of Bahia Hariri, head of the Parliamentarian Committee for Education and Culture, the network works to overcome challenges for schools, harmonize norms and values across different types of schools, and reduce gaps in access to resources and financial means among schools. The school network created a platform for dialogue on common ground, values, and ways to share experiences and work together to improve education quality. Equity in access to a high-quality education is a core pillar of the network. The network started with 68 schools in 2004 and now consists of 110 entities, as it expanded its membership to include vocational and technical schools and UNRWA schools.

The activities under the network include the following:

1. A monthly working forum for school principals to develop unified strategic plans to meet shared goals and implement them in schools.

2. Resource creation and sharing, such as the development of a unified parents' and students' handbook.

3. Financial and material support, such as transportation for students.

4. Exchange of teacher expertise.

5. Technology sharing and collaboration.

6. Shared activities and programs.

cost-effective, and institutionalized manner while drawing lessons from previous experiences in implementation. Examples of activities that show innovations in the system are:

1. Pedagogical counseling to teachers performed by counselors from Direction d'Orientation Pédagogique et Scolaire (DOPS). Counselors conduct observations of teachers and provide individualized feedback and coaching to help teachers identify their learning needs and work on improving their classroom practices. DOPS counselors also provide guidance on the design and use of learning assessments to measure learning outcomes of students. They also conduct school and regional gatherings to encourage knowledge sharing and peer-to-peer support for teachers and school administrators.

2. Health and psychosocial counseling for schools led by DOPS provides essential support to extremely vulnerable students to overcome social tensions, bullying, harassment, and violence in schools. They promote good mental and physical health and implement the newly established child protection framework.

3. ALPs and remedial programs developed by the CERD and the MEHE. Many of these programs were developed as a response to the Syrian refugee crisis to provide the necessary academic support for refugee children to be able to compensate for lost school years and integrate formal education with their Lebanese peers. The MEHE's first inclusive education pilot is also an important innovation to transform the way schools integrate children with special needs and disabilities. The vision behind these programs and the methodology which focuses on differentiated instruction and teaching at the learner's level can be expanded and scaled up to serve all students as a permanent

feature of the system (for example, adaptive teaching and tailored approaches for vulnerable children).

4. School grants under the SIP supported the process of increasing school-level autonomy and accountability for results. It consists of having the school management in consultation with all school stakeholders to assess needs and prepare a SIP which would then be financed through a grant from the Ministry of Education. This initiative has a strong focus on school management capacity building, as school grants can only be effective in improving the school learning environment and student learning outcomes when the leadership skills of the school principal and administrators are strengthened.

STRENGTHENING THE REGULATORY FRAMEWORK GUIDING SCHOOL PERFORMANCE

Freedom of education provision was not meant to transfer the responsibility for accountability to the parents. To improve education in Lebanon, both public and private schools must achieve their best performance within a strong oversight and accountability framework. Competition between schools might lead in general to better quality based on well-defined standards and norms. However, competition alone cannot guarantee good quality. The Ministry of Education, in its interaction with private schools, has so far been focused on administrative compliance for issues such as legal requirements, curriculum standards, examinations and certification, and fair tuition and teacher salary scales. However, the MEHE should have a stronger oversight and regulatory role when it comes to quality of education and learning outcomes.

Establishing a quality assurance system intended to ensure that services delivered meet agreed-upon standards is thus a necessity. Given the variety of providers and stakeholders in education in Lebanon, there is a need for modern and professionally crafted standards, evidence-based practices, and public policies that specify outcomes and lay out processes to ensure quality implementation. The quality oversight is critical and should consist of measurement, comparison of findings to standards, and feedback to practitioners and authorities for reflection and calibration. The framework for quality standards and oversight should be developed in consultation with all stakeholders and implemented by an oversight body under the umbrella of the ministry. There are many examples of such systems in OECD countries, which could serve as a reference. Additionally, some private school associations have introduced such systems to monitor and support their own schools; and lessons learned from their experience can be scaled up to cover the whole system. For such a system to work, the following should be taken into consideration:

1. The oversight body needs to be institutionalized with enough political and community support.
2. The quality assurance framework needs to have clear, objective, systematic, and streamlined criteria and processes for establishing and regulating education institutions.
3. The quality assurance and regulatory system should be designed with a focus on school improvement. It should be providing feedback not only to the central administration but also to schools and all service delivery arms.

The system should provide feedback and information of school performance compared with other schools in the country, but its focus should not be on ranking schools, as this will exacerbate inequity and will distract from the actual areas of development for each school.

4. Engagement with parents is essential, as they will greatly benefit from such a system, which will provide them with inputs to inform their selection of schools and will give them a better understanding of the quality of education their children are receiving in schools.

5. The system should accommodate differences in delivery models and be sensitive to schools and associations to which those schools belong.

6. The system should not be used to shame and blame schools but should be aimed at identifying needs for support and monitoring progress across schools in the country.

7. The use of data- and evidence-driven school improvement initiatives should be enhanced, as they are essential for the success of the regulatory framework.

8. The introduction of incentives and models for capacity building at the MEHE will be essential to be able to implement and manage the regulatory system.

9. Lessons could be learned on setting up regulatory frameworks from country examples from the region (for example, Dubai in the United Arab Emirates) and other regions with a similar development level, such as Chile in Latin America.

STRENGTHENING DATA SYSTEMS TO TRACK BUDGETS, PERSONNEL, AND INFRASTRUCTURE

Ensuring the fiscal and financial sustainability of the system is crucial. The education system in Lebanon is overstretched financially and sometimes beyond the capacity of the country's economy. The system is in urgent need of systematic public financial management. Data systems to monitor inputs into the education system could help in providing evidence for policy makers to maximize the use of resources using principles of efficiency, effectiveness, economy, and value for money. Adequate financing keeps the system going and allows for innovations. For example, a salary and benefits package for teachers—that is positively comparable with those of other professional occupations—is an essential ingredient to attract and motivate competent teachers to the profession. However, the execution of such compensation plans needs to be evidence-based and data-driven, with a focus on results and high performance. Both monetary and nonmonetary incentives encourage educators to maintain high standards and to continue improving their skills. A well-established professional development system aligned with their needs is also crucial to ensure better productivity of teachers and higher returns on investment.

Some of the key functions and data to be monitored are related to (1) school-level expenditures, (2) school assets management and school maintenance and rehabilitation needs, (3) teaching and learning material procurement including textbooks, and (4) teacher management and deployment, including the management of teacher working load, the distribution and sharing of teachers between schools, and the recruitment of contractual teachers.

The following are main recommendations for strengthening data and monitoring systems:

Infrastructure and assets

1. Monitoring and tracking the status of school infrastructure and assets, as well as rehabilitation needs, including in rented schools. This information should be the basis for any rehabilitation activities and to close infrastructure gaps between schools.
2. Cost-effective and targeted budget allocation for schools' infrastructure, equipment, and furniture maintenance.
3. Development of guidelines and rules for the maintenance of school infrastructure and assets.

Personnel and human resources

1. Furthering the development of and ensuring compliance with norms for hiring contractual teachers based on school teaching needs by subject and level.
2. Utilizing unified data systems to track teachers and human resources at schools, including distribution and sharing of teachers between schools and the central administrative units, in addition to the tracking of teacher qualifications, teaching load, teacher absenteeism and substitutions, and teacher contractual arrangements.
3. Improving the tracking of teacher support activities, including all preservice and in-service activities for school staff, the identification of teachers' professional development needs based on a diagnosis of teacher competencies and skills, funding for these activities, and a system for accountability to align teacher professional development with evaluations and incentives.

Budgets, accounting, and school-level activities

1. Streamlining and harmonizing budget execution at the central, regional, and school levels, including increasing efficiency in procurement and financial management processes.
2. Using data systems to approve and monitor school budgets, expenditures, and procurements.

IMPROVING INSTITUTIONAL CAPACITY

Improving education outcomes on a substantial scale requires the country to engage in bold, holistic, systematic, and sustainable institutional capacity improvement at the central, regional, and school levels. Capacity building should be comprehensive in scope and should directly address the emerging needs of the system. The R4R program has identified capacity needs around the following areas:

- **Leadership and management** to involve all the institutional units and stakeholders in systemic collaborations and in the setting and execution of a unified vision for desired change. The leadership should focus on institutional improvement activities, which lead to schools' improvement and student success.

- **Strategy and planning** to align education institutions with national education goals on student success and with the operational processes for translating the desired future into defined goals and objectives and executing the actions to achieve them. This includes technical planning and developing theories of change, as well as financial planning, costing, and budgeting.
- **Monitoring and evaluation** to build a culture of evidence and use of information in daily activities and decisions; to this end, the institution's capacity to collect, access, analyze, and use data to inform decisions should be strengthened. Capacity should also be strengthened in the evaluation of activities and interventions.
- **Teaching and learning** to engage teachers in the examination of pedagogy methods, student support, professional development, and the central role of teachers as change agents within schools. This engagement should also focus on facilitating student learning and success through the continuous monitoring of learning outcomes and increased support inside and outside of the classroom. The system should also be strengthened in the use of assessment results for improvement. Capacity in leveraging technology for teaching and learning should also be reinforced.
- **Equity** to reinforce the commitment, capabilities, and experiences of the institution to equitably serve vulnerable, low-income, and at-risk students, including students with disabilities and with learning difficulties, and to provide them with improved access, support, learning conditions, and learning climate.
- **Communication and strategic partnerships** with key factors such as private schools, universities, employers, community-based organizations, and public sector stakeholders to participate in the education agenda and improvement of outcomes.
- **Research capacity** to lead, engage in, and interpret actionable research on pressing issues to inform decisions and support the education reform agenda.

LONG-TERM INSTITUTIONALIZATION OF RESEARCH AND RESEARCH UPTAKE

The R4R program has shown an important shift into high-quality research underpinned by good research governance. The program created a strong platform to invest in longer-term research to guide Lebanon's progress toward the 2030 SDG for quality education. However, a 3-year research program is short in the life cycle of education sector reform. The role of the CERD, which is the primary institution mandated to lead education research in the country, should be strengthened to set up a full portfolio of high-quality research and rigorous impact evaluations over the coming decade. The CERD should be supported by a network of public and private stakeholders, who can help in raising funds for educational research, guiding priorities for the research agenda, and reinforcing policy uptake of research findings. The R4R Steering Committee served as a good example of such a network and could thus be expanded into a Research Governance Committee with leadership by the CERD and MEHE and membership from both the public and private sectors. A protocol for policy uptake of research is detailed in appendix C.

REFERENCES

Bronfenbrenner, U. 2009. *The Ecology of Human Development: Experiments by Nature and Design*. Cambridge, MA: Harvard University Press.

Newman, J. L., E. M. King, and H. Abdul-Hamid. 2016. "The Quality of Education Systems and Education Outcomes." Background Paper, *The Learning Generation: Investing in Education for a Changing World*, International Commission on Financing Global Education Opportunity, New York.

APPENDIX A

Bibliography

EDUCATION POLICY

El-Habbal, J. 2011. "The Institutional Dynamics of Sectarianism Education and Personal Status Laws in Postwar Lebanon." Unpublished Master's Thesis, Lebanese American University, Beirut.

Issa, J. E. 2012. "Investing in, Maintaining and Retaining Intellectual Capital in Education: Study in Lebanon." Unpublished Doctoral Thesis, Holy Spirit University of Kaslik, Jounieh.

Robalino, D., and S. Haneed. 2012. "Republic of Lebanon—Good Jobs Needed: The Role of Macro, Investment, Education, Labor and Social Protection Policies ("Miles")." World Bank, Washington, DC. https://openknowledge .worldbank.org/handle/10986/13217.

World Bank. 2010. "Lebanon—Second Education Development Project." World Bank, Washington, DC. http://documents.worldbank.org/curated /en/613671468263697818/Lebanon-Second-Education-Development -Project.

أبودية، مروة. 2013. نحو معالجة الفساد في القطاع التربوي في لبنان دعم البرلمان واللجنة النيابية للتربية والتعليم العالي والثقافة -تلامذة وطلاب لبنان ضحايا فساد التربية وغياب الارادة السياسية. برنامج الأمم المتحدة الإنمائي. بيروت. لبنان. (الرقم التسلسلي 112)

الأمين، عدنان. 2000. الوضع التربوي في لبنان ومعالم السياسة التربوية فيه. الأوضاع الاقتصادية والتربوية والبيئية في لبنان. وزارة الشؤون الاجتماعية. بيروت. لبنان.(الرقم التسلسلي 682)

الأمين، عدنان. 2007. السياسة التربوية: حول التعليم الثانوي الرسمي. التعليم الثانوي الرسمي: واقعه وشروط تطويره. رابطة أساتذة التعليم الثانوي في لبنان. بيروت. لبنان. ص.ص. 59–66 (الرقم التسلسلي 18)

الأمين، عدنان. 2012. سياسة تعيين المتعاقدين في الوظيفة العامة في لبنان: مثال المعلمين الرسميين. مجلة الدفاع الوطني، عدد 82. مديرية الجيش اللبناني. بيروت. لبنان. (الرقم التسلسلي 400)

بلوط، علي. 2013. واقع الاعداد في كلية التربية بين النسق المؤسساتي والسياسة التربوية.الأبحاث التربوية، عدد 23. كلية التربية في الجامعة اللبنانية. بيروت. لبنان. ص.ص. 9–51 (الرقم التسلسلي 410)

ريشا، ليليان. 2014. الهوية الوطنية من خلال السياسة التربوية في مناهج التّعليم العامّ في لبنان (1997) (التربية الوطنية والتنشئة المدنية واللغة العربية وآدابها نموذجا). أطروحة دكتوراه غير منشورة. الجامعة اللبنانية. بيروت. لبنان. (الرقم التسلسلي 204)

السوالي، محمد. 2011. السياسات التربوية؛ الأسس والتدابير. دار العربية للعلوم. بيروت. لبنان. (الرقم التسلسلي 3007)

شرارة، ريتا ألبير. 2007. الرؤية التربوية في نصوص تشريعية لبنانية بعد الطائف (1992–2002). رسالة ماجستير غير منشورة. جامعة القديس يوسف. بيروت. لبنان. (الرقم التسلسلي 620)

عامل، مهدي. 2007. في قضايا التربية والسياسة التعليمية. دار الفارابي. بيروت. لبنان. (الرقم التسلسلي 251)

عبد الباقي، سليمة. 2004. السياسة التربوية للدولة اللبنانية من خلال كتاب التربية المدنية للصف الثالث ثانوي بين النظرية والتطبيق. منطقة البقاع نموذجا. رسالة ديبلوم غير منشورة. الجامعة اللبنانية. بيروت. لبنان. (الرقم التسلسلي 522)

القواص، عصمت. 2006. التعليم الثانوي الرسمي: البعد الوطني والسياسة التربوية الرسمية. التعليم الثانوي الرسمي: واقعه وشروط تطويره. رابطة أساتذة التعليم الثانوي في لبنان. بيروت. لبنان. ص.ص. 67–73 (الرقم التسلسلي 77)

EDUCATIONAL ADMINISTRATION

Assaf, G. 2013. « L'effet de la motivation et des performances sur l'implication de personnel administratif, d'un établissement scolaire libanais, dans le cadre d'une démarche qualité : cas d'une congrégation catholique. » Mémoire non publié, Université Saint Joseph, Beyrouth.

El Badri, N. 2015. "Public Administration Education: The Case of Lebanon." Unpublished Master's Thesis, American University of Beirut, Beirut.

Hamadeh, N. 2006. "Understanding Leadership Practice in a Lebanese School: A Director's Experience." Unpublished Master's Thesis, American University of Beirut, Beirut.

Saad, M. 2012. "School Principals' and Counselors' Perspectives of the Ideal Profile, Facilitators, and Obstacles of the Professional School Counselor: A Case Study of the Public and Private Schools in Lebanon." Unpublished Master's Thesis, American University of Beirut, Beirut.

Wazen, C. E. 2007. "The Leadership and Management Styles and Behaviors of Subject Coordinators in a Sample of Lebanese Secondary Schools." Unpublished Master's Thesis, American University of Beirut, Beirut.

دور المدراء والمشرفين في تحسين أداء العاملين التربويين. دار المحجة البيضاء، بيروت. لبنان. (رقم تسلسلي: 3003)

الصيداوي، أحمد. 2001. القيادة التحويلية التربوية. الأمين، عدنان (تحرير): الإدارة التربوية في البلدان العربية. (ص ص. 29–58) الهيئة اللبنانية للعلوم التربوية. بيروت. لبنان. (رقم تسلسلي 702)

الطويل، هاني عبد الرحمن. 2001. التقييم والمساءلة كمدخل في إدارة النظم التربوية. الأمين، عدنان (تحرير): الإدارة التربوية في البلدان العربية. (ص ص. 131–58). الهيئة اللبنانية للعلوم التربوية، بيروت. (رقم تسلسلي 704)

عبد، علي محسن؛ غالي، حيدر نعمة. 2010. القيادة التربوية: مدخل استراتيجي. المؤسسة الحديثة للكتاب. لبنان (رقم تسلسلسي: 986)

فريحة، نمر. 2003. المركز التربوي في 1017 يوما. لا ناشر. بيروت. لبنان. (رقم تسلسلي: 793)

فلحة، حسان محمد. 2008. المركزية واللامركزية في الإدارة التربوية اللبنانية 1943-2007. أطروحة غير منشورة. جامعة القديس يوسف. بيروت. لبنان. (رقم تسلسلي 627)

نصر الله، محمد؛كلاكش، ريما. 2014. مسار علمي في تطوير الإدارة.رحلة في التطوير التربوي: تجربة المبرات. دار الشفق للنشر والتوزيع. لبنان. ص 99–145: (رقم تسلسلي: 361)

SCHOOL ADMINISTRATION

Habli, F. 2006. "Effective Leadership Practices in Schools Facing Challenging Contexts." Unpublished Master's Thesis, Lebanese American University, Beirut.

Harb, S. 2014. "Identification and Alignment of Lebanese Teachers' and Principals' Perspectives of Effective Leadership." Unpublished Master's Thesis, American University of Beirut, Beirut.

Osman, D. 2003. "An Exploration of Role and Perceptions of Public School Principals in the City of Saida." Unpublished Master's Thesis, American University of Beirut, Beirut.

Sioufi, H. 2002. "The Leadership Orientations of Division Directors in a Lebanese Private School." Unpublished Master's Thesis, American University of Beirut, Beirut.

جابر، عبير عادل. 2000. الدور القيادي لمدير المدرسة الرسمية والخاصة في مدينة بيروت. رسالة ماستر غير منشورة. الجامعة اللبنانية. بيروت. لبنان. (رقم تسلسلي 155)

جدعون، أندريه قيصر. 2014. السمات القيادية لدى مديري المدارس الثانوية الرسمية والخاصة في محافظة بيروت الكبرى. رسالة ماستر غير منشورة. الجامعة اللبنانية. بيروت. لبنان. (رقم تسلسلي 161)

حمود، ليانة. 2012. نمط الإدارة المدرسية وأثره في رضا المعلم الوظيفي من وجهة نظر معلمي الحلقة الأولى والثانية ومعلماتها في بعض مدارس بيروت الرسمية والخاصة. رسالة ماستر غير منشورة. جامعة القديس يوسف. بيروت. لبنان. (رقم تسلسلي 660)

سبعأعين، ندى. 2008. دراسة أثر النمط القيادي لرؤساء الدوائر الأكاديمية على تحفيز المعلمين في بعض مدارس محافظة بيروت. رسالة ماستر غير منشورة. الجامعة اللبنانية. بيروت. لبنان. (رقم تسلسلي 116)

العرابي، مروان. 2014. تأثير النمط القيادي لمديري المدارس الرسمية على دافعية المعلمين. رسالة ماستر غير منشورة. الجامعة اللبنانية. بيروت. لبنان. (رقم تسلسلي 63)

غانم، شربل. 2013. دور المدير كقائد تربوي في عملية التدريب المستمر للمعلمين وتنميتهم مهنيا في المدارس الانطونية. رسالة ماستر غير منشورة. الجامعة اللبنانية. بيروت. لبنان. (رقم تسلسلي 276)

فهد، عبدو الخوري أنطوان. 2002. مدير المدرسة الرسمية في قضاءي المتن وكسروان، اختياره، اعداده، مسؤولياته بين النص والواقع. رسالة ماستر غير منشورة. الجامعة اللبنانية. بيروت. لبنان. (رقم تسلسلي 297)

كعكي، جميلة ابراهيم. 2004. النمط القيادي في الادارة المدرسية وعلاقته بإدراك المعلمين لسلوك المدير. رسالة ماستر غير منشورة. الجامعة اللبنانية. بيروت. لبنان. (رقم تسلسلي 316)

كعكي، جميلة إبراهيم. 2011. خصائص الشخصية القيادية عند المديرة في المدارس المتوسطة الرسمية والخاصة في بيروت وضاحيتها الجنوبية وأثرها في فعالية المدرسة. أطروحة دكتوراه غير منشورة. جامعة القديس يوسف. بيروت. لبنان. (رقم تسلسلي 646)

موسوي، سمية سادات لوح. 2013. أثر النمط القيادي لمدير المدرسة في الرضا الوظيفي من وجهة نظر معلمي الحلقة الثالثة ومعلماتها في بعض مدارس الضاحية الجنوبية لمدينة بيروت. رسالة ماستر غير منشورة. جامعة القديس يوسف. بيروت. لبنان. (رقم تسلسلي 663)

CLASSROOM MANAGEMENT

Baghjajian, N. 2011. "The Effect of Classroom Placement on Self-Esteem: The Case of Lebanese Middle School Students with Dyslexia." Unpublished Master's Thesis, Notre Dame University, Loueize.

Farhat, A. 2011. "The Impact of Clinical Supervision on Teachers' Performance in Classroom Managerial Skills." Unpublished Master's Thesis, Lebanese University, Beirut.

Iskandarani, M. 2008. "Views on Classroom Management Issues: A Case Study." Unpublished Master's Thesis, Lebanese American University, Beirut.

Kashani-Kavlakian, S. 2014. "Developing Student-Teachers' Emotional Intelligence to Promote an Efficient Classroom: An Exploratory Study in a Lebanese University." Unpublished Master's Thesis, Université Saint-Esprit de Kaslik, Jounieh.

Matta, M. 2015. "The Effects of Well-Trained Teachers in Grades 6, 7, and 8 on Creating a Positive Classroom Environment in Lebanese Schools in Mount Lebanon: Meten El Shemali and Kesrwan." Unpublished Doctoral Thesis, Lebanese University, Beirut.

Tabsh, N. 2013. "The Effect of Training Grades 5 and 6 Elementary School Students in Skillstreaming Program on Classroom Survival Skills." Unpublished Master's Thesis, American University of Beirut, Beirut.

Zaiter, N. 2005. "The Relationship between Classroom Interaction and Success." Unpublished Master's Thesis, Lebanese University, Beirut.

أبو خليل، فادية. 2011. إدارة السلوك وتعديل السلوك الصّفي. دار النهضة العربية. بيروت. لبنان. (رقم تسلسلي 3004)

توق، محي الدين. 2014. إدارة الصف. وقائع مؤتمر التجديد التربوي: عبر تدريب المعلمين. مؤسسة رفيق الحريري. بيروت. لبنان. ص. ص. 19-31 (رقم تسلسلي 154)

دكاش، سليم. 2001. وثيقة الصّف للعمل والعيش المشترك. القيم والتعليم. الهيئة اللبنانية للعلوم التربوية. بيروت. لبنان. ص.ص. 339-52 (رقم تسلسلي 681)

رعد، مريم. 2002. خريطة العلاقات التواصلية في صف الروضة. رسالة ماستر غير منشورة. الجامعة اللبنانية. بيروت. لبنان. (رقم تسلسلي 201)

زرزور، راوية نزير. 2013. مفهوم الإدارة الصفية وصعوباتها من وجهة نظر معلمي الحلقة الثانية من التعليم الأساسي في منطقة إقليم الخروب. رسالة ماستر غير منشورة. جامعة القديس يوسف. بيروت. لبنان. (رقم تسلسلي 658)

الشامي، رنا مصطفى. 2013. واقع الإدارة الصفية والصعوبات التي تواجهها من وجهة نظر معلمي الحلقة الثانية من التعليم الأساسي ومعلماتها في بعض مدارس بيروت. رسالة ماستر غير منشورة. الجامعة اللبنانية. بيروت. لبنان. (رقم تسلسلي 659)

محمود، لما محمود. 2011. إدارة الصف لدى معلمات رياض الأطفال وأثرها قي سلوكهم في بعض مدارس صيدا (لبنان). (رقم تسلسلي 651)

يموت، سوسن. 2008. الإدارة الصفية في الحلقة الأولى من التعليم الأساسي في مدارس بيروت: الواقع والمرتجى. رسالة ماستر غير منشورة. جامعة القديس يوسف. بيروت. لبنان. (رقم تسلسلي 617)

CURRICULUM

Al Khatib, L. 2015. "The Relationship of Teacher's Transformational Leadership Behavior and Process-Based Curriculum with Democratic Classroom Climate and Participatory Citizenship." Unpublished Master's Thesis, Haigazian University, Beirut.

El Hayek, B., and Pascale, E. 2013. "Financial Literacy: A Possible Shortcoming of the Economics Curriculum in Lebanese Schools." Unpublished Master's Thesis, Notre Dame University, Loueize.

Frayha, N., A. Youness, and J. Hassan. 2001. *Contenu de l'education et stratégies d'enseignement adoptées au 21e siècle : Problèmes et solutions*. Beyrouth : CRDP / UNESCO.

Negrel, I. 2013. "L'interdisciplinarité." وقائع مؤتمر التجديد التربوي: تجارب في التطوير المدرسي. Rafic Hariri Foundation, 107–23.

UNICEF (United Nations Children's Fund). 2015. *Curriculum, Accreditation and Certification for Syrian Children in Syria, Turkey, Lebanon, Jordan, Iraq and Egypt*. Amman: UNICEF.

Yammine, A. 2006. "Rôle des pouvoirs sociopolitiques et religieux dans la réforme des programmes d'enseignement scolaires libanais : La transposition didactique externe : exemple de la reproduction humaine en EB8." Mémoire de Master non publié, Université Libanaise, Beyrouth.

الأمين، عدنان وجرداق، مراد. 2005. إصلاح التعليم العام: دراسة حالة إصلاح المناهج اللبنانية. إصلاح التعليم العام في البلدان العربية، (عدنان الأمين تحرير)، أعمال حلقة دراسية. الهيئة اللبنانية للعلوم التربوية. بيروت. لبنان. ص ص. 55–76 (رقم تسلسلي 689)

ريشا، ليليان. 2014. الهوية الوطنية من خلال السّياسة التّربوية في مناهج التّعليم العامّ في لبنان (1997) (التربية الوطنية والتنشئة المدنية واللغة العربية وآدابها نموذجا). أطروحة دكتوراه غير منشورة. الجامعة اللبنانية. بيروت. لبنان. (رقم تسلسلي 204)

سعادة، جودت أحمد وابراهيم، عبد الله محمد. 2001. تنظيمات المناهج وتخطيطها وتطويرها. دار الشروق. دار الشروق للنشر والتوزيع. بيروت. لبنان. (رقم تسلسلي 851)

عبدالباقي، سليمة. 2014. المناهج التربوية الحديثة تنشئة ام تطبيع بحث نظري وميداني في المناهج التربوية اللبنانية، علم الاجتماع مثالًا. أطروحة دكتوراه غير منشورة. الجامعة اللبنانية. بيروت. لبنان. (رقم تسلسلي 523)

كوراني، حسن. 2014. التقييم التربوي الواقعي، رؤيته التربوية وأثره في «أسس تقييم» مناهجنا الجديدة: دراسة نظرية تحليلية. رسالة ماجستير غير منشورة. جامعة القديس يوسف. بيروت. لبنان. (رقم تسلسلي 670)

المركز التربوي للبحوث والإنماء. 2003. تطبيق المناهج الجديدة: مشكلات ومستلزمات وحلول مقترحة من خلال آراء مديري الثانويات الرسمية ومعلّميها. المركز التربوي للبحوث والإنماء. (رقم تسلسلي 86)

المركز التربوي للبحوث والإنماء. 2006. آراء أهالي الطلاب حول إدراج قضايا الصحة الإنجابية والنوع الاجتماعي في المدارس، بالتعاون مع صندوق الأمم المتحدة للسكان. المركز التربوي للبحوث والإنماء. (رقم تسلسلي 114)

النادي الثقافي العربي. 2001. تطوير مناهج اللغة العربية في لبنان. النادي الثقافي العربي. (رقم تسلسلي 710)

ناصر الدين، راغدة. 2001. تفاعل مديري المدارس الثانوية الرسمية مع المناهج التعليمية الجديدة في لبنان. رسالة ماستر غير منشورة. الجامعة اللبنانية. بيروت. لبنان. (رقم تسلسلي 357)

STUDENT ACHIEVEMENT AND LEARNING

Aboulmona, I. H. 2001. "The Effect of Mind Mapping on Student Achievement in a Grade 8 American High School General Science Class." Unpublished Master's Thesis, American University of Beirut, Beirut.

Al Kabbi, Y. A. 2015. "To What Extent Does the Use of Concept Map among Eighth Graders Increase Their Achievement in Chemical Reactions." Unpublished Master's Thesis, Lebanese University, Beirut.

Assi, S. E. 2013. "Effect of Peer Tutoring on Achievement of Grade 8 Students in Chemistry." Unpublished Master's Thesis, Lebanese University, Beirut.

Attieh, M. F. 2003. "The Effect of Using Concept Maps as Study Tools on Achievement in Chemistry on Secondary Students." Unpublished Master's Thesis, American University of Beirut, Beirut.

Dhamsiddine, M. 2007. "The Effect of Demonstrations and Activities on the Students' Attitude toward Chemistry and Their Achievement in Middle East." Unpublished Master's Thesis, Lebanese American University, Beirut.

Dhatila, N. A. 2004. "Effect of Inquiry Strategies on Students' Acquisition as well as Retention of Basic Concepts in Electricity." Unpublished Master's Thesis, Lebanese American University, Beirut.

Fayad, E. 2014. "The Effect of Role Play on the Academic Achievement, and Motivation of Tenth Graders while Teaching the Synaptic Cleft." Unpublished Master's Thesis, Lebanese University, Beirut.

Fayyad, N. Y. 2015. "The Effect of Hands-on Modeling Activities on the Achievement, Attitude, and Self-Efficacy of Different Learning Style, Opposite Gender and Different Kind of School Biology Students." Unpublished Master's Thesis, Lebanese University, Beirut.

Hannoun, S. V. 2010. "The Effect of Using Concept Maps as Learning Tools under Cooperative and Individualistic Structures on Middle School Students' Achievement in Biology." Unpublished Master's Thesis, American University of Beirut, Beirut.

Jarjoura, C. 2013. "The Effect of Using Team-Based Learning on the Achievement and Attitude of Grade 7 Biology Students." Unpublished Master's Thesis, Lebanese University, Beirut.

Kameh, L. M. 2009. "The Effect of Cooperative Learning on Science Achievement and Attitudes toward Science in the Third Grade." Unpublished Master's Thesis, American University of Beirut, Beirut.

Karadaghlian, S. B. 2014. "The Effect of Computer-Based Games on the Academic Achievement and Motivation towards Biology of Grade 8 Students." Unpublished Master's Thesis, Lebanese University, Beirut.

Karkar, L. 2013. "ر تدريس علم الأحياء باستخدام اللوح التفاعلي في تحصيل طلاب الصف الأول ثانوي في ثانوية الازهر في طرابلس." Unpublished Master's Thesis, Lebanese University, Beirut.

Sawma, Y. 2014. "The Roles of Figures of Speech in the Process of Conceptual Change in the Physics Classroom." Unpublished Master's Thesis, Lebanese American University, Beirut.

Sleem, F. 2013. "The Impact of Using Teacher-Guided Facebook in Biology Teaching on Students' Motivation and Achievement in Biology." Unpublished Master's Thesis, Lebanese University, Beirut.

Zeidan, M. 2014. "The Effect of Self-Regulation (Checklist as a Tool of Learning) on Students' Motivation and Achievement in Biology." Unpublished Master's Thesis, Lebanese University, Beirut.

ARABIC LANGUAGE TEACHING

Demachkie, M. 2008. "The Collaborative Strategic Reading Strategy to Improve Students' Reading Comprehension in Arabic." Unpublished Master's Thesis, American University of Beirut, Beirut.

El Rayshouny, L. 2014. "Contribution d'un dispositif de didactique intégrée à la prise de parole des élèves en arabe classique : Recherche action menée dans une école privée au Liban." Mastère non publié, Université Saint Joseph, Beyrouth.

بدر الدين، حسين. 2014. أثر استعمال اللّغة المعاصرة في تعليم البلاغة. ماستر غير منشورة. الجامعة اللبنانية. بيروت. لبنان. (رقم تسلسلي 123)

بلوط، زينب. 2014. فعاليّة برنامج تعليم حروف الأبجديّة العربيّة بإدخال الحواس في تحسين القراءة لدى تلاميذ الصفّ الأوّل الأساسيّ يعانون من صعوبات في القراءة. رسالة ماستر غير منشور. الجامعة اللبنانية. بيروت. لبنان. (رقم تسلسلي 136)

حجازي، رشا. 2015. فعاليّة برنامج الحرف الملوّن في اكتساب مهارة القراءة والكتابة لدى تلاميذ الصّف الأساسيّ الأوّل الذين يعانون من عسر في القراءة والكتابة. رسالة ماستر غير منشور. الجامعة اللبنانية. بيروت. لبنان. (رقم تسلسلي 173)

دمشقية، رندة منير. 2011. تدريس اللّغة العربيّة للتلاميذ اللّبنانيّين العائدين من بلد أجنبيّ. رسالة ماستر غير منشور. جامعة القديس يوسف. بيروت. لبنان. (رقم تسلسلي 649)

شاتيلا، ندى شفيق. 2014. أثر الحوافز والإبداع في التعبير الشفويّ والكتابيّ في تعزيز انتماء المتعلّم إلى اللّغة العربيّة (الصفّ الأوّل الثانويّ). رسالة ماستر غير منشور. الجامعة اللبنانية. بيروت. لبنان. (رقم تسلسلي 227)

شعيب، حسيب عبد الحليم. 2011. مرجع المعلّم في طرائق تدريس اللّغة العربيّة في المراحل الابتدائيّة والمتوسّطة والثانويّة. دار الكتب العالميّة. بيروت. لبنان. (رقم تسلسلي 3000)

عسّاف، محمد يوسف. 2013. أثر الكومبيوتر في تعليم قواعد اللّغة العربيّة على تحصيل الطلّاب (الصفّ الاساسيّ الثامن). رسالة ماستر غير منشور. الجامعة اللبنانية. بيروت. لبنان. (رقم تسلسلي 258)

علامة، سامية محمد. 2000. نقل الطفل من العاميّة إلى العربيّة الفصيحة في رياض الأطفال. رسالة دبلوم غير منشور. جامعة القدّيس يوسف. بيروت. لبنان. (رقم تسلسلي 677)

فرحات، درية كمال. 2013. دور تعليم القواعد في تنمية التحصيل اللّغويّ (المرحلة المتوسّطة). رشاد برس. بيروت. لبنان. (رقم تسلسلي 3029)

المعلوف، منير. 2005. الطرائق الناشطة في تعليم اللّغة العربيّة وآدابها في الحلقة الثالثة من التعليم الأساسيّ. رسالة ماستر غير منشور. جامعة الروح القدس. كسليك. لبنان. (رقم تسلسلي 601)

مكرزل، الياس خليل. 2005. تعلّم اللّغة العربيّة في الحلقة الثالثة من التعليم الأساسيّ وفي المرحلة الثانويّة (مشاكل وحلول). دبلوم غير منشور. جامعة الروح القدس. الكسليك. لبنان. (رقم تسلسلي 602)

الهاشم، نهاد. 2003. تطوّر تعليم القراءة العربيّة في المرحلة المتوسّطة (الصف السابع الأساسيّ). رسالة ماستر غير منشور. جامعة اللبنانية. بيروت. لبنان. (رقم تسلسلي 99)

الهاشمي، عابد توفيق. 2000. طرائق تدريس مهارات اللغة العربية وآدابها للمراحل الدراسية. مؤسسة الرسالة للطباعة. بيروت. لبنان. (رقم تسلسلي 841)

CITIZENSHIP EDUCATION

Daccache, S. J. 2013. *Pluralisme, vivre-ensemble et citoyenneté au Liban : Le salut vient-il de l'école ? Etude comparative des finalités, des objectifs et des valeurs transcommunautaires des écoles libanaises chrétiennes, musulmanes et laïques*. Paris : L'Harmattan.

Khalifé, A. 2013. "Une école *extra-muros*: l'impact de la pédagogie du voyage sur l'acquisition des compétences communicationnelles et sociales du civisme." *Recherches pédagogiques* 23: 45–73.

Kiwan, F. 2007. "La citoyenneté, histoire, différentes acceptions et enjeux actuels au Liban." *Travaux et jours* 79.

Moghaizel-Nasr, N. 2007. "Education à la citoyenneté." *Travaux et jours* 79.

الأعور، لبنى. 2014. دور الفلسفة في تعزيز عناصر المواطنية لدى طلاب الثالث الثانوي. رسالة ماستر غير منشورة. الجامعة اللبنانية. بيروت. لبنان. (رقم تسلسلي 13)

الأمين، عدنان، وأبو شديد، كمال. 2008. التربية والمواطنة المعارف المفاهيم المواقف والأعمال - نتائج دراسة لطلبة الصف التاسع في لبنان من منظور دولي. برنامج الأمم المتحدة الإنمائي / مجلس الإنماء والاعمار / وزارة التربية والتعليم العالي. بيروت. لبنان. (رقم تسلسلي 131)

بو فياض، ناديا. 2013. حقوق المواطن وواجباته بين النصوص الدستورية ومناهج ومحتوى كتب التربية الوطنية والتنشئة المدنية للمرحلة الثانوية في لبنان. رسالة ماستر غير منشورة. الجامعة اللبنانية. بيروت. لبنان. (رقم تسلسلي 401)

بيضون، بثينة. 2015. دور المشرف التربوي في تفعيل التربية على المواطنية في المدرسة: مدارس المصطفى(ص) نموذجا.

حلاق، حسان. 2012. إشكالية المشاريع التربوية وتوحيد كتب التاريخ في لبنان: مشاريع للتوحيد أم للتفرقة؟ تعلم مادة التاريخ وتعليمها: دروس من لبنان وللبنان. الهيئة اللبنانية للعلوم التربوية. بيروت. لبنان. ص.ص. 131–39 (رقم تسلسلي 751)

شعيب، مها. 2014. دلالات تأثير تهميش التماسك الاجتماعي في المدارس الثانوية في اتجاهات التلامذة السياسية والاجتماعية والمدنية في لبنان. عمران، عدد 10. المركز العربي للأبحاث ودراسة السياسات. ص.ص. 7–24 (رقم تسلسلي 401)

العكرة، أدونيس العكره. 2007. المواطنية في مبادئها وقيمها. دار الطليعة. بيروت. لبنان. (رقم تسلسلي 65)

فريحه، نمر. 2002. فعالية المدرسة في التربية على المواطنية. شركة المطبوعات للتوزيع. بيروت. لبنان. (رقم تسلسلي 861)

فريحة، نمر. 2005. التربية الوطنية، منهاجها وطرائق تدريسها. دار الفكر اللبناني. بيروت. لبنان. (رقم تسلسلي 903)

فريحة، نمر. 2012. من المواطنة إلى التربية المواطنية: سيرورة وتحديات. المركز الدولي لعلوم الانسان — بيبلوس. جبيل. لبنان. (رقم تسلسلي 794)

ياسين، فاطمة. 2012. التاريخ الموحد والمتعدد: أثر كل منهما في بناء المواطنية. تعلم مادة التاريخ وتعليمها: دروس من لبنان وللبنان. الهيئة اللبنانية للعلوم التربوية. بيروت. لبنان. ص.ص. 147–51 (رقم تسلسلي 823)

ICT IN EDUCATION

Alameh, S. 2013. "The Impact of Using Computers as Cognitive Tools on Grade 10 Lebanese Students' Attitudes and Conceptual Understanding in Physics." Unpublished Master's Thesis, American University of Beirut, Beirut.

Aoun, A. 2013. "Les élèves du cycle 3 au sein de situations de production technique: quelles expériences techniques, relationnelles et éducatives." Mémoire non publié, Université Libanaise, Beyrouth.

Bogharian, T. 2004. "Technology-Based Unit in Middle School Science." Unpublished Master's Thesis, Lebanese American University, Beirut.

Eid, N. 2008. "L'intégration des TICE dans l'enseignement des sciences de la vie et de la terre : avantages et limites : cas des concepts reliés au système nerveux en classe de seconde." Mémoire non publié, Université Saint-Joseph, Beyrouth.

Hage, C. 2015. "Le tri des déchets et le recyclage : changement de comportement des élèves de EB6 à travers le blog." Mémoire non publié, Université Libanaise, Beyrouth.

Halawi, S. 2014. "Le tableau blanc interactif (TBI) : un outil technologique pour répondre à un besoin pédagogique." Mémoire non publié, Université Libanaise, Beyrouth.

Karadaghlian, S. 2014. "The Effect of Computer Based Games on the Academic Achievement and Motivation towards Biology of Grade 8 Students." Unpublished Master's Thesis, Lebanese University, Beirut.

Kazan, S. 2015. "The Effect of Assistive Technology (AT) Training on Science Teachers' Self-Efficacy and Attitude in Inclusive Schools." Unpublished Master's Thesis, Lebanese University, Beirut.

Mcheik, M. 2015. "Impact des TICE sur l'acquisition des apprenants en Biologie de la première année secondaire au lycée officiel de Tamnin, et sur le développement de leurs réflexivités." Mémoire non publié, Université Libanaise, Beyrouth.

Rabaa, M. 2015. "The Impact of E-Learning Using IWB on 8th Grade Students' Achievement in Chemistry at an Intermediate School in Beirut." Unpublished Master's Thesis, Lebanese University, Beirut.

Sleem, F. 2013. "The Impact of Using Teacher-Guided Facebook in Biology Teaching on Students' Motivation and Achievement in Biology." Unpublished Master's Thesis, Lebanese University, Beirut.

عبد الخالق، فؤاد. 2005. التكنولوجيا التعليمية في تعليم العلوم في المدارس الثانوية. التربية والتعليم وتكنولوجيا المعلومات في البلدان العربية: قضايا واتجاهات. الهيئة اللبنانية للعلوم التربوية. بيروت. لبنان. ص.ص. 329–55 (الرقم التسلسلي 784)

علوية، دانيال علي. 2013. أثر تكنولوجيا الألواح التفاعلية في تحصيل مادة الفزياء لدى تلميذات الصف الثانوي الأول في إحدى ثانويات الغبيري الرسمية. رسالة ماجستير غير منشورة. جامعة القديس يوسف. بيروت. لبنان. (الرقم التسلسلي 662)

عواضة، هاشم. 2013. تعليم وتعلم مهارات استعمال الحاسوب صف البداية ولغة التعليم. أوراق جامعية، العدد 38. رابطة الأساتذة في الجامعة اللبنانية. بيروت. لبنان. (الرقم التسلسلي 425)

فقيه، ريما. 2005. اتجاهات المعلمين نحو تكنولوجيا التعليم المعتمدة في مواد العلوم (نموذج محافظة النبطية). رسالة دبلوم غير منشورة. الجامعة اللبنانية. بيروت. لبنان. (الرقم التسلسلي 546)

TEACHERS PREPARATION

أبو رجيلي سوزان. 2012. الاعداد التربوي العام في برامج التربية في الجامعات في لبنان. مجلة الأبحاث التربوية العدد 22. كلية التربية في الجامعة اللبنانية. بيروت. لبنان. ص ص. 41–63. (رقم تسلسلي 407)

أمبو سعيدي، عبدالله بن خميس والحجيري بنت حمدان فاطمة. 2009. نماذج في تغير برامج إعداد المعلم: دورة انتاج المعرفة SECI. مؤتمر المؤسسات الجامعية لإعداد المعلمين في البلدان العربية. الهيئة اللبنانية للعلوم التربوية. بيروت. لبنان. ص. ص. 241–64 (رقم تسلسلي 350)

الأيوبي، زلفا. 2009. نحو معايير عربية لضمان جودة إعداد المعلم الجامعي. مؤتمر المؤسسات الجامعية لإعداد المعلمين في البلدان العربية. الهيئة اللبنانية للعلوم التربوية. بيروت. لبنان. ص. ص. 99–116. (رقم تسلسلي 350)

بتلوني، ناصر. 2014. واقع خرجي الجامعة اللبنانية كلية التربية في سوق العمل: اختصاص تربية بدنية ورياضية. مجلة الأبحاث التربوية، عدد 24. كلية التربية الجامعة اللبنانية، بيروت، 2014، 9–57. (رقم تسلسلي 412)

بلوط، علي، واقع الاعداد في كلية التربية بين النسق المؤسساتي والسياسة التربوية. مجلة الأبحاث التربوية، عدد 23. كلية التربية الجامعة اللبنانية. بيروت. لبنان. ص. ص. 1–9. (رقم تسلسلي 410)

جرار، سمير. 2009. اعداد المعلم العربي للألفية الثالثة: تحديات واتجاهات. مؤتمر المؤسسات الجامعية لإعداد المعلمين في البلدان العربية. الهيئة اللبنانية للعلوم التربوية. بيروت. لبنان. ص. ص. 13–33. (رقم تسلسلي 350)

جرار، سمير ووهبه، نخلة. 2009. الاتجاهات العالمية في ضمان جودة إعداد المعلمين والمعلمات وفي الترخيص للمهنة والترقي بها. مؤتمر المؤسسات الجامعية لإعداد المعلمين في البلدان العربيّة. الهيئة اللبنانية للعلوم التربوية. بيروت. لبنان. ص. ص. 37–97. (رقم تسلسلي 350)

خورا، سانجيان مارسيل. 2012. شروط القبول والتخرج في شهادة الاجازة في التربية. مجلة الأبحاث التربوية عدد 22. كلية التربية في الجامعة اللبنانية. بيروت. لبنان. ص. ص. 97–102. (رقم تسلسلي 409)

دواني، كمال. 2009. نظرة مستقبلية حول اعداد المعلمين في العالم العربي. مؤتمر المؤسسات الجامعية لإعداد المعلمين في البلدان العربيّة. الهيئة اللبنانية للعلوم التربوية. بيروت 2009، 297–318. (رقم تسلسلي 350)

الروادي، نعيم. 2009. التنمية الشاملة للمجتمع وإعداد المعلم المستقبلي: معادلة مطلوبة. مؤتمر المؤسسات الجامعية لإعداد المعلمين في البلدان العربيّة. الهيئة اللبنانية للعلوم التربوية. بيروت. لبنان. ص. ص. 265–95. (رقم تسلسلي 350)

زكريا نورما. 2012. دراسة المقررات في مكوني الاعداد العام والخاص في برامج التربية في الجامعات اللبنانية. مجلة الأبحاث التربوية عدد 22. كلية التربية في الجامعة اللبنانية. بيروت. لبنان. ص. ص. 21–40. (رقم تسلسلي 406)

السمراء، سامي. 2014. الاجازة في التربية في جامعة سيدة اللويزة. قضايا النوعية في التعليم العالي في البلدان العربيّة. الهيئة اللبنانية للعلوم التربوية. بيروت. لبنان. ص. ص. 485–93. (رقم تسلسلي 701)

سنجقدار، أحمد. 2002. تطوير المعلمين لحاجاتهم في مجال الاعداد في لبنان. إعداد المعلمين في البلدان العربيّة. الهيئة اللبنانية للعلوم التربوية. بيروت. لبنان. ص.ص. 127–51. (رقم تسلسلي 770)

غيث غازي. 2013. اعداد المعلمين والمعلمات في مؤسسات التعليم العالي مواكبة لتطور مناهج التعليم العام في لبنان. المركز التربوي للبحوث والانماء. بيروت. لبنان. (رقم تسلسلي 285)

كبّة، إبراهيم، ومروة، مازن. 2008. آراء أساتذة التربية في الجامعة اللبنانية لدور ومهام الكلية الحالية والمستقبلية. أوراق جامعية عدد 30، س 16. رابطة الأساتذة في الجامعة اللبنانية. بيروت. لبنان. ص.ص. 179–96. (رقم تسلسلي 420)

TEACHERS PROFESSIONAL DEVELOPMENT

Hoyek, S. 2007. "Représentations indentitaires et rapport à la formations continue : cas des enseignants de français du Liban." *La revue de l'ILE* 3.

Mahfouz, S. 2014. "The Impact of a One Year School-Based Induction Program on Elementary Beginning Teachers." Unpublished Master's Thesis, Lebanese University, Beirut.

Matta, M. 2015. "The Effects of Well Trained Teachers in Grades 6, 7, and 8 on Creating a Positive Classroom Environment in Lebanese Schools in Mount Lebanon: Meten El Shemali and Kesrwan." Unpublished Master's Thesis, Lebanese University, Beirut.

Shoufani, E. 2005. "The Effects of a Professional Development Programs of the Implementation of a Mathematical Problem Solving in the Classroom." Unpublished Master's Thesis, Haigazian University, Beirut.

الأمين، عدنان. 2002. الدراسة التقييمية لبرامج تدريب المعلمين. تقييم المناهج التعليمية الجديدة في لبنان. الهيئة اللبنانية للعلوم التربوية. (رقم تسلسلي 3060)

الحويك، سمير. 2002. كيفية إدخال المعلمين في ثقافة التدريب المستمر. اعداد المعلمين في البلدان العربية. الهيئة اللبنانية للعلوم التربوية. بيروت. لبنان. ص.ص. 251–67 (رقم تسلسلي 755)

الحويك، سمير. 2009. إعداد وتدريب المعلمين. كلية العلوم التربوية تمهين التعليم في لبنان : وثائق المؤتمر الذي نظمته كلية العلوم التربوية، 28 آذار 2009. جامعة القديس يوسف. بيروت. لبنان. ص.ص. 107–41 (رقم تسلسلي 34)

داغر، أنطوان. 2004. تجربة في تدريب معلمي الرياضيات: تغيّر في تصورات المعلمين حول حل المسائل وفي ممارساتهم التعليمية. مجلة الأبحاث التربوية، العدد 21. كلية التربية، الجامعة اللبنانية. بيروت. لبنان. (رقم تسلسلي 403)

رضوان، رفاه رمزي. 2014. دور المدير في دعم المعلم المبتدىء غير المعد تربوياً. رسالة ماستر غير منشورة. الجامعة اللبنانية. بيروت. لبنان. (رقم تسلسلي 200)

عقل، أنور. 2007. دورة تدريبية للمعلمات في أساليب التقويم الحديثة. دار النهضة العربية. (رقم تسلسلي 261)

عقيل، ريما. 2015. دور المشرف التربوي في تدريب معلم اللغة العربية على بناء خطة التطوير المهني. رسالة ماستر غير منشورة. الجامعة اللبنانية. بيروت. لبنان. (رقم تسلسلي 263)

غانم، شربل. 2013. دور المدير كقائد تربويّ في عمليّة التّدريب المستمرّ للمعلّمين وتنميتهم مهنيًا في المدارس الأنطونيّة. رسالة ماستر غير منشورة. الجامعة اللبنانية. بيروت. لبنان. (رقم تسلسلي 276)

كبريت، سمير. 2011. التدريب والتدرب على التعليم. دار النهضة العربية. 2011 (رقم تسلسلي 3009)

كفوري، كارول. 2001. إدارة الجودة الشاملة وتدريب المعلمين. الإدارة التربوية في البلدان العربية. الهيئة اللبنانية للعلوم التربوية. 2001. ص.ص. 273–94 (رقم تسلسلي 802)

المقابلة، محمد قاسم. 2011. التدريب التربوي والأساليب القيادية الحديثة وتطبيقاتها التربوية. دار الشروق. (رقم تسلسلي 996)

TEACHERS PROFESSIONAL PRACTICE

Al-Asmar, L. 2008. "The Effect of Teacher Corrective Feedback on Student Intrinsic Motivation, Time On-Task, and Achievement." Unpublished Master's Thesis, American University of Beirut, Beirut.

Ayoub, K. 2014. "The Effect of Implementing Diverse Evaluation on Teachers' Performance in Class Environment and Instruction Domains in a Private School in Mount Lebanon." Unpublished Master's Thesis, Lebanese University, Beirut.

Azar, A. 2014. "Exploring Leaderships Capabilities and Implication on Teachers' Performance." Unpublished Master's Thesis, Lebanese American University, Beirut.

Farhat, A. 2011. "The Impact of Clinical Supervision on Teachers' Performance in Classroom Managerial Skills." Unpublished Master's Thesis, Lebanese University, Beirut.

Farhat, K. R. 2012. "Effet de l'auto-efficacité de l'enseignant sur les élèves à risque de décrochage scolaire." Mémoire non publié, Université Saint Joseph, Beyrouth.

Papazian-Zohrabian, G. 2010. "Les effets de la maltraitance sur la vie socio-affective et la performance scolaire des enfants." *Revue de l'Institut libanais d'éducateurs* 4: 11–24.

Soubra, A. 2015. "Empowering Teachers as Leaders." Unpublished Master's Thesis, Lebanese American University, Beirut.

بو زين الدين، أمل. 2002. آلية تقييم أداء المعلمين وتقنياته. إعداد المعلمين في البلدان العربية. الهيئة اللبنانية للعلوم التربوية. بيروت. لبنان. ص. ص. 237–49 (رقم تسلسلي 737)

خنيصر، ماري تريز. 2015. أثر تطبيق الإشراف التربوي التطوّري في تحسين الممارسات التدريسيّة. رسالة ماستر مهني غير منشورة. الجامعة اللبنانيّة. بيروت. لبنان. (رقم تسلسلي 190)

زيتوني، مهى. 2015. أثر استعمال الإشراف الإكلينيكي على تحسين أداء المعلّم في مدرسة خاصة في منطقة جبل لبنان. رسالة ماجستير غير منشورة. الجامعة اللبنانيّة. بيروت. لبنان. (رقم تسلسلي 207)

الشدياق، لمى. 2014. إشراف الأقران وأثره في تحسين أداء معلمة في مدرسة خاصة في بيروت. رسالة ماستر مهني غير منشورة. الجامعة اللبنانيّة. بيروت. لبنان. (رقم تسلسلي 54)

الطفيلي، ندى. 2011. تقويم أداء المعلمين في الثانويات الخاصة ضمن منطقة النبطية. رسالة ماجستير غير منشورة. الجامعة الإسلاميّة. بيروت. لبنان. (رقم تسلسلي 591)

عواضة، هاشم. 2008. تطوير أداء المعلمين: كفايات التعليم والتأهيل المتواصل والإشراف. دار العلم للملايين. بيروت. لبنان. (رقم تسلسلي 962)

قاسم، آمال. 2015. دور الإشراف المتنوّع في تنمية أداء معلمات المرحلة الأساسيّة (الحلقة الثانية) في مدرسة خاصة في ضاحية بيروت. رسالة ماجستير غير منشورة. الجامعة اللبنانيّة. بيروت. لبنان. (رقم تسلسلي 300)

الموعد، ياسمين. 2014. دور المشرف التربوي في تطوير كفايات المعلّم التكنولوجيّة في المرحلة التعليميّة الأساسيّة بما يتوافق مع اقتصاد المعرفة. رسالة ماستر مهني غير منشورة. الجامعة اللبنانيّة. بيروت. لبنان. (رقم تسلسلي 95)

INSTITUTIONAL ASSESSMENT

Imad, G. 2006. "Evaluating the Department of English in French Medium School." Unpublished Master's Thesis, Lebanese American University, Beirut.

Khatib, I. 2002. "An Assessment of Distance Learning Perceptions in Lebanon." Unpublished Master's Thesis, Lebanese American University, Beirut.

أبو رجيلي، سوزان. 2002. تقييم برامج إعداد المعلمين. إعداد المعلمين في البلدان العربية. الهيئة اللبنانية للعلوم التربوية. ص ص. 211–36. بيروت. لبنان. (رقم تسلسلي 717)

اسماعيل، رنا. 2014. منهجية دراسة التقويم الذاتي لأثر برنامج التطوير الإداري. رحلة في التطوير التربوي: تجربة المبرات. دار الشفق للنشر والتوزيع. ص ص. 55–91. بيروت. لبنان. (رقم تسلسلي 6)

بديع، منى. 2012. تقويم المؤسسة المدرسية وأثره في رفع مستوى الجودة في التحصيل العلمي: نماذج من مدارس صيدا الخاصة. رسالة ماستر غير منشورة. جامعة القديس يوسف. بيروت. لبنان. (رقم تسلسلي 653)

بوزين الدين، أمل. 2002. آلية تقييم أداء المعلمين وتقنياته. إعداد المعلمين في البلدان العربية. الهيئة اللبنانية للعلوم التربوية. ص ص. 237-49. بيروت. لبنان. (رقم تسلسلي 737)

رزق الله، دلال. 2015. تطوير معايير التقييم الذاتي التشاركي وإجراءاته بحسب مبادىء «مجتمع التعلُم المهني»: نموذج لتجذير التجربة في واقع المدرسة اللبنانيّة. أطروحة دكتوراه غير منشورة. الجامعة اللبنانية. بيروت. لبنان. (رقم تسلسلي 1)

سلامة، رمزي & وهبة، نخلة. 2009. تقييم مؤسسات تكوين أعضاء الهيئات التعليمية في سبع دول عربية أفريقية. المؤسسات الجامعية لإعداد المعلمين في البلدان العربية. الهيئة اللبنانية للعلوم التربوية. ص ص. 152-86. بيروت. لبنان. (رقم تسلسلي 766)

شبارو، ريما أحمد. 2007. المدارس المعززة للصحة: تقويم واقع الصحة المدرسية في عدد من مدارس بيروت. رسالة ماستر غير منشورة. جامعة القديس يوسف. بيروت. لبنان. (رقم تسلسلي 619)

طفيلي، ندى سعيد. 2011. تقويم أداء المعلمين في الثانويات الخاصة ضمن منطقة النبطية. رسالة غير منشورة. الجامعة الاسلامية. بيروت. لبنان. (رقم تسلسلي 591)

عكاري، ريما كرامي & رزق الله، دلال سمير. 2014. تطوير تقييم الأداء التربوي للمدرسة اللبنانية مقاربة لبناء معايير التقييم الذاتي وإجراءاته وتجذيرها في واقع السياق المحلي. إضافات: المجلة العربية لعلم الاجتماع ع. 25، شتاء. الجمعية العربية لعلوم الاجتماع. ص.ص: 158-81. بيروت. لبنان. (رقم تسلسلي 385)

قانصو، عائدة محمد. 2013. دور التقويم الشامل في إنماء الفرد اقتصاديا واجتماعيا: دراسة مقارنة لنماذج من مجتمعات ريفية أمية ومجتمعات مدنية متعلمة في منطقة النبطية. رسالة ماستر غير منشورة. جامعة القديس يوسف. بيروت. لبنان. (رقم تسلسلي 654)

كوراني، حسن. 2014. التقييم التربوي الواقعي: رؤيته التربوية وأثره في «أسس تقييم» مناهجنا الجديدة : دراسة نظرية تحليلية. رسالة ماستر غير منشورة. جامعة القديس يوسف. بيروت. لبنان. (رقم تسلسلي 670)

نخلة، وهبة. 2008. الأضرار المؤسسية التي سببتها حرب تموز في المدارس. آثار حرب تموز 2006 على القطاع التربوي في لبنان: أعمال الحلقة الدراسية التي عقدت في 2007/01/13 في المعهد الألماني، بيروت. المركز الدولي لعلوم الإنسان. ص ص. 10-24. بيروت. لبنان. (رقم تسلسلي 375)

النقيب، عصام. 2009. تقييم نوعي لبرامج التربية في الجامعات العربية: تجربة مشروع التعليم العالي لبرنامج الأمم المتحدة الإنمائي. المؤسسات الجامعية لإعداد المعلمين في البلدان العربية. الهيئة اللبنانية للعلوم التربوية. ص ص. 187-207. بيروت. لبنان. (رقم تسلسلي 711)

STUDENT ASSESSMENT

Ayoub, K. 2014. "The Effect of Implementing Diverse Evaluation on Teachers' Performance in Class Environment and Instruction Domains in a Private School in Mount Lebanon." Unpublished Master's Thesis, Lebanese University, Beirut.

Bohsali, L. 2010. "Research-Based Design for Informal Assessment Techniques." Unpublished Master's Thesis, Lebanese American University, Beirut.

El-Hage, F. 2013. "L'approche par compétences: de méthodes d'enseignement aux modalitésd'évaluation." وقائع مؤتمر، التجديد التربوي: تجارب في التطوير المدرسي. 95–106." Rafic Hariri Foundation, Beirut.

El-Hassan, K. 2014. "Modern Student Evaluation Practices." *Educational Innovation: Teacher Training*, 39–51. Hariri Foundation, Beirut.

Itani, H. 2004. "Causes of Low Academic Achievement in the Official Exams in a Public School: A Case Study." Unpublished Master's Thesis, Lebanese American University, Beirut.

Kandil, B. 2008. "Pedagogical Guide for Using Technology in Formative Assessment." Unpublished Master's Thesis, Lebanese American University, Beirut.

MEHE (Ministry of Education and Higher Education)/CERD (Center for Educational Research and Development). 2012. "Évaluation diagnostique des acquis scolaires." MEHE/CERD, Beyrouth.

World Bank. 2013. "Lebanon Student Assessment." SABER Country Report, World Bank, Washington, DC.

الحسن، كرمة. 2002.، تقييم نظام التقييم، دراسة، تقييم المناهج التعليمية الجديدة في لبنان، تقرير غير منشور، بيروت، الهيئة اللبنانية للعلوم التربوية (رقم تسلسلي 3059)

الخوري، توما جورج. 2008. القياس والتقويم في التربية والتعليم. المؤسسة الجامعية للدراسات. (رقم تسلسلي 961)

الشَّامي، منى. 2004. التقييم التربوي في مرحلة الروضة واقع ومشكلات-محافظة الشمال. رسالة ماستر غير منشورة. الجامعة اللبنانية. بيروت. لبنان. (رقم تسلسلي 49)

عبد الخالق، رشراش أنيس. 2007. طرائق النشاط في التعليم والتقويم التربوي: فصل خاص عن التقويم في لبنان. دار النهضة العربية. بيروت. لبنان. (رقم تسلسلي 253)

مارون ، جورج. 2010. أسس التقويم التربوي ومعاييره. المؤسسة الحديثة للكتاب. بيروت. لبنان. (رقم تسلسلي 984)

المركز التربوي للبحوث والانماء / وزارة التربية والتعليم العالي / الهيئة الوطنية للمدرسة الرسمية. 2015. التقرير العام النهائي بنتيجة ورش العمل الوطنية الموسعة التي نفذت حول الامتحانات الرسمية «مضمون، آليات ونتائج» بين 2009-12-16 الى 2010-3-6. المركز التربوي للبحوث والإنماء / وزارة التربية والتعليم العالي / الهيئة الوطنية للمدرسة الرسمية. بيروت. لبنان. (رقم تسلسلي 82)

مقلد، سمر. 2002. التقييم والعلاقة مع الأهل في مرحلة الروضة. رياض الأطفال في لبنان. الهيئة اللبنانية للعلوم التربوية. بيروت. لبنان. ص. ص: 301–31 (رقم تسلسلي 809)

PARENTS AND COMMUNITY ENGAGEMENT

Abdul-Ahad, D. M. 2008. "The Relationship between Parental Attitude towards Homework and Students' Academic Achievement at the Upper Elementary Level." Unpublished Master's Thesis, American University of Beirut, Beirut.

Awad, R. 2006. "The Effect of Parental Involvement on the Reading Achievement of a Selected Group of Grade Two Students." Unpublished Master's Thesis, American University of Beirut, Beirut.

Cofsky, M. B. 2005. "The Effects of Parental Involvement at Home and Parent Education Level on Student Achievement in Elementary School." Unpublished Master's Thesis, Haigazian University, Beirut.

El hajjeh, M.-N. "La collaboration éducateurs-parents contribuant à l'acquisition du projet individuel de l'enfant éficient physique." Mémoire de Mastère non publié, Université Libanaise, Beyrouth.

Hajj, L. 2003. "Parents' Perceptions of Science and Science Teaching." Unpublished Master's Thesis, American University of Beirut, Beirut.

Issa, M.-A. S. 2007. "Parental Involvement and Health Risk Behaviors among Lebanese High School Students." Unpublished Master's Thesis, American University of Beirut, Beirut.

Khater, C. 2009. "Test Anxiety as a Mediating Variable between Parenting Styles and Academic Achievement." Unpublished Master's Thesis, Haigazian University, Beirut.

Rouhana, S. 2013. "Exploring Lack of Parental Involvement in a School for Special Needs." Unpublished Master's Thesis, Lebanese University, Beirut.

أديب، سليم / شليطا، فيفيان. 2006. آراء اهالي الطلاب حول ادراج قضايا الصحة الانجابية والنوع الاجتماعي في المدارس. المركز التربوي للبحوث والانماء. بيروت. لبنان. (رقم تسلسلي 114)

الحلبي، لارا جهاد. 2014. دور مدير المدرسة في تفعيل العلاقة بين المدرسة والأهل والمجتمع المحلي من خلال الانشطة اللاصفية (مدرسة عماطور المتوسطة الرسمية). رسالة ماستر غير منشورة. الجامعة اللبنانية. بيروت. لبنان. (رقم تسلسلي 32)

ديب، ميرنا أنطونيوس. 2007. علاقة مديري المدارس بلجان الأهل في المدارس الخاصة غير المجانية (المدارس الكاثوليكية في مدينة جونيه نموذجاً). رسالة ماستر غير منشورة. الجامعة اللبنانية. بيروت. لبنان. (رقم تسلسلي 193)

فضول، سيمون. 2006. المدرسة والاهل: من المصلحة المشتركة الى الشراكة في التربية. الهيئة اللبنانية للعلوم التربوية. بيروت. لبنان. (رقم تسلسلي 795)

كلوت، قاسم. 2007. أثر الاعلام التلفزيون والاسرة والمدرسة في تكوين الوعي السياسي عند اطفال الصف السادس الاساسي في مدارس ضاحية بيروت الجنوبية. رسالة دبلوم غير منشورة. الجامعة اللبنانية. بيروت. لبنان. (رقم تسلسلي 553)

مقلد، سمر. 2002. التقييم والعلاقة مع الأهل في مرحلة الروضة. كتاب رياض الاطفال. الهيئة اللبنانية للعلوم التربوية. بيروت. لبنان. ص.ص. 301–31 (رقم تسلسلي 809)

موصللي، رشا. 2004. العوامل المؤثرة في نجاح ورسوب التلاميذ في بداية الحلقة الثانية بين العائلة والمدرسة. رسالة دبلوم غير منشورة. الجامعة اللبنانية. بيروت. لبنان. (رقم تسلسلي 567)

Public Perception Study Methodology

To study the public perception of education in Lebanon, the World Bank worked with the Consultation and Research Institute (CRI) on a tailored sampling approach to gather the sampling base. One of the main challenges in conducting household surveys in Lebanon is the lack of a recent population census; additionally, available official statistics either do not reflect the resident population or do not have a contact list or addresses (that is, they do not have a sampling base). To mitigate this challenge, this study adopts a tailored sampling approach, which was designed in consultation with the Lebanon Central Administration of Statistics (CAS) and international partners with technical expertise in household surveys (the World Bank, UN agencies) and was applied previously in several national surveys supported by international partners and UN agencies.

The tailored sampling methodology covers all Lebanese territories, except for Palestinian camps, formal and informal refugee camps, and a limited number of clusters for security reasons (for example, Arsal in the Bekaa). The statistical unit in this approach was the "household" representing the individuals permanently residing in their primary dwelling. The sample size was set to 1,500 questionnaires, with one questionnaire per household. The sample of household units was distributed geographically per governorate according to the latest official statistics. Table B.1 displays the three national official surveys that were published by the Lebanon CAS covering, respectively, 1997, 2004, and 2009. The study used the latest official distribution (2009).

Within each governorate, the household sample was distributed by district (*caza*) following the population distribution published by CAS in 1997.[1] Within every caza, the questionnaires were also distributed by *circonscription foncière* (CF), the smallest administrative unit in Lebanon. The determination of the number of questionnaires per CF followed was proportional to the demographic weight of each CF in a caza. Three additional conditions were used to determine the number of questionnaires: (1) number of households should not be below a limited number (for example, four); (2) an acceptable coverage of densely populated areas versus semi-deserted areas was needed; and (3) the sample should cover a minimum of 15 percent of the existing CFs (not less than 200 CFs from all over the Lebanese territories).

There were no "filters" or "exclusion criteria" based on nationality, and all permanent residents could be included in the sample regardless of their nationality. Moreover, the sample did not "filter out" or "exclude" units based on the number of children enrolled in schools, as all households were covered, including households with no children enrolled in schools.

TABLE B.1 **Distribution of the resident population in Lebanon per governorate (three national studies)**

GOVERNORATE	CAS 1997 SURVEY (%)	CAS 2004 SURVEY (%)	CAS 2009 SURVEY (%)	SAMPLE-97 (NUMBER OF HOUSEHOLDS)	SAMPLE-04 (NUMBER OF HOUSEHOLDS)	SAMPLE-09 (NUMBER OF HOUSEHOLDS)
Beirut	11.06	11.56	10.82	166	173	162
Mount Lebanon	39.97	42.20	42.81	600	633	642
North Lebanon	17.48	18.45	17.54	262	277	263
Bekaa	12.69	11.68	11.75	190	175	176
South Lebanon	11.30	10.16	10.37	170	152	156
Nabatieh	7.50	5.94	6.70	112	89	101
Lebanon	**100.00**	**100.00**	**100.00**	**1,500**	**1,500**	**1,500**

Source: Data provided by CAS, http://cas.gov.lb/index.php/demographic-and-social-en.
Note: CAS = Central Administration of Statistics.

TABLE B.2 **Final sample distribution per governorate, district, and CF**

GOVERNORATE	DISTRICT/CAZA	TOTAL CFs	EMPTY CFs	TOTAL NON-EMPTY CFs	TOTAL POPULATION 1997	TOTAL POPULATION 1997 (%)	INITIAL DISTRIBUTION (NUMBER OF HOUSEHOLDS)	ACTUAL DISTRIBUTION (NUMBER OF HOUSEHOLDS)
Beirut	Beirut	13	1	12	403,338	100	162	167
Beirut total		**13**	**1**	**12**	**403,338**	**100**	**162**	**167**
Bekaa	Baalbek	99	22	77	227,758	42	74	74
	Hermel	12	4	8	36,002	7	12	13
	Rachayya	43	15	28	33,146	6	11	11
	West Bekaa	44	8	36	65,520	12	21	21
	Zahle	65	8	57	177,037	33	58	58
Bekaa total		**263**	**57**	**206**	**539,463**	**100**	**176**	**177**
Mount Lebanon	Aley	83	16	67	163,869	11	70	71
	Baabda	57	2	55	520,164	35	222	221
	Shouf	109	19	90	153,317	10	65	65
	El Metn	103	4	99	428,166	28	182	181
	Jubail	107	15	92	80,501	5	34	35
	Kasrouane	84	12	72	161,291	11	69	68
Mount Lebanon total		**543**	**68**	**475**	**1,507,308**	**100**	**642**	**641**
Nabatiye	Bint Jubail	38	3	35	66,119	24	24	24
	Hasbaiya	23	3	20	31,003	11	11	11
	Marjaayoun	34	5	29	52,926	19	19	19
	Nabatiye	52	5	47	125,321	46	46	46
Nabatiye total		**147**	**16**	**131**	**275,369**	**100**	**101**	**100**
North Lebanon	Akkar	168	4	164	253,170	31	83	83
	Batroun	76	6	70	46,124	6	15	15
	Bcharre	24	1	23	21,242	3	7	8
	Koura	43	0	43	48,215	6	16	16
	Minieh-Danieh	63	10	53	118,681	15	39	39

continued

TABLE B.2, *continued*

GOVERNORATE	DISTRICT/CAZA	TOTAL CFs	EMPTY CFs	TOTAL NON-EMPTY CFs	TOTAL POPULATION 1997	TOTAL POPULATION 1997 (%)	INITIAL DISTRIBUTION	ACTUAL DISTRIBUTION
	Tripoli	17	1	16	264,894	33	86	88
	Zgharta	52	5	47	55,129	7	18	18
North Lebanon total		443	27	416	807,455	100	263	267
South Lebanon	Jezzine	80	17	63	20,248	4	7	7
	Saida	79	7	72	250,898	53	83	82
	Sour	75	2	73	200,949	43	66	66
South Lebanon total		234	26	208	472,095	100	156	155
Grand total		1,643	195	1,448	4,005,028		1,500	1,507

Source: Data provided by CAS, http://cas.gov.lb/index.php/demographic-and-social-en.
Note: CF = *circonscription foncière.*

The error margin corresponding to a sample size of 1,500 respondents was estimated at ±2.53 percent for an observed frequency of 50 percent at a level of confidence of 95 percent. It should be noted that the margin of error could vary according to (1) the observed frequency of each variable; (2) the standard deviation, when the variable is numeric; and (3) the adopted level of confidence.

To avoid sample biases, some preliminary results were generated from basic sociodemographic and economic variables (for example, average family size, education level, gender distribution, and age distribution) and then compared with the results published in previous studies implemented by official national bodies or international organization. The sample was found to match similar samples in other studies.

The quality control process was composed of several levels. The questionnaire design was an essential factor of the quality control. The questionnaire itself had clear definitions/sentences, indications, and filters to facilitate the work of surveyors and reduce the risk of errors. Professional surveyors, supervisors, and data entry officers with extensive experience in similar field surveys were recruited for the study. Supervisors double-checked the filled questionnaires, assisted surveyors, and conducted callbacks (or revisits) for a sample of households. The questionnaires were then rechecked at the central office of the CRI, where coding and data entry were completed. Second-round of callbacks were also conducted. To reduce survey errors even further, the questionnaire program (KOBO), which has several built-in safety nets and alerts, was used, and the CRI statisticians performed consistency checks on the data. Table B.2 presents the final sample for the study.

NOTE

1. The 2004 and 2009 surveys are limited only to the governorate level. Subcategories of geographic units are only available in the 1997 survey.

Dialogue and Protocol for Policy Uptake

The Ministry of Education and Higher Education (MEHE), the Center for Educational Research and Development (CERD), and Lebanese stakeholders can benefit from this research to inform policy and improve service delivery in Lebanon's education system. R4R is the largest and most ambitious education research program in Lebanon to date. It is also the first program to establish a strong research governance structure, which included the Technical Committee led by the CERD and including members from academia and education experts, and the Steering Committee led by the MEHE's Director General of Education and including participation of key officials from the MEHE, CERD, academia, and international partners (the World Bank, DFID, USAID). Furthermore, in-depth consultation and engagement of the full spectrum of Lebanese stakeholders has been prioritized at every stage of the program: the MEHE, CERD, other government officials, Parliamentary Committee for Education, teacher unions, schools, parents and students, private schools associations, faith groups, and the private sector. This in-depth, wide-ranging stakeholder engagement has a special importance in Lebanon, given the confessional nature of the political system and the high proportion of private and faith-based schools alongside public schools.

Research uptake requires real-time links with the national education plan and reform programs to ensure that there are live entry points to inform policy and service delivery. Institutionalizing research uptake and changing cultures around using evidence to inform policy, programs, and budgets takes time. Countries which benefit from longitudinal research or long-term series of research of 10–15 years create ecosystems and a culture of research informed policy (for example, Brazil, Vietnam, and Canada). The R4R program represents an initial step for setting up an ecosystem of research to be led by the government education institutions.

Research uptake is usually conceived of as four related strands: stakeholder engagement, capacity building, communication, and monitoring and evaluation of uptake (figure C.1).

There is case study evidence which demonstrates that research results can and do contribute to policy and/or practice impacts. The framework in figure C.2 is helpful in delineating the specific and general ways research can influence policy, practice, and capacity.

The R4R program's research uptake model in Lebanon includes the following:

1. Engagement of the Steering Committee and Technical Committee to ensure these top-priority policy makers and stakeholders are engaged and excited

FIGURE C.1

Strands of research uptake (from the United Kingdom Government)

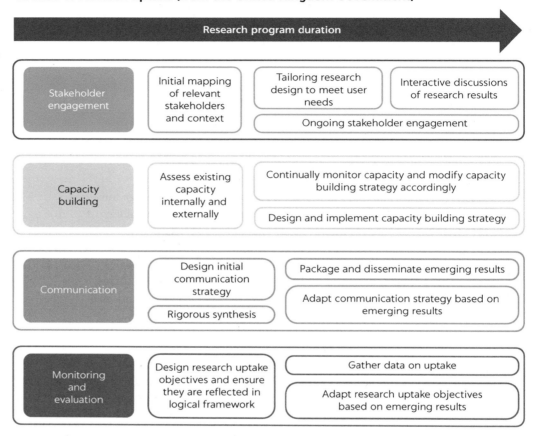

Source: UK DFID 2016 © Crown copyright 2016.
Note: The activities shown in the diagram are illustrative and will vary among programs. UK DFID = U.K. Department for International Development.

about the research products and feed in real-time reflections from policy and practice.

2. Effective engagement with the MEHE and the CERD as institutions by involving all directors and ensuring links with service providers. These directors have key policy-making and practice-making roles in each area of the system (for example, assessment, teachers, and professional development) centrally and regionally.

3. High-quality consultations with the full range of Lebanese stakeholders at each key milestone of the program.

4. Strong understanding of the political economy as it affects the education sector, including in key areas such as teachers' pay and workforce management.

5. Highly professional research management to ensure that the project is implemented with precision on deadlines and with effective management of contractors to keep client confidence.

6. A strong communications plan with timely, well-targeted communications products for stakeholders. Specific communications methods will combine findings from a number of studies to provide the information most applicable to each stakeholder group.

FIGURE C.2

"The Punton Framework": A model of how research leads to change (from the United Kingdom government)

Type of change		Symbolic	Indirect	Direct
	Instrumental	Research being used to legitimize a decision that has already been made	General ideas from research being used to influence a specific policy, practice, piece of research, etc.	Specific research influencing a specific policy, practice, piece of research, etc.
	Conceptual	Not applicable	General ideas from research feeding into general enlightenment about particular concepts	Specific research influencing the way people think about or understand an issue
	Capacity	Not applicable	General ideas from research or relationships from a research partnership improving the capacity of individuals or organizations	Specific research activities or ideas improving the capacity of individuals or organizations

How change happened

Source: UK DFID 2014 © Crown copyright 2014.
Note: UK DFID = U.K. Department for International Development.

This research will benefit from involving and sustaining participation of the following stakeholders:

1. **The MEHE/national government** in decision-making positions to shape policy more directly. Also, because the MEHE does not have final decision-making authority on many educational issues, it needs to utilize such research findings to engage and gain support from a number of other political actors, such as the Council of Ministers, the Parliament, the Council for Development and Reconstruction (CDR), and the General Inspectorate of Education. The research also identifies (a) areas for technical assistance for reform, (b) alignment with existing programs, (c) compliance with funding requirements, (d) incentives for the MEHE staff who have a proven track record in pushing forward similar educational agendas, and (e) clear comparison with international education practices and spending that can inspire motivation and action.

2. **The CERD** needs to take this opportunity to lead such research efforts in close coordination with the MEHE and use the findings in providing teacher training, setting teacher competencies, setting curricula, drafting textbooks, conducting educational research, pushing for actual learning versus curriculum with student learning profiles, aiming for fewer political constraints on change, increasing the availability of instructional resources, reducing achievement gaps using international evidence, and reaching the best ways to build teacher-student and teacher-parent relationships.

3. **Teachers** could benefit from engaging in this research for better classroom practices, favorable teacher-student relationships, positive teacher-parent relationships, awareness of dropout warning signs, and appropriate teacher working conditions.

4. **Teacher unions'** engagement in this research will contribute to better policies, more convenient teacher management and working conditions, and better teacher performance management and remuneration.

5. **School administrators'** engagement in this research will lead to better school performance and more investment in schools, focus on actual learning versus curriculum with student learning profiles; increased opportunities for decentralized school management; higher accessibility/student support; more decision-making transparency; use of international evidence on reducing achievement gaps between schools; and awareness of local best practices for school finance, management, teachers, and the physical and learning environment.

6. **International donors and multilateral agencies** can benefit from this research in funding and coordination, collecting more evidence on educational best practices to scale up programs in Lebanon and worldwide and designing programs based on the evidence/results provided to ensure relevancy and more accurate solutions to existing educational challenges.

7. **Researchers/academics/NGOs/civil society groups engagement in the research** to better affect and advocate for national policy reform.

8. **Parents' engagement** is important for better knowledge on learning outcomes, insight on school financing, familiarity with best ways to coordinate with schools on behalf of their children, and learning how to prevent dropping out and promote learning in their homes.

9. **Students** most directly affected by educational reform and who directly experience school and teacher quality.

REFERENCES

UK DFID (Department for International Development). 2014. "What Is the Evidence on the Impact of Research on International Development?" A DFID Literature Review. London, DFID, © Crown copyright 2014, London. https://assets.publishing.service.gov.uk /media/57a089aced915d622c000343/impact-of-research-on-international-development .pdf.

———. 2016. "Research Uptake: A Guide for DFID-funded Research Programmes." DFID, © Crown copyright 2016, London. https://assets.publishing.service.gov.uk/government /uploads/system/uploads /attachment_data/file/514977/Research_uptake_guidance.pdf.